MARYLAND SUPPLEMENT FOR
Modern Real Estate Practice

H. WARREN CRAWFORD
JOHN F. RODGERS, III

Fourth Edition

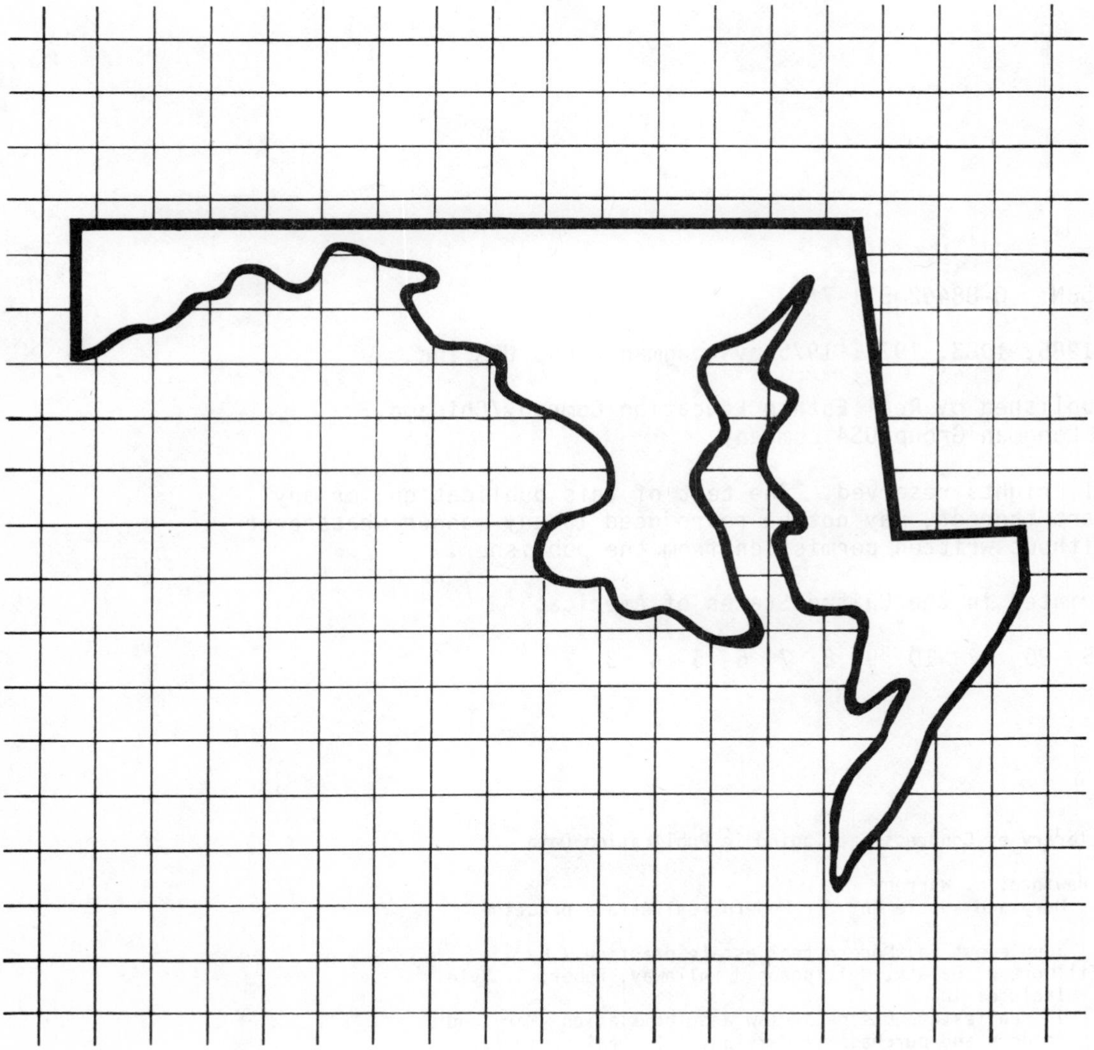

REAL ESTATE EDUCATION COMPANY/CHICAGO
a Longman Group USA company

While a great deal of care has been taken to provide accurate and current information, the ideas, suggestions, general principles, and conclusions presented in this book are subject to local, state, and federal laws and regulations, court cases, and any revisions of same. The reader is thus urged to consult legal counsel regarding any points of law--this publication should not be used as a substitute for competent legal advice.

ISBN: 0-88462-511-7

Published by Real Estate Education Company/Chicago,
a Longman Group USA company

Printed in the United States of America.

85 86 87 10 9 8 7 6 5 4 3 2

Library of Congress Cataloging in Publication Data

Crawford, H. Warren.
Maryland supplement for Modern real estate practice.

Supplement to: Modern real estate practice / by Fillmore W. Galaty, Wellington J. Allaway, Robert C. Kyle.
Includes index.
1. Real estate business--law and legislation--Maryland. 2. Vendors and purchasers--Maryland. 3. Real property--Maryland. 4. Real estate business--Maryland. I. Rodgers, John F. II. Galaty, Fillmore W. Modern real estate practice. III. Title.
KF2042.R4G34 1982 Suppl. 13 346.75204'37 84-27749
ISBN 0-88462-511-7 347.5206437

Contents

Preface

Real estate practice in every state is based upon state laws and regulations as well as federal input. Each state has its own constitution, legislation, courts, commissions, laws, and regulations that govern activities in that particular state.

The Maryland State Legislature meets in January of each year and remains in session for 90 days. Thereafter, it may be called into special session by order of the governor. In any of these sessions, new laws may be passed or changes made in existing laws that affect real estate practice. The practice of real estate in any specific location in Maryland may also be influenced by local agencies, bureaus, and organizations, such as county and city governments or local boards of Realtors®, and by the controls and customs that these organizations initiate.

The purpose of this supplement is to discuss the laws and operating procedures concerning real estate applicable to the State of Maryland. This supplement builds on the basic information that is presented in the text, Modern Real Estate Practice, by Galaty, Allaway, and Kyle. Every effort has been made not to duplicate information that has been presented in Modern Real Estate Practice. Therefore, you should first cover each subject area in the basic text and then refer to the same subject area in this book. Throughout this supplement, references may be made to numbered articles and sections of the Annotated Code of Maryland. Some chapters in the basic text have no related chapter in the supplement because the subject matter does not involve laws or practices that vary significantly from state to state, such as appraisal or property management.

Following each chapter are tests. They can be both an evaluative and a teaching device. As you finish each chapter, and before you go on to the next, be certain that you understand and are able to answer each question in the test. An answer key for all of the tests is included at the end of this supplement.

Throughout your real estate course, you'll be studying and taking tests in preparation for the Maryland Real Estate Examination. This examination is prepared and administered for the Maryland Real Estate Commission by an independent testing service, Assessment Systems Incorporated (ASI) of Philadelphia, Pennsylvania. The Maryland Supplement for Modern Real Estate Practice has been designed to familiarize you with the kinds of items you'll find on that examination. The questions at the end of each chapter are prepared in a format similar to those in the licensing examination. In addition, the "Maryland Real Estate License Examination" section is designed to help you do your best on the state exam.

The fourth edition of this text has been expanded to increase its usefulness to students taking an advanced real estate course. Details of the new Maryland Real Estate Time-Sharing Act are included, as well as revisions to the Maryland Condominium Act and the Real Estate License Law. While care has been exercised in providing information pertaining to the laws governing the practice of real estate in Maryland, the reader is urged to consult with legal counsel regarding any statutory enactment and should not rely solely on this publication as legal authority for compliance with any statute. Additional changes to the real estate license law and other laws pertaining to the practice of real estate in Maryland can be expected between printings of this supplement. Such changes will be contained in update sheets.

The authors appreciate the constructive suggestions on the updating and revision of this text provided by Brian Swartwood, Swartwood & Associates; Donald A. Gabriel, University of Baltimore & Catonsville Community College; Wanda Nesbitt, Coldwell Banker Russell T. Baker; Ronald L. Forman, Montgomery College, George Washington University, and Century 21 Forman Realty, Inc.

In addition, the authors acknowledge reviewers of previous editions: Sally Broadbent, Lu Fischbeck, Frank Harman, Charles Harrision, Martin Kandel, John Kohlaway, Donald Martin, Albert Meyer, Jeffrey Miller, John Miller, Alvin Monshower, Ronald N. DeBonis, John Chester, and Lee Frew Platt.

Thanks are extended to the staff at Real Estate Education Company, including David Walker, Project Editor, and Bobbye Middendorf, Sponsoring Editor.

Special thanks to Lu Fischbeck, G.R.I., Senior Lecturer at Catonsville Community College and Associate Director of the National Real Estate Institute, Inc. for her assistance in preparing the sample final examination.

Suggestions for improving this supplement are welcomed; they should be sent to the publisher and labeled for the Maryland Supplement.

The Maryland Supplement has been prepared by H. Warren Crawford of Ocean City, Maryland, and John F. Rodgers III of Catonsville, Maryland.

Mr. Crawford is a partner in the law firm of Crawford and Crawford, which operates a title insurance agency. He is also president of Peninsula Properties, Realtors®. He has been licensed to practice real estate in Maryland since 1948, a Realtor® since 1953, and is also a licensed broker in the District of Columbia, Virginia, and Delaware. Mr. Crawford was the first Realtor® in Maryland to earn the professional designation of CRB (Certified Residential Broker), awarded by the National Institute of Real Estate Brokers. He has a juris doctorate from the University of Baltimore, where he taught real estate brokerage courses. He has also taught at Ocean City College. Mr. Crawford is past president of the Maryland Association of Realtors® as well as dean of the Realtors® Institute of Maryland, of which he was a founder.

Mr. Rodgers is associate professor of business and real estate, responsible for the real estate program at the Catonsville Community College. He has been active in real estate education since 1963, and has developed, lectured, and taught courses for a number of colleges and organizations. He has a baccalaureate degree in real estate and is a graduate of the Realtors® Institute with the G.R.I. designation. He has been licensed since 1959, and maintains a Maryland broker's license. Mr. Rodgers was the founding president of the National Real Estate Institute, Inc., the founding secretary of the Maryland Real Estate Educators Association, Inc., and the founding president of the Greater Baltimore Association of Realty Educators, Inc. He is a member of the National Association of Realtors®, the Maryland Association of Realtors®, and the Greater Baltimore Board of Realtors®, having served on various committees. He is also member of the Real Estate Education Association. Mr. Rodgers serves on the educational advisory committee for the Maryland Real Estate Commission. He is the author of Elements of Real Estate and Handbook of Real Estate Terms, as well as numerous study guides.

Special credit is extended to The Greater Baltimore Board of Realtors®, the Central Maryland Multiple Listing Service, Inc., and the Maryland Association of Realtors® for permission to use their material and forms.

5

Real Estate Brokerage

In Maryland, a person must be licensed as a real estate broker, associate broker or salesperson in order to perform, offer, attempt, or agree to perform for a fee, commission, or any other valuable consideration, or the promise of expectation of a fee or commission, any of the following real estate activities in whole or in part:

1. selling
2. purchasing
3. exchanging
4. leasing
5. renting
6. collecting rent
7. locating residential property for rent or purchase
8. subdividing and selling lots or sites
9. promoting the sale of real estate through a publication issued primarily for the purpose of subdividing and selling lots
10. dealing or trading in real estate or leases and options thereon.

In other words, unless specifically exempted, a person must be licensed as a real estate broker or salesperson in order to perform real estate activities for others for a fee.

Some activities, such as a private owner selling his or her own real estate or a person selling property under court order, are exempted from the regulations of the Maryland Real Estate License Law. These exemptions, along with other provisions of the license law, will be discussed in detail in Chapter 14.

REAL ESTATE LICENSE LAW

Maryland real estate licenses are issued and administered by the Maryland Real Estate Commission under the provisions of the Maryland Real Estate License Law, Article 56, Sections 212 through 232, of the Annotated Code of Maryland. In addition to the basic statute, the commission has adopted a number of regulations and a Code of Ethics to elaborate on the basic law and provide additional guidelines for brokers and salespeople.

Definitions. Under the license law, a real estate broker is defined as a person who operates a real estate business under his or her own name (or an authorized trade name), or a person who has been designated as the broker of record, who is responsible for the real estate activities of a copartnership, association, or corporation. A real estate salesperson is defined as any person who is licensed to perform any real estate activities on behalf of a licensed broker.

The law also authorizes a third type of license, the associate broker's license. An associate broker's license is required for every member of a partnership or association or any officer of a corporation (other than the broker of record or salespeople) who performs brokerage acts for the firm. Note, however, that such activities may also be performed by a person licensed as a broker of record.

Mobile Home Sales. Although Maryland law stipulates that a person must obtain a special license to sell automobile trailers, the Motor Vehicle Code states that a person need not be licensed as a trailer dealer to sell "special mobile equipment." This has been defined as vehicles not used primarily for highway transportation of persons or property but those that can be readily operated or moved over a highway to facilitate their stationary use. In practice, this means that a real estate licensee may not need to obtain a special license as a trailer dealer to sell mobile homes that will be used primarily in fixed locations as residences.

THE BROKERAGE BUSINESS

Agency Relationships

A listing agreement, as described in the main text, creates an agency between a broker (the agent) and the seller of real estate (the principal). Maryland law provides that such agreements must be in writing (for residential sales), signed, and state the commission a broker is to receive in either a specific amount or a specific percentage and contain a definite termination date. Listing agreements will be discussed in detail in Chapter 16 of the text and this supplement.

Dual agency. A broker may not legally collect a commission from more than one party to a transaction without the full knowledge of all parties to the transaction. This dual agency is a violation of both the law of agency, as discussed in the text, and the Code of Ethics of the Maryland Real Estate Commission. According to the Code of Ethics, the obligation of absolute fidelity to the client's interest is primary, but it does not relieve the licensee from the obligation of dealing fairly with all parties to the transaction. The broker is primarily loyal to the principal and must explain this position to the other party. A broker cannot obtain the highest price for the seller and the lowest price for the buyer in the same transaction; one broker cannot fulfill both of these obligations.

Place of Business

A real estate broker is required by law to have a definite office or place of business in which to transact brokerage business. Local zoning ordinances in some jurisdictions prohibit the use of the broker's residence for such business.

Small Business - Litigation Expenses

Litigation expenses up to $10,000 may be recovered by a small business (less than 50 employees) when a State agency brings action against the business without substantial justification or in bad faith. This procedure was established by the State legislature to assure that a State agency has sufficient proof of wrongdoing by a business before charges are brought.

Workers Compensation: Real Estate Salespersons and Brokers

Real estate salespersons and associate real estate brokers have been held exempt from the worker's compensation requirements if they are on a commission-only basis under a written agreement with the broker, and otherwise qualify as independent contractors for Federal tax purposes.

QUESTIONS

1. A licensed real estate salesperson:

   a. must work for a licensed associate real estate broker.
   b. may only list real estate on behalf of a licensed broker.
   c. is exempt from the licensing requirement.
   d. may operate a real estate business under his or her own name.

2. A person NOT exempt from real estate licensure could be:

   a. a private owner.
   b. a person selling property under a court-ordered sale.
   c. someone collecting a fee or commission.
   d. someone acting gratuitously.

3. Which of the following statements about Maryland real estate licenses are NOT correct?

   a. They are regulated by Article 56 of the Maryland Annotated Code.
   b. They are issued and administered by the Maryland Real Estate Commission.
   c. They are not issued to corporations or associations.
   d. They are required for every person who sells real estate.

4. In Maryland, a residential listing agreement:

   a. does not create an agency.
   b. may be oral.
   c. must be in writing.*
   d. need not contain a definite termination date.

5. Real estate broker Joe Phillips has Enid Wilcox's home listed for sale with his firm. David and Kelly Greene are looking for a home and have offered broker Phillips $2,000 cash as a finder's fee if he can find them a suitable residence. Phillips has shown the Wilcox home to the Greenes, and they seem interested in buying it. What must broker Phillips do in this situation?

    a. not go through with the transaction, since it would violate the law of agency
    b. inform buyer and seller that he is collecting compensation from both
    c. not accept the finder's fee from the Greenes
    d. reduce the amount of commission he would receive from Wilcox by $2,000--the amount of the Greenes' finder's fee

6

Listing Agreements

Maryland brokers use the various types of listing agreements discussed in the text--open listings, exclusive agency listings, exclusive-right-to-sell, and multiple listing agreements. Note that net listings, as described in the text, are prohibited by the Maryland Real Estate License Law.

Listing Requirements

In Maryland, all contracts listing residential real property for sale, rental, lease, or exchange, whether exclusive or open, must be in writing and signed by the parties to the agreement. The listing agreement must state the commission the licensee will charge, either as a percentage or as a specific amount. In addition, a copy of the agreement must be given to the seller (owner) before the real estate licensee may begin to advertise, show, or offer the listed property. A definite termination date must be contained in the listing agreement.

Listing information. The Maryland Real Estate Commission's Code of Ethics requires a licensee to make a reasonable investigation to ascertain all material facts about each listed property to prevent errors, misrepresentation, or concealment of material facts.

Signatures of married persons. When listing property owned by a married couple, a licensee should obtain the signatures of both spouses if the property is held as tenants by the entirety. Tenancy by the entirety is a special form of real estate ownership granted to married couples and will be discussed in Chapter 8 of the text and this supplement.

Broker Cooperation

The Commission's Code of Ethics states that a licensee shall cooperate with other brokers on property listed exclusively by the licensee's firm whenever it is in the best interests of the client. The licensee must share commissions with a cooperating licensee on a previously agreed-upon basis. Negotiations concerning property listed exclusively with one broker, however, must be carried on solely with that broker.

MULTIPLE LISTING SERVICE

A number of boards offer multiple listing service covering specific geographical areas. The Central Maryland Multiple Listing Service, Inc., for example, covers Baltimore City and the counties of Baltimore, Carroll, Harford, and Howard. It is not unusual to have a property listed with several multiple listing services. Each service and board provides forms to their members to cover the various types of properties likely to be listed, including residential sale, condominium, cooperative, multi-family income, farms, residential lots and unimproved land, commercial/industrial sale or lease, business opportunity and residential rental. Board or MLS forms may be used only by members of the issuing organization. Use by non-members is a violation of the license law and could result in suspension or revocation of license in addition to a $2,000 penalty.

Since the listing contract forms vary with each geographical area and multiple listing service and are frequently changed, licensees should familiarize themselves with the current local forms. A form used by the Central Maryland Multiple Listing Service, Inc., is reproduced on the next two pages. Particular attention should be paid to the portion of the contract containing the terms at the bottom of the second page. The blanks are completed after negotiating the terms with the principal.

Use of Listing Forms

Notice the word Realtor® used in the printed portion of a number of listing forms. If the broker using such a form is not a member of a local board of Realtors®, the word Realtor® cannot be used. Improper use of this term could result in suspension or revocation of the broker's license by the Commission and a possible lawsuit by the local board of Realtors®. Using any contract form that includes the name of an association or organization of which the broker is not a member is prohibited by the license law and is grounds for suspension or revocation of the broker's license.

Termination of Listing

Chapter 5 of the text sets out seven means by which a listing may be terminated. These are based on actions of either the principal or the agent. It should be noted that the agency created by a listing may also be terminated by "operation of law." This will usually include the death, incompetency, or bankruptcy of either party. (But note that death of one tenant by entirety may not terminate.) Some listing contracts contain a clause making the listing contract binding on the sellers' estate in case of the sellers' death. A foreclosure/trustee sale also terminates.

CENTRAL MARYLAND
MULTIPLE LISTING SERVICE, INC.
CENTRAL OFFICE
1501 MOUNT ROYAL AVENUE • BALTIMORE, MARYLAND 21217
(301) 462-5100

CLASS 1

RESIDENTIAL SALE

PUBLISHED BY THE CENTRAL MARYLAND MULTIPLE LISTING SERVICE, INC.
THIS DESCRIPTIVE INFORMATION, THOUGH BELIEVED ACCURATE, IS NOT GUARANTEED

(CHECK ONE)

☐ BROKER LOAD ☐ CENTRAL LOAD AREA ☐ LIST NO. ☐☐☐☐☐☐☐☐

FEATURES:

Underline at least one descriptive item for each of the features that is designated by an "R" (Required). Multiple selections are permitted (unless specified).

A. (R) DESIGN OF HOME (SELECT ONE)
1. Bi-Level
2. Bungalow
3. Cabin
4. Cape Cod
5. Colonial
6. Contemporary
7. Cottage
8. Duplex/2 Apt.
9. End-of-Group
10. Estate
11. Farm House
12. Group/Townhouse
13. Raised Rancher
14. Rancher
15. Semi-Detached
16. Split Foyer
17. Split Level
18. Traditional
19. Tri-Level
20. Tudor
21. Victorian
22. Mobile Home
23. House of Worship
24. Shell

B. LEVELS (EXCLUDING BASEMENT)
1. 1 Level
2. 1½ Levels
3. 2 Levels
4. 2½ Levels
5. 3 Levels
6. 4+ Levels

C. EXTERIOR WALL
1. Brick
2. Block
3. Frame
4. Stone
5. Log
6. Asbestos Shingle
7. Wood Siding
8. Cedar Shake
9. Aluminum Siding
10. Vinyl Siding
11. Masonite Siding
12. Brick Veneer
13. Stucco
14. Formstone
15. Alum/Vinyl Soffits/Trim

D. ROOF
1. Asphalt Shingle
2. Wood Shingle
3. Slate
4. Tile
5. Metal
6. Built Up/Tar
7. Composite
8. Other

E. LIVING AREA
1. Formal Living Room
2. Sunken Living Room
3. Great Room
4. Family Room
5. Den
6. Rec Room
7. Study/Office
8. Library
9. Solarium/Atrium
10. Entry Hall
11. Entry Hall w/Closet
12. Powder Room
13. Cathedral Ceiling(s)
14. Skylight(s)
15. French Doors

F. DINING
1. Formal Dining Room
2. Living/Dining Combo.
3. Living/Dining "L"

KITCHEN

4. Eat in Kitchen
5. Country Kitchen
6. Modern Kitchen
7. Efficiency Kitchen
8. Breakfast Bar
9. Cooking Island
10. Pantry
11. Laundry
12. Breakfast Room
13. Mud Room
14. Intercom

G. MASTER BED/BATH
1. Fireplace/Master Bed
2. Walk-in Closet(s)
3. Linen Closet(s)
4. Cedar Closet
5. Updated Bath
6. Master Bath
7. Dressing Room
8. Sunken Tub
9. Hot Tub
10. Whirlpool Bath
11. Sauna
12. Shower/Tub Combo
13. Separate Shower
14. Bidet
15. Tub Only

H. (R) BASEMENT
1. Slab
2. Crawl Space
3. Half, Improved
4. Half, Unimproved
5. Full, Improved
6. Full, Unimproved
7. Full, Partially Improved
15. Not Applicable

I. IN BASEMENT
1. Clubroom
2. Laundry
3. Half Bath
4. Full Bath
5. Rough In Bath
6. Workshop
7. Utility Room
8. Bedroom(s)
9. Kitchen
10. Bar
11. Outside Entrance
12. Walk Out
13. Flush
14. Fireplace/Stove

J. (R) MAIN FUEL
1. Electric
2. Gas
3. Oil
4. Coal
5. Solar
6. Liquid Petroleum
7. Kerosene
8. Wood
9. Other
10. None

K. HEATING
1. Forced Hot Air
2. Hot Water Baseboard
3. Hot Water Radiator
4. Steam Radiator
5. Radiant
6. Baseboard (Elec.)
7. Heat Pump
8. Floor Furnace

COOLING

9. Central Air
10. Window Air
11. Window Fans
12. Ceiling Fan
13. Attic Fan
14. Window Screens

L. AUXILIARY HEAT
1. 1 Fireplace
2. 2+ Fireplaces
3. Gas Fireplace
4. Fireplace w/Insert
5. Firepl. w/Heatalator
6. Wood Stove
7. Wood/Coal Stove
8. Coal Stove
9. With Heat Ducts
10. Space Heater(s)
11. Solar
12. See Remarks
13. Flue Hook-Up
14. Radiant Heat

M. ENERGY SAVING
1. Existing Storm Windows
2. Existing Replace. Windows
3. Existing Dual Glaze Windows
4. Existing Storm Doors
5. Solar Water Heater
6. Additional Attic Insulation
7. Additional Insul./Exterior Wall
8. Awnings
9. Existing Dual Glazed Doors

N. APPLIANCES
1. Gas Range
2. Electric Range
3. Self Clean Oven
4. Cont. Clean Oven
5. Wall Oven
6. Microwave
7. Refrigerator
8. Freezer
9. Washer
10. Gas Dryer
11. Electric Dryer
12. Dishwasher
13. Disposal
14. Trash Compactor
15. Food Center

O. INTERIOR AMENITIES
1. Hardwood Floors
2. Partial Hardwd. Flrs.
3. Parquet Floor(s)
4. Quarry Tile/Slate Floor(s)
5. No Wax Kitch. Floor
6. Existing W/W Carpet
7. W/W - Subfloor only
8. Existing Curtain Rods
9. Existing Shades
10. Existing Blinds
11. Existing Interior Shutters
12. Jalousie Windows
13. Some Draperies
14. Existing Light Fixtures
15. Some Built-Ins

P. EXTERIOR FEATURES
1. Patio
2. Deck
3. Balcony
4. Porch
5. Screened Porch
6. Sun Porch
7. Inground Pool
8. Above Ground Pool
9. Tennis Court
10. Storage Shed
11. Green House
12. Gazebo/Summer Hse
13. Outbuildings
14. Exterior Lighting

Q. PARKING
1. 1 Car Attch. Garage
2. 2+ Car Attch. Garage
3. 1 Car Detach. Garage
4. 2+ Car Detach. Garage
5. Carport (1 Car)
6. Carport (2+ Cars)
7. Parking Pad
8. Driveway
9. Off Street Parking
10. Breezeway
11. Auto. Garage Opener
12. Permit Parking

R. SITE INFORMATION
1. Corner Lot
2. Inside Lot
3. Cul-de-Sac
4. Dead End Street
5. Wooded Lot
6. Part. Wooded Lot
7. Tree Studded Lot
8. Fenced Yard
9. Part. Fenced Yard
10. Level Lot
11. Landscaped
12. Subject to Agric. Transfer Tax

S. (R) UTILITIES
1. Public Water
2. Public Sewer
3. Public Gas
4. Well
5. Well w/Water Conditioner
6. Well Test Required
7. Septic
8. Pub. Water Avail.
9. Pub. Sewer Avail.
10. Priv. Water System
11. Priv. Sewer System
12. Cable T.V.
13. 220 V Service

T. WATER SITUATION
1. Pond
2. Stream
3. Waterfront
4. Water View
5. Water Privilege
6. Private Dock
7. Private Beach
8. Community Dock
9. Community Beach
10. Bulkhead
11. Pier

U. FINANCING
1. Assumption
2. Assumpt./% Increase
3. Assumpt./Vet Only
4. Assumpt./FNMA
5. Owner Take Back
6. Owner Holds Second
7. Will Pay Points
8. Limited Buy Down
9. WRAP Available
10. Pre-Appraised
11. Prior Financing
12. Rent/Option to Buy
13. Will Rent w/Sale
14. Will Rent
15. Other/See Remarks

V. CURRENT LOAN
1. Paid in Full
2. Conventional
3. VA
4. HUD203B
5. HUD245
6. HUD221D2
7. HUD222
8. PMI
9. MHF
10. FHL
11. Renegotiable
12. Blended Rate
13. GEM
14. Private
15. None

W. SHOW INSTRUCTIONS
1. Call Office/Appt.
2. Key in Office
3. Keybox
4. Call Listing Associate
5. L.A. must Accompany
6. Restricted Hours

POSSESSION

7. Possess.: 30-60 Days
8. Possess.: 60-90 Days
9. Possess.: 90-120 Days
10. Possess.: 120+ Days
11. Possess.: Immediate
12. Possess.: Negotiable
13. Contingent on Finding Home

X. SPECIAL NOTE
1. Master Listing
2. Package Listing
3. To Be Built
4. T.B.B. Your Lot
5. Historic District
6. Rehab.
7. Model Unit
8. Under Construction
9. Duplicate Represent.
10. Suit./Handicapped
11. Sign Posted
12. Excluded Party on File in Office
13. L.A. is Principal
14. Home Owner Warranty
15. Flood Ins. May be Req.

Y. EXCLUSIONS
1. Some Light Fixtures
2. Some Appliances
3. Some Draperies
4. Some Curtain Rods
5. Some Shades/Blinds
6. Some Interior Shutters
7. Ceiling Fan
8. Bookcase(s)
9. Washer
10. Refrigerator
11. Dryer
12. Microwave
13. Exterior Shed
14. Tagged Shrubs
15. See Remarks

Z. MISCELLANEOUS
1. In Law Apt./Quarters
2. Includes 1+ Apt.
3. Incl. Doctors Office
4. Farmette
5. Handy Man's Special

INCLUDES:

6. Security System
7. T.V. Antenna
8. Instant Hot
9. Range Hood/Exhaust Fan
10. Humidifier
11. Dehumidifier
12. Central Vacuum
13. Green House Window
14. Expandable Attic
15. Some Updated Plumbing

KEYWORDS: When Adding a Listing (AL), enter the Keyword information as prompted by the computer. (R)'s denote required entries.

ADDRESS

(R) NO: ☐☐☐☐☐ St. Number — DN: ☐ (Direct. N,S,E,W) — (R) ST: ☐☐☐☐☐☐☐☐☐☐☐☐☐☐☐☐☐☐☐☐ Street Name — (R) ZP: ☐☐☐☐☐ Zip Code — (R) MP: ☐☐☐☐☐☐☐ (Map Coordinates) County Page Grid

NB: ☐☐☐☐☐☐☐☐☐☐☐☐☐☐☐ Neighborhood — (R) LP: ☐☐☐☐☐☐☐ $ List Price — (R) GR: ☐☐☐☐☐ $ Gr. Rent (Annual) — CV: ☐☐☐☐☐ $ Capitalized Value of Gr. Rent

Realtor	Owner	Date
Agency	Owner	Date

PAGE 1 OF A 2 PAGE AGREEMENT

ADDRESS: ____________________

RESIDENTIAL SALE **1**

THIS PROPERTY IS OFFERED WITHOUT REGARD TO RACE, COLOR, CREED, SEX, AGE, NATIONAL ORIGIN OR MARITAL STATUS.

HOME DESCRIPTION

BD: Beds — BA: Full / Half Baths — AG: Age — FR: (Family Room or other Special Room Dimensions)

LR: Living Room — DR: Dining Room — KT: Kitchen

NOTE: Show dimensions in feet only — Round down.

MB: Master Bedroom / (level) — B2: 2nd Bedroom / (level) — B3: 3rd Bedroom / (level) — B4: 4th Bedroom / (level)

BASEMENT IS LEVEL O

LOT INFORMATION

LT: Lot Size (Acres) — PD: Lot Dimensions or Description

LI: Liber

FO: Folio

DD: Date of Deed (Yr/Mo)

ANNUAL FEES

(R) TX: $ Taxes

FS: $ Fees

HE: $ Heat Cost

GE: $ Gas & Elec.

OT: $ Other (See Remarks)

MORTGAGE DATA*

(R) ME: Mortgagee

(R) MG: $ Mortgage Balance

(R) IR: Interest Rate %

(R) PI: $ P + I Only

(R) YR: Yrs./Remaining

*NOTE: Mortgage data is only required on assumptions.

LISTING INFORMATION

(R) ID: Associate Identification No.

(R) LA: Name of Listing Associate — (R) PH: L.A. Home Phone — (R) BN: Broker No.

(R) LD: List Date (Yr/Mo/Da) — (R) ED: Expir. Date (Yr/Mo/Da) — (R) CO: Commission to SR — MLS NUMBER (Office Use)

REMARKS OR DIRECTIONS

L1: (Line # 1)

L2: (Line # 2)

L3: (Line # 3)

MULTIPLE LISTING CONTRACT

Published by the Central Maryland Multiple Listing Service, Inc.

Date________________19_____

____, Realtor®, is hereby authorized exclusively to sell the property described above. This authority shall continue for a period of______months from the date hereof, except that either party, by giving______ days' prior written notice, may cancel this contract so that it will terminate at the end of ________ months from the date hereof, or at any time thereafter. The descriptive information shown above is to be considered as a part hereof. Such information, though believed accurate, is not guaranteed.

The undersigned owner agrees to pay Realtor® a commission for services rendered in the amount set forth below, (1) if during the term of this contract, or any extension thereof, Realtor® produces a customer to purchase said property at the listing price and on the terms shown above or at such other price or on such other terms as shall be accepted by the owner or agreed upon in writing between the owner and Realtor®, or (2) if said property is sold or exchanged directly by the owner or through Realtor® or others, during the term of this contract or any extension thereof, or within _______ months thereafter, to anyone who, with the knowledge of the owner, inspected or made inquiry about the property during the term of this contract or any extension thereof; except that Realtor® shall have no claim upon the owner for any commission if the property is so sold or exchanged by any other licensed Real Estate broker after the expiration of this contract or any extension thereof.

The amount of Realtor® compensation is not prescribed by Law nor established by any membership organization with which the Realtor® is affiliated.

Realtor® shall not be responsible for the care of the physical condition of the property involved under this agreement. Realtor® agrees to Multiple List this contract and this contract shall be void, (1) if Realtor® is not a Participant of the **Central Maryland Multiple Listing Service, Inc.** at the time of the signing hereof, or (2) if this contract is not multiple listed. Realtor® is hereby granted the right to report promptly any contract of sale and the sales price set forth therein to the Multiple Listing Service for dissemination to Participants of the Service. This property is offered without respect to race, color, creed, sex, national origin or marital status. This agreement shall be binding upon the respective heirs, personal representatives, assignees and/or successors of the parties hereto.

In the event of a sale or exchange the commission is to be ______ % of sales price, or of listing price in event of an exchange, plus ______ months ground rent, if any.

If a deposit made on any contract of sale shall be forfeited to owner or if all or part of a deposit shall be received by the owner as a settlement made by and between the owner and purchaser, the commission for Realtor's® services shall be ______________% of the amount forfeited or of the amount received as a settlement, but in no event to exceed an amount equal to the full commission specified herein.

WITNESS ______________________ OWNER ______________________(SEAL)
WITNESS ______________________ OWNER ______________________(SEAL)
REALTOR ______________________(SEAL) OWNER'S ADDRESS ______________________
OR AUTHORIZED REPRESENTATIVE OWNER'S PHONE ______________ ZIP CODE ________

PAGE 2 OF A 2 PAGE AGREEMENT

LISTING THE PROPERTY

It is important to list property correctly. The listing should include an appropriate price for the property, all pertinent data about the property, and the seller's terms. A listing may be thought of as containing five parts: (1) the actual listing terms, the rate of commission, and the termination date of the listing; (2) a detailed description of the property, including ground rent and other facts required by the listing form being used; (3) any special situations, including such requirements as surveys or termite inspection; terms of occupancy; construction problems; unpaid bills; title or estate problems; (4) any special financing available through the seller or other sources; and inclusions and/or exclusions; and (5) the signatures of the owners or their authorized representatives.

In obtaining the details of the property from the seller, the listing salesperson may ask the seller questions to which the seller does not know the answer. This may involve the age of the house, the actual footage of the lot, the zoning of the property, taxes, or other detailed information. Any such missing information should be obtained by the salesperson from records.

The salesperson should find out about any special situations involving the property. A good listing salesperson will always try to foresee every possible circumstance that may develop and provide for it accordingly. For example, if the seller is moving to a new residence that is not yet complete, there could be a problem with possession. There may also be a problem if the seller is moving to a property where the present occupants are waiting to take possession of their new property. It may be desirable to establish in advance a daily occupancy rate--the rent for the seller's occupancy of the property--after the buyer becomes the new owner. This becomes more important if the property is presently occupied by tenants.

The salesperson should also inquire about any existing survey of the property. What information does it show regarding property lines and improvements? Is it thorough and up-to-date? Every circumstance that is identified in advance is one less hurdle to overcome when the property is shown.

Maryland real estate license law requires licensees to disclose any material fact, data, or information relating to the property which the licensee knows or should have known. It behooves the licensee to pay close attention to the details of the property he or she is listing.

Condition of property. When describing the condition of the property, the licensee is cautioned against using such words as "excellent," "perfect," "in mint condition," etc. These words, if construed as an implied warranty, could lead to legal action against the licensee by the Commission, as well as civil liability.

Square footage. Misrepresenting the size of a listed property can result in license suspension as well as court action. The licensee must be able to compute square footage, which is determined by measuring the outside dimensions of the house and multiplying by the number of floors. Crawl spaces and unfinished attics do not count--only usable space. The square footage shown in listing contracts is not intended to be definitive and should never be quoted as absolute in showing or selling a property.

Zoning information. There is no legal requirement to disclose the zoning classification of residential property being sold, or that of property adjacent to it. However, such information should be disclosed to the buyer by the seller or his or her agent. Care should be taken not to mislead buyers as to the zoning of a listed or adjacent property. When selling individual homes that contain an apartment, licensees are well advised to ascertain that the apartment in the dwelling conforms to existing zoning. There have been cases where buyers have purchased what they thought were two-family dwellings only to find that such use was illegal.

Suitable for handicapped. Some listing forms include a "Suitable for Handicapped" block. A property must meet a substantial portion of the following criteria in order to qualify as "Suitable for Handicapped."

- Parking and Outside Travel
  - --Adjacent off-street parking available
  - --Paved, level 36" walkways without steps or steep inclines from parking area to building
  - --Outside lighting adequate for safe passage
  - --Curbs which are cut or ramped for wheelchair
- Building Entry
  - --Main entry at ground level or steps, if present, with sufficient adjacent ground space to install a wheelchair ramp at front or side of stoop
  - --Entrance door opening minimum of 32" wide and door opening inward
  - --Wheelchair clearance (minimum 32" x 48") in entry hall beyond door swing
- Living Quarters
  - --Entrance doorway a minimum of 32" wide when open
  - --At least one bedroom and bathroom accessible by direct entry (no right turn) or hall wide enough (48") for turn into doors of bedroom and bath
  - --Room doorways a minimum of 30" wide when doors are fully open
  - --Most windows accessible from a wheelchair (sill maximum of 30" from floor)
- Bathroom
  - --Fixtures separated by at least one foot of space
  - --Lavatory space open beneath fixture
  - --Bathroom at least 5' wide with no floor-standing heater
  - --Mirrors low enough (over sink) to see
- Kitchen
  - --All appliances and cabinets clear of entry door swing
  - --Shelves wheelchair level
  - --A minimum of 48" open floor space down the center of the kitchen cabinets and appliances
  - --Electric stove

Available financing. Particularly important to the listing is any financing available to the buyer, as discussed in Chapter 15 of the text. Any owner financing possibilities should be described in the listing--they may make the difference between a sale and just another showing.

The agent taking a listing should also make every attempt to discuss in detail the seller's financing needs. When balancing equity in the property against debt, the seller may realize that it is not economically feasible to sell the property at the present time. By helping the seller determine this before the selling process has begun, the salesperson performs a service for the owner and avoids wasting time and energy on a listing that may never be converted into a sale.

Signatures. When the listing form is completed and all possible information has been included, it must be signed. Only those persons with an interest in the property or who have proper authorization from such persons may sign the contract. However, it is the responsibility of the listing agent to make sure that all parties who have an interest do sign the contract. In Maryland, married couples may hold property in a special kind of co-ownership called tenancy by the entirety. When listing property so held by married couples, the licensee must obtain the signatures of both spouses. (The details of this form of ownership are discussed in Chapter 8 of the text and this Supplement.) The date on the listing should reflect the effective date when the last necessary signature is obtained.

ADVERTISING REAL ESTATE

Agent Identification

The Maryland Real Estate License Law (Section 224j) requires a licensee to disclose in all advertising whether he or she is a broker or a salesperson. This disclosure must be made even when the licensee is selling his or her personal real property. Furthermore, a salesperson may not use his or her own name in an ad without also naming the sponsoring broker or firm. In many cases violation may be unintentional or careless, but may result in a suspension or loss of license and/or fine.

The Code of Ethics prohibits the broker from permitting a salesperson's name or telephone number to appear in advertising unless the connection with the broker is obvious.

Use of Trade Names

In 1979, the Commission dealt with problems regarding the use of trade names in advertising. A trade name is a trademark or service mark irrespective of whether the licensee must obtain permission to use it. A licensee using a trade name on a for-sale sign, business card, office sign, sales contract, listing contract, or other document is required to clearly and unmistakably include his or her name or trade name as registered with the Commission. The same information must be included in oral communcation, whether in person or by telephone. This is intended to ensure that his or her identity is made known to that person.

Brokers may advertise properties only if they have the listing, and only with the owner's permission.

Ground Lease Disclosure

A broker's advertisements or signs posted on any property for sale that is subject to ground lease must state the annual ground rent and capitalization if the price of the leasehold property is included on the sign--and all these statements must be in lettering of equal size. The capitalization is the sum for which the land could be purchased outright if owned in fee and not held under a ground lease. Ground rents, including capitalization, will be covered in detail in Chapter 16.

"For Sale" Signs

The Commission's Code of Ethics requires that a licensee obtain an owner's permission before placing signs on a property. A licensee may now keep a "for sale" sign up as long as the homeowner and local ordinances permit.

Note that certain areas of Maryland have adopted prohibitions against the posting of "for sale" signs; the Real Estate Commission has declared some areas of the state to be "conservation areas" in which no signs may be posted. A licensee should check local laws regarding the use of "for sale" signs to ensure his or her full compliance with the law.

Directional signs. Baltimore County zoning regulations prohibit display of "sold" signs and of "sold" strips on "for sale" signs on real estate. Temporary signs directing prospects to real estate that is for sale, for lease, or open for inspection are permitted in Baltimore County under the following strict requirements:

1 Only one sign for each purpose (sale, lease, open) may be displayed at the intersection of two roads, regardless of the number of homes listed on one sign.
2 The size of such signs is limited to 6 inches by 24 inches, with the height not to exceed 4 feet above the ground.
3 Only the words "for sale," "for lease," or "open for inspection" may appear on the sign. No advertising and no company names or logos may be used; however, the REALTOR® logo may be used when applicable.
4 Signs may be displayed only between the hours of 10:00 A.M. Saturday to 8:00 P.M. Sunday.

Baltimore City sign restrictions. Chapter 10, Baltimore City Zoning Ordinances, deals with signs. Directional signs are now allowed in Baltimore City; no signs are allowed within 100 feet of the right-of-way line of an expressway; no sign may be placed so as to obstruct free and clear vision of traffic flow lines or traffic signs; signs will not consist of any moving, rotating, or otherwise animated part or any flashing, blinking, fluctuating, or animated lights; no roof or wind signs are permitted; no sign shall extend above the roof line of a building; no sign shall project beyond the street line into the public way; "for sale" or "for lease" signs cannot exceed a height of five feet or an area of six square feet for residential dwellings and maximum eight feet high, 36 square feet for multiple-family dwellings and apartments.

Real Estate Conservation Areas

As just mentioned, the Maryland Real Estate Commission has designated 16 areas in the northeast and western portions of Baltimore City as Real Estate Conservation Areas and has suspended all methods of advertising real estate dealer or brokerage services and all methods of soliciting listings for houses in these areas.

Included among the acts prohibited by this suspension are the following, but all may not apply in a given area:

1 door-to-door solicitation in person or by telephone calls to or within the designated areas
2 distribution of circulars, cards, or advertisements

This suspension does not prohibit a real estate broker or salesperson from responding in a proper manner to offers or announcements made by a homeowner who wishes help in selling his or her own home.

Advertising in regularly distributed newspapers, magazines, and telephone directories, and on radio and television, is permitted.

Suspension in each of these Real Estate Conservation Areas is in force for the 24 months following its effective date. Other areas may be added. A licensee is cautioned to know where all of these areas are; unauthorized acts could result in the suspension or revocation of a license. In addition, a licensee who violates the conservation areas would be exposed to a criminal misdemeanor charge. Conviction for such could result in a fine of up to $1,000, imprisonment for up to one year, or both.

Raffles of Real Property

In some counties, bona fide charitable organizations can conduct a raffle for the exclusive benefit of the charitable organization when the prize awarded is real property to which the organization holds title or has the ability to convey title. An organization may not conduct more than two raffles of real property in any calendar year. The Secretary of State has the statutory authority to adopt regulations governing this kind of raffle.

Out-of-State Listings

Even though an out-of-state property is multiple listed in the State of Maryland and properly advertised, Maryland licensees may not show the property unless licensed in the state where the property is located.

QUESTIONS

1. Which type of listing agreement is illegal in Maryland?

   a. net listing
   b. exclusive agency listing
   c. open listing
   d. exclusive-right-to-sell listing

2. Residential listing agreements:

   a. must be in writing.
   b. need not state the amount of broker's commission.
   c. may omit the date or time of termination.
   d. may only be signed by the owner(s).

3. Frank Ralston has just signed a listing agreement to sell his Maryland home with broker Jan Baker. Broker Baker must give Ralston a copy of the agreement:

   a. if the seller requests it.
   b. before advertising the seller's property in a local newspaper.
   c. within 15 days after acceptance by the broker.
   d. only when a buyer is found.

4. Salesperson Joe Davidson is listing a home for sale that is subject to a ground rent. In the advertising posted on this property, Davidson, by law, must include which of the following information?

   a. the annual ground rent and capitalization for the property, and sales price
   b. the zoning classification of the property
   c. his broker's name
   d. a and c

5. Which statement about "For sale" signs is false?

   a. are prohibited in conservation areas
   b. must not be placed on listed property without the owner's permission
   c. need not conform to deed restrictions
   d. are exempt from zoning ordinances

6. The amount or rate of commission on a real estate sale:

   a. must be stated in the listing agreement.
   b. is established by the Real Estate Commission.
   c. is established by the local real estate board.
   d. is regulated by law.

7. A listing agreement form published by a multiple listing service may be used by:

   a. any member of the service publishing the form.
   b. any member of any Board of Realtors®.
   c. any member of the Board of Realtors® that operates the service.
   d. any licensee.

8. A licensee who violates the conservation areas:

   a. is committing a misdemeanor.
   b. is committing a felony.
   c. could be fined up to $5,000 per violation.
   d. could be imprisoned up to two years per violation.

9. In a four-month period, salesman Frank made sales of property totaling $140,000 and received $6,100 in commissions. He earned 5 percent commission on his first $50,000. His commission rate on the balance of his sales was:

   a. 3%
   b. 3-1/2%
   c. 4%
   d. 4-1/2%

10. A broker charges a 6 percent commission for her services and pays her salesmen 15 percent of the commission for a listing and 40 percent for a sale. One salesman lists a $20,000 house and sells a $35,000 property, so he will earn:

   a. $ 955
   b. $1,020
   c. $1,065
   d. $1,135

7

Interests in Real Estate

ESTATES IN LAND

Freeholds in fee simple, fee simple determinable, fee simple conditional, life estates, remainder, and reversion all are recognized in Maryland as described in the text. Leasehold estates for years, from period to period, at will, and at sufferance are also recognized in Maryland. In addition, a ground rent system is prevalent in some areas of the state. Leasehold estates will be discussed in detail in Chapter 16 of this supplement.

Legal Life Estates

Both dower and curtesy have been abolished in Maryland. Likewise, there is no homestead exemption in Maryland.

Easement by prescription. An easement by prescription may be acquired in Maryland by an adverse user of another's land for a continuous period of 20 years, under certain specified conditions. Consult an attorney.

Riparian Rights

An owner of real estate bordering a navigable body of water (estuaries, bays, or rivers) in Maryland has the common-law right to make a landing, wharf, or pier for his or her own use or for the use of the public, subject to state rules and regulations. However, regardless of whether or not the owner's title extends beyond the dry land, the title of land below the high-water mark of navigable waters, as well as the waters themselves, belong to the public. Thus, an owner may legally own only the property up to the mean high-water mark. High-water mark is defined as the highest elevation of water in the course of the usual, regular, periodical ebb and flow of the tide, excluding the advance of waters above that line by winds, storms, or floods.

Agricultural Land Preservation Easement

The Maryland Agricultural Land Preservation Foundation has been established to purchase easements on land in certain areas for the purpose of restricting land to agricultural use. Details are contained in the Agricultural Article of the Annotated Code of Maryland. The state is purchasing development rights and limiting residential subdivision of agricultural land.

QUESTIONS

1. Which of the following is recognized in Maryland?

   a. dower
   b. homestead exemption
   c. curtesy
   d. easement by prescription

2. In Maryland, real property may be owned under <u>all but which</u> of the following estates in land?

   a. fee simple determinable
   b. estate for years
   c. fee simple
   d. life estate

3. A person may acquire an easement by prescription over another person's property:

   a. after 20 years' continuous use.
   b. after 25 years' continuous use.
   c. after 30 years' continuous use.
   d. only if it is an easement by necessity.

4. Owen McCarver owns several acres of land in Maryland. His property is divided into two nearly equal halves by a navigable river that runs through the land. McCarver has the right:

   a. to build a pier on one of the riverbanks, subject to state laws.
   b. to construct a dam across the river to divert the waters into a man-made lake on his property.
   c. to construct a wharf without state approval.
   d. to access only to the dry land.

5. In the situation above, Owen McCarver is said to own the land bordering the river:

   a. above the mean high-water mark.
   b. below the mean high-water mark.
   c. to the center of the river.
   d. to the riverbed and across to the other side.

8

How Ownership Is Held

FORMS OF OWNERSHIP

Maryland statutes permit estates in severalty and co-ownership--tenancy-in-common, joint tenancy, tenancy by the entirety, partnership, and trust, all described in the text.

Co-ownership

According to Maryland law, a conveyance of real estate to two or more persons automatically establishes a tenancy-in-common unless the deed expressly creates a joint tenancy, or is a conveyance to a married couple (which would create a tenancy by the entirety, as will be discussed below). To create a joint tenancy, it is customary to use such wording as, "To Harry Waller and Sue Skilling as joint tenants and not as tenants-in-common."

Tenancy by the entirety. In Maryland, only a legally married husband and wife can own property under a tenancy by the entirety, as discussed in the text. (Common-law marriages cannot be established in Maryland but will be recognized as valid in Maryland if they were established in jurisdictions that permit them.) Such a tenancy is automatically created when title passes to persons described as husband and wife. Sale or conveyance of the property during both spouses' lifetimes requires both signatures on the deed. A tenancy by the entirety is terminated and converted to a tenancy in severalty upon the death of either spouse and/or upon divorce or other legal termination of the marriage to a tenancy-in-common, unless other arrangements have been made. If one spouse dies, the surviving spouse will own the property in severalty by operation of law.

Although Maryland has not actually declared itself a community property state, the new Property Disposition in Divorce and Annulment Statute has much the same effect as community property rulings in other states. In domestic cases filed after January 1979, the court may prevent a partition proceeding for a period not to exceed three years if the property is occupied as the "family home" by a custodial spouse and any unemancipated children, when an operation of law has changed the property ownership from tenants by the entireties to tenants-in-common. Furthermore, while actual title cannot be transferred by judicial decree, the court has the right to render a monetary judgment against a spouse which, if not paid, could be used to cloud title or force the sale of real property.

Partnership. The provisions of the Uniform Partnership Act apply in Maryland; by statute, a corporation (as well as an individual) can become a member of a partnership.

Trusts. Real estate investment trusts (REITs) have been recognized in Maryland since 1963 as a permitted form of unincorporated trust or association that may conduct business in compliance with Annotated Code of Maryland, Corporations and Trusts, Title 8.

A declaration of trust must be filed, providing, among other things, the total number of shares to be issued, the classification of shares, and the date of the annual shareholders' meeting and election of trustees.

The powers and restrictions of REITs include:

1 making contracts, incurring liabilities, and borrowing money;
2 selling, mortgaging, leasing, pledging, exchanging, conveying, transferring, and disposing of all or any assets;
3 issuing bonds, notes, and other obligations and securing them by mortgage or deed of trust;
4 acquiring by purchase or in any other manner receiving, holding, using, employing, improving, encumbering, and otherwise dealing with any interest in real and personal property except land for farming, agriculture, horticulture, or similar purposes;
5 at least 75 percent of the value of assets must be real property assets, government securities, cash, and receivables;
6 beneficial ownership must be held by 100 or more persons for at least 75 percent of each year;
7 fifty percent or more of the shares may not be held directly or indirectly by five or fewer shareholders.

The details in state statute concerning formation, bonds required, mergers, proceedings for dissolution, required reports, and the general powers and liabilities thereof are so complex in nature that legal counsel should be obtained before creating a REIT.

Maryland Securities

The Maryland Securities Act, Maryland Corporations and Associations Articles, Section 11-101 through 11-805, requires licensing of persons engaged in the selling of real estate-related securities. This is covered in more detail in Chapter 14.

CONDOMINIUMS

In 1963 Maryland enacted the Horizontal Property Act, now called the Condominium Act, providing for condominium projects. Effective July 1972, this law was restated and recodified and it was further revised as of July 1976, July 1981, July 1982, July 1983, and July 1, 1984. The detailed provisions are contained in Title 11 of the Real Property Article of the Annotated Code of Maryland. The following pages highlight the main points of the Act; any licensee involved with condominium sales or development should obtain a complete copy of the article. Note that persons building or selling condominiums are subject to the provisions of the Real Estate License Law as explained in Chapter 14.

Definitions

Some of the more important terms defined in Section 11-101 of the Real Property article known as the Condominium Act are:

Common elements All of the condominium except the units.

Limited common elements All those common elements identified in the declaration or on the condominium plat as reserved for the exclusive use of one or more, but less than all, of the unit owners.

General common elements All the common elements except the limited common elements.

Common expenses; common profits The expenses and profits of the council of unit owners.

Condominium Property subject to the condominium regime.

Council of unit owners The legal entity described in Section 11-109 of the Act. May be incorporated as a nonstock corporation, or unincorporated, but if so, shall be subject to certain provisions of the Corporation article.

Developer Any person who subjects his or her property to the condominium regime established by the Act.

Occupant Any lessee or guest of a unit owner.

Rental facility Property containing dwelling units intended to be leased to persons who occupy the dwellings as their residences.

Unit A three-dimensional space identified as such in the declaration and on the condominium plat, including all improvements within the space except those excluded in the declaration or master deed.

Unit owner The person (or combination of persons) who holds legal title to a unit.

Establishment

In order to create a condominium, as discussed in the main text, an owner or co-owners must expressly declare the desire to convert real estate to condominium ownership through the recording of a declaration, bylaws, and condominium plat. These documents, including a plat of survey in proper form, must comply with the requirements detailed in Title 11. Property is then said to be under the condominium regime and the owners are known as the developer. The declaration is indexed on the county records under the name of the developer and under the name of the condominium. The condominium regime must be registered with the Secretary of State before a condominium unit may be sold or offered for sale.

Amendments to the declaration or master deed or the plat may be made only with written consent of every unit owner and every mortgagee. The declaration may be amended with the written consent of 80 percent of the unit owners. An amendment to the declaration may not change the boundaries of any unit, the undivided percentage interest in the common elements of any unit, the liability for common expenses or rights to common profits in any unit, or the number of votes in the council of unit owners of any unit without the written consent of every unit owner and mortgagee. An amendment to the declaration may not modify rights expressly reserved for the benefit of the developer or provisions required by any governmental authority or for the benefit of any public utility.

Except to the extent expressly permitted by the declaration, an amendment to the declaration may not change residential units to nonresidential units or change nonresidential units to residential units or redesignate general common elements as limited common elements without the written consent of every unit owner and mortgagee.

Amendments become effective when recorded. Such amendments are indexed in the public records only under the name of the condominium.

Public Offering Statement

A contract for the initial sale of a condominium unit to a member of the general public is not enforceable by the seller unless the purchaser is given a Public Offering Statement, which must contain the following information.

1 A copy of the proposed contract of sale, which includes notice of the purchaser's rescision rights.
2 A copy of the proposed declaration, bylaws and rules and regulations.
3 A copy of the proposed articles of incorporation of the council of unit owners, if it is to be incorporated.
4 A copy of any proposed management contract, employment contract, or other contract affecting the use of, maintenance of, or access to all or part of the condominium to which it is anticipated the unit owners or the council of unit owners will be a party.
5 A copy of the actual annual operating budget for the condominium or, if no actual operating budget exists, a copy of the projected annual operating budget for the condominium.
6 A copy of any lease to which it is anticipated the unit owners or the council of unit owners will be a party following closing.
7 A description of any contemplated expansion of the condominium with a general description of each stage of expansion and the maximum number of units that can be added to the condominium.
8 A copy of the floor plan of the unit or the proposed condominium plats.
9 A description of any recreational or other facilities and a statement as to whether or not they are to be part of the common elements.
10 A statement as to whether streets within the condominium are to be dedicated to public use or maintained by the council of unit owners.
11 A statement of any judgments against the council of unit owners and the existence of any pending suits to which the council of unit owners is a party.

12 In the case of a condominium containing buildings substantially completed more than 5 years prior to the filing of application for registration with the Secretary of State, a statement of the physical condition and state of repair of the major structural, mechanical, electrical, and plumbing components of the improvements, to the extent reasonably ascertainable, and estimated cost of repairs presently needed and a statement of repairs which are intended to be made.
13 A description of any provision in the declaration or bylaws limiting or providing for the duration of developer control or requiring the phasing in of unit owner participation, or a statement that there is no such provision.
14 If the condominium is one which will be created by the conversion of a rental facility, a copy of the notice and the materials required before converting a residential rental facility to a condominium regime.
15 Any other information required by regulation duly adopted and issued by the Secretary of State.

A contract for the initial sale of a unit to a member of the public may not be entered into until the Public Offering Statement for the proposed condominium regime has been registered with the Secretary of State and until 10 days after all amendments then applicable to the Public Offering Statement have been filed with the Secretary of State.

The purchaser has the right to approve any changes in the foregoing material that would materially affect his or her interest and the right to cancel the contract within five days of receipt of the changes (with the exception of changes required by governmental authority or public utility). In addition, the buyer may rescind the purchase contract in writing within 15 days after receipt of the above-listed papers for any reason. He or she will then be entitled to have all deposits returned.

It should be noted that these rights are for prospective purchasers, because the right to cancel or rescind a purchase terminates when a purchaser closes the sale. However, a seller remains liable to a purchaser for one year for any damages the latter suffers as a result of the seller's omission of, or false or misleading statements of, material facts. The purchaser's right to rescind or cancel under the Condominium Act may not be waived in the contract of sale. The disclosure requirements apply to the initial sale of any new condominium unit offered for sale in Maryland.

Leasehold Estates

The fee simple owner or lessee under a lease that exceeds 60 years of any property in the State may subject the property to a condominium regime.

Developer's Progress Report

A developer of a condominium is required to file a written statement with the Secretary of State as well as the council of unit owners which describes the progress of construction, repairs, and all other work on the condominium which the developer has completed or intends to complete in a certain manner. The progress report must be filed within 30 days after completion of 80 percent of the units in the condominium or 2 years after the creation of the condominium, whichever is sooner.

CONVERSION OF RESIDENTIAL RENTAL FACILITY

Notice of Conversion

Before a residential rental facility is subject to a condominium regime, the tenant must be given a notice in the form prescribed by law. This notice is given after registration with the Secretary of State, along with the Public Offering Statement. A tenant may not be required to vacate the premises prior to the expiration of 180 days from the giving of notice. The tenant may terminate the lease without penalty for termination upon at least 30 days' written notice to the landlord.

Moving Expenses

The developer must pay tenants who choose not to purchase their units, and who meet certain income requirements, $375 when they vacate the apartments. In addition, the developer must pay for moving expenses in excess of $375, up to $750, which are actually and reasonably incurred. To receive reimbursement, the tenant must make a written request accompanied by proof of expenses within 30 days after moving. The tenant is entitled to receive reimbursement within 30 days after the request is received.

Extended Leases

The developer who converts rental facilities to a condominium must offer extended leases to qualified tenants. To qualify, a member of the tenant's household must be a handicapped or senior citizen, must be living in the tenant's unit as of the date of the notice, and must have been a member of the household for at least 12 months preceding the date of the notice. In addition, the annual income of all members of the household cannot exceed 80 percent of the applicable median income for the year. The tenant must also be current in rental payments and otherwise in good standing under the existing lease. Up to 20 percent of the units in the rental facility must be offered if there are qualified tenants, with preference given to those who rented the longest time.

Tenants receiving extended leases have the right to continue renting their residences for at least 3 years from the date of the notice. A tenant may cancel an extended lease by giving 3 months' written notice if more than 1 year remains on the lease, and 1 month's written notice if less than 1 year remains. Rents under extended lease may be increased only once a year and are limited by increases in the cost of living index.

Right of First Refusal

Where required by local law, an owner of a rental facility may not grant the rental facility to a purchaser for the purpose of subjecting it to a condominium regime unless the county, incorporated municipality, or housing agency has first been offered in writing the right to purchase the rental facility on substantially the same terms and conditions offered by the owner to the purchaser.

OWNERSHIP OF UNIT AND INTEREST IN COMMON ELEMENTS

In addition to exclusive ownership of his or her condominium unit, each unit owner has a right to share a definite percentage of the undivided interest in the common elements of the property, as set forth in the terms of the recorded declaration or master deed. The percentage is usually determined from the unit's market value at the time of creation of the condominium regime.

The unit owners' undivided interest in the common elements cannot be partitioned or separated from the unit to which the shares are assigned. However, unit owners may subdivide or consolidate units or parts of units and allocate those respective percentage interets in the common elements. This action requires the written consent of all unit owners and their mortgagees, and such consent must be evidenced by an amendment to the declaration or master deed that is properly recorded. Any removal of walls in a consolidation of units must be authorized by the council of unit owners.

The use of the common elements must be in accordance with the intended purposes stated in the recorded declaration or master deed. The declaration or master deed may state that, within seven years after the recording, a portion of the common elements may become limited common elements for the exclusive use of certain unit owners.

Co-ownership. Any condominium unit may be held and owned by one owner or by more than one person as joint tenants, tenants-in-common, or tenants by the entirety.

ORGANIZATION

The Declaration

The recorded declaration must contain at least the following items:

1 the name by which the condominium is to be identified, including or followed by the phrase "a condominium"
2 a description of the land and buildings, with a statement of the owners' intent to establish a condominium regime
3 a general description and number of each unit, its perimeters, location, and other identifying data; condos created after July 1, 1981 must be described in great detail regarding designation of unit boundaries and as to limited common elements (awnings, balconies, etc.) that are outside the unit's boundaries but allocated exclusively to the unit
4 a general description of the common elements together with a designation of any portions that are limited common elements and the units to which their use is restricted initially
5 the percentage interest appurtenant to each unit
6 the number of votes at meetings of the council of unit owners appurtenant to each unit.

Bylaws

The bylaws are required to express at least the following:

1. the form of administration, whether the council is to be incorporated, whether the council's duties may be delegated to a board of directors or manager, and what powers the owners have in their selection and removal
2. the council's mailing address
3. the procedure followed in council meetings
4. the manner of assessing and collecting unit owners' respective shares of the common expenses.

The bylaws may also contain any of the following provisions:

1. other provisions for the management and operation of the condominium, including any restrictions or requirements concerning the use and maintenance of the units and common elements
2. a provision rescinding the council meeting voting right of any unit owner who has an outstanding debt for common expenses and against whom the council has recorded a lien which has not been paid by the time of the meeting.

Unless a higher percentage is required in the bylaws, the bylaws may be amended by the affirmative vote of unit owners having at least 66-2/3 percent of the votes in the council of unit owners.

Condominium Plat

The condominium plat recorded with the declaration and bylaws should contain the following items:

1. the name of the condominium
2. a survey showing the location of all buildings
3. floor plans showing the measured dimensions, floor area, and location of each unit, and diagrams of the common elements
4. the elevation of the upper and lower boundaries of each unit.

The plat must be certified by a registered surveyor. In the declaration, a condominium developer may reserve the right for ten years to expand a condominium. When additions are made to the condominium regime, the percentages of common elements held by the old and new unit owners are adjusted appropriately. Any registered surveyor who is authorized to practice his or her profession in the State of Maryland is authorized to certify a condominium plat.

Except for such expansion plans disclosed by the developer or a court-ordered reformation, the plat can be amended only by written consent of 80 percent of unit owners listed on the current roster; all amendments must be recorded.

Termination

Unless taken by eminent domain, a condominium regime may be terminated only by agreement of at least 80 percent of the unit owners, or more if specified in the declaration.

Upon termination, and unless otherwise provided in the deed of termination, the unit owners become tenants-in-common, each owning an interest equal to the former percentage interest in the common elements.

Council of Unit Owners

The council of unit owners is made up of all unit owners. It is considered a legal entity even if unincorporated.

Meetings. A meeting of the council of unit owners must be held within 60 days from the date that 50 percent of the percentage interests in the condominium have been conveyed by the developer to the initial purchasers of units. Officers or a board of directors for the council of unit owners are to be elected, as provided in the condominium declaration or bylaws.

Voting, proxies, elections. Unit owners may vote by proxy, but the proxy is effective only for a maximum period of 180 days and may be revoked at any time at the pleasure of the issuing owner. A unit owner may nominate himself or any other unit owner to be an officer or member of the board of directors. Only nominations made at least 15 days before the notice of election are listed on the election ballot. (See details in the Condominium Act [Section 11-109].)

Records. The council of unit owners keeps the books and records. On the request of unit owners of at least 5 percent of the units, the council of unit owners is required to have an independent certified public accountant audit the books and records. The cost of the audit is considered to be a common expense. An audit need not be made more than once in any consecutive 12-month period.

Every record, including insurance policies kept by the council of unit owners, must be maintained in Maryland or within 50 miles of its borders, and must be available at some place designated by the council of unit owners within the county where the condominium is located for examination and copying by any unit owner, the owner's mortgagee, and their respective duly authorized agents or attorneys, during normal business hours, and after reasonable notice.

Rulemaking procedure. Effective July 1, 1984 new rulemaking procedures were established. These are detailed in the Condominium Act (Section 11-111), which specifically provides that the council of unit owners or the body delegated in the bylaws of a condominium may adopt rules for the condominium under certain circumstances. Provisions are made for notice, comment, voting, and appeal procedures.

Granting easements, etc. The Board of Directors may, by majority vote, grant easements, rights-of-way, licenses, leases in excess of 1 year, or similar interests for the provision of utility services or communications systems. These actions are subject to a number of requirements detailed in the Condominium Act (Sections 11-109 and 11-125).

COMMON EXPENSES, ASSESSMENTS, AND LIENS

Each unit owner is responsible for his or her percentage share of the common expenses of the council of unit owners. Assessments against unit owners for common expenses become liens on the unit when a statement of lien is recorded within two years after the assessment becomes due. This lien may be foreclosed the same as a mortgage or deed of trust if foreclosure is brought within three years of recording the lien.

A mechanic's lien for the cost of repairs, materials, or improvements made to a unit upon the individual owner's order creates a lien against that unit. A mechanic's lien arising from repairs, materials, or improvements to the common elements, authorized by the council of unit owners, attaches to each unit in proportion to its percentage of common elements. (Mechanics' liens will be discussed in Chapter 10.)

A unit owner's liability for damages that result from injuries incurred in connection with the common elements is restricted to his or her percentage interest in the common elements, lacking negligence by the owner. This also applies to liabilities incurred by the council of unit owners. A unit owner may pay the proportionate share of any judgment and be entitled to a release of his or her unit from the judgment lien.

A declaration, master deed, or bylaws providing for an annual assessment payable in regular installments may also require full payment of the remaining annual assessment by a unit owner who fails to make a payment when due. For such a demand to be enforceable, the council, within 15 days of a unit owner's failure to pay an installment, must notify the delinquent owner that failure to pay within 15 days of the notice will make due full payment of the remaining annual assessment, which will constitute a lien on the unit. This is detailed in the Condominium Act, Section 11-110.

Insurance

The council of unit owners is required to maintain property insurance on common elements and units, and comprehensive general liability insurance, including medical, in amounts set by the declaration, master deed, or council. The insurance is to be effective no later than the date of the first conveyance of a unit to anyone other than the developer, and all policies must be available for inspection. This requirement applies only to condos intended for residential use.

The bylaws may provide for insurance of the building against risks without prejudice to the rights of individual owners who wish to insure their own units. If the entire condominium is not repaired or replaced, the insurance proceeds attributable to the damaged common elements are to be used to restore the damaged area to a condition compatible with the remainder of the condominium. Insurance proceeds attributable to the units and limited common elements which are not rebuilt are to be distributed to owners of those units and the owners of the units to which the limited common elements were assigned. The remainder of the proceeds are to be distributed to all the unit owners in proportion to their percentage interests in the common elements.

Real Estate Taxation

Each unit is taxed as a separate and distinct entity on the county tax records. Tax assessments are based on the value of a unit and on its percentage interest in the common elements. Any foreclosure or sale for delinquent taxes or special assessments will involve only the unit on which taxes are delinquent. A delinquent tax on a specific unit will never affect the title to any other unit on which all taxes and assessments are paid.

Resident Agent

The developer of each condominium regime must file with the Department of Assessments and Taxation, in the same manner as now provided for corporations, and provide the name of its resident agent, who must be either a resident and citizen of Maryland or a corporation qualified to do business in the state. If the council of unit owners is incorporated, the resident agent must also be the resident agent for the corporation. Following the first annual meeting, and annually thereafter, the council must provide the Department with the names of the resident agent and managing agent, and of the officers and directors, and pay an annual fee of ten dollars.

RESALE OF UNIT

A contract for the resale of a unit by a unit owner other than a developer is not enforceable unless the contract of sale contains in conspicuous type a notice in the form specified in the Condominium Act (Section 11-135). The unit owner is required to furnish to the purchaser not later than 15 days prior to the closing (1) a copy of the declaration (other than the plat); (2) the bylaws; (3) the rules or regulations of the condominium; and (4) a certificate containing statements concerning such things as monthly expenses, proposed capital improvements, fees payable by unit owners, financial statements of the condominium, insurance coverage, etc. These contracts should contain the required clauses and disclosures to assure compliance with the Act. Some of the local boards have available for their members "Condominium Contract of Sales" and "Condominium Listing Contract." The contract of sale is voidable by the purchaser for seven days after the certificate has been provided or until conveyance of the unit has been made, whichever comes first.

TIMESHARE OWNERSHIP

A type of ownership known as timesharing is a relatively new industry that originated in Europe and has been utilized in the United States for the last ten years. The two principal kinds of timesharing are either the right-to-use method or the purchase-of-fractional-interest method. In the former, owners of interest in vacation properties, including condominiums, hotels, motels, marinas, and boats may trade their vacation periods and facilities either directly or indirectly through space banks, which are maintained by firms established to help timesharers to swap vacation facilities.

The latter kind is that which has been established in Maryland in the Ocean City and western Maryland areas, by which the customer buys a fractional interest, usually for one or two weeks, in a resort condominium on a long-term basis. The buyer receives a deed for a share of the property. Mortgages or deeds of trust are accepted for the unpaid portion of the purchase price. Contracts, settlements and all other matters are similar to purchase of a condominium unit.

In 1982, a major allegation of fraudulent practices in timesharing sales in a condominium unit in Ocean City resulted in filing of a civil suit jointly by the Maryland Real Estate Commission and the State of Maryland Consumer Protection Division, whereby a receiver was appointed to prevent complete financial disaster affecting up to 1,500 buyers (Maryland Real Estate Commission, et al. v. Seatime Associations, Inc., Circuit Court for Worcester County, Chancery No. 13,604). Some of the buyers either loaned money to the developer, were sold timeshare intervals that had already been purchased by others, or were sold units with encumbrances that prevented receipt of clear title. The Consumer Protection Division for the Attorney General of Maryland took part in the investigation and subsequent litigation.

The State Securities Commission requires that anyone offering most types of part ownership or interest in condominiums must disclose the inherent risks of such an investment. Limited-use resort securities must comply with the registration and antifraud requirements of the State Securities Act.

THE TIME-SHARING ACT

In 1984 the Maryland Real Estate Time-Sharing Act was passed, to become effective January 1, 1985. The Act provides for the creation, sale, lease, management, and termination of timeshare interests; registration of certain documents; registration of timeshare developers with the Real Estate Commission; and certain bonding requirements. Certain advertising and promotion practices are prohibited. Developers are required to prepare public offering statements describing timeshare projects that are regulated by the Secretary of State. Certain protections to purchasers are provided which include sales contract cancellation periods and disclosure of certain information, including warranties and exchange programs. Terms generally relating to timeshare interests in real estate are defined. The detailed provisions are contained in Title 11A of the Real Property article of the Annotated Code of Maryland. The following pages highlight the main points of the Act. Any licensee involved in timeshare sales or development should obtain a complete copy of the article. The 1984 edition of the Real Estate Law and Regulations booklet published by the Real Estate Commission includes this Act. Timeshare developers and persons selling timeshare estates are also subject to the provisions of the License Law as explained in Chapter 14. It is expected that the 1985 session of the Maryland General Assembly will pass legislation to correct any mistakes and inconsistencies in the Act.

Definitions in the Act

Association A nonstock corporation consisting of timeshare estate owners (as opposed to timeshare licensees). Unless all units in the project are timeshare estates, this association will be a different entity than the condominium association created under the Maryland Condominium Act.

Common elements All of the timeshare project except for the timeshare units.

Common expenses The costs of management and operation plus maintenance of the units and common elements in the timeshare project.

Conversion building A building that was occupied by any person other than the timeshare purchaser prior to the disposition of the timeshare.

Developer Any person in the business of creating or disposing of that person's timeshares in timeshare projects.

Developer control period The time during which the developer controls and manages the timeshare project.

Exchange company Any person operating an exchange program.

Exchange program Any arrangement for the exchange of occupancy rights of timeshare owners.

Facility fees Fees charged for recreational and other facilities on a per-use basis.

Managing entity The person or entity who manages the timeshare project.

Occupancy expenses The costs occasioned by use of individual timeshare units; for example, housekeeping or cleaning.

Project Real property (usually a condominium), all or a portion of which is devoted to timeshare units.

Project instrument The recordable document or documents applying to the project and containing restrictions or covenants regulating the use, occupancy, enjoyment, or disposition of units or amenities or other aspects of the timeshare project.

Purchaser Any person, other than the developer, who by means of a voluntary transfer acquires a legal or equitable interest in a timeshare other than as security for an obligation.

Sales contract Any agreement transferring the rights and obligations of the timeshare to a purchaser.

Timeshare Consists of either a timeshare estate or a timeshare license.

Timeshare estate The ownership during separated time periods, over a period of at least five years, of a timeshare unit, whether the ownership is by deed (a freehold or fee simple estate) or by lease (an estate for years).

Timeshare expenses Consists of common expenses and occupancy expenses, but does not include facilities fees.

Timeshare instrument A document that describes the timeshare.

Timeshare license The right to use or occupy one or more timeshare units over a period of at least five years, without the benefit of lease or deed. Note that the word license refers to the real property and not that of a real estate broker or salesperson.

Timeshare plan Any arrangement other than an exchange program, including membership, agreement, tenancy in common, sale, lease, license, or right to use agreement, or by any other means whereby the timeshare purchaser, in exchange for a consideration, receives a timeshare and the rights and obligations to the timeshare.

Timeshare project The portion of the project that is subject to timeshare arrangements.

Timeshare unit A unit that is subject to a timeshare arrangement.

Unit Real property, or a portion thereof, designated for separate use.

Creation

The recordation of a timeshare instrument creates a timeshare estate either as a freehold estate or an estate for years, as specified in the timeshare instrument. Each timeshare estate is considered, for the purposes of title, a separate estate or interest in the unit.

Public Offering Statement

At or prior to the execution of the sales contract, the developer or any other person in the business of selling real estate who offers timeshares for their own account must deliver to each purchaser a public offering statement. This could apply to any real estate licensee who sells his or her own timeshare.

Extensive disclosure requirements are set forth in Section 11A-112(f) of the Time-Sharing Act. The requirements for disclosure under the Time-Sharing Act differ substantially from those required under the Condominium Act. It is possible that developers of joint timeshare-condominium projects could file a single public offering statement that would satisfy the requirements of both acts.

The Time-Sharing Act provides for a fine of not more than $10,000 and 6 months imprisonment, or both, for persons convicted of providing or disseminating any false or misleading statement or for any omission of material fact in the public offering statement. Real estate licensees are cautioned to thoroughly read the public offering statement and to refrain from selling any units in the timeshare project until they are satisfied that the requirements of the Time-Sharing Act have been complied with.

Timeshare Conversions

The developer desiring to convert a building which is more than five years old into a timeshare project is required to include an engineer's report in the public offering statement, and give each tenant or subtenant at least 120 days' notice of the intention to convert the building to a timeshare project.

Cancellation Rights

Purchasers of timeshares have the right to cancel the sales contract until midnight of the tenth calendar day following whichever occurs latest: (1) the contract date; (2) the day on which the timeshare purchaser received the last of all documents required to be provided as part of the public offering statement; or (3) the timeshare unit meets all building requirements and is ready for occupancy. However, item 3 does not apply if the developer obtains a payment and performance bond from a surety to insure completion of the project as represented in the public offering statement and contract of sale and files the bond with the Commission.

The right of cancellation cannot be waived. No closing can occur until the purchaser's cancellation period has expired. If closing is held prior to the cancellation period, the closing is voidable at the option of the purchaser for a period of one year after the expiration of the cancellation period.

Resale Disclosures

An owner selling his or her timeshare is required to furnish to the purchaser before execution of the contract or transfer of title or use, (1) a copy of the timeshare instrument and (2) a resale certificate containing the information required by Section 11A-115(a) of the Time-Share Act. The purchaser may cancel the contract to purchase at any time within seven days after receipt of the resale certificate without reason and without liability. Upon cancellation, the purchaser is entitled to the return of any deposits made under the contract.

Deposits

All purchase money received by a developer from a purchaser must be deposited in an escrow account designed solely for that purpose with a financial institution whose accounts are insured by a government agency. The funds remain there until the end of the 10-day cancellation period or any later time provided for in the contract. Purchase money may be released to the developer, provided the developer maintains a surety bond for the benefit of each purchaser. No claim can be made against the Real Estate Guaranty Fund (described in Chapter 14) if the claim is covered by the surety bond.

Warranties

All timeshare units sold by developers have implied warranties of 3 years for common elements and 1 year for units. In addition, the developer must warrant to a purchaser of a timeshare that any existing use of the timeshare unit that will continue does not violate any law.

Sales Contract

Requirements for sales contracts used by developers are described in Section 11A-118, where specific language to be used in disclosing the cancellation right appears. Other information required includes the estimated completion date of the unit and each common element, and estimates of the timeshare expenses and facility fees. This is intended to disclose the total financial obligation being incurred by the purchaser.

Advertising

The advertisement of timeshares is now regulated by Section 11A-119 of the Time-Sharing Act.

Exchange Programs

The Time-Sharing Act requires detailed information concerning each exchange program the developer makes available for the purchaser's use. In order to comply with the Act (Section 11A-120), each exchange company offering an exchange program is required to file certain information with the Commission on an annual basis.

Registration with Real Estate Commission

The Time-Sharing Act (Section 11A-121) requires the developer to register with the Real Estate Commission. A developer may not offer a timeshare to the public until such time as the developer has received a certificate of registration as a timeshare developer. The developers are required to file certain documents and material with the Commission, thereby permitting the Commission to monitor the developers' compliance with the regulatory provisions the Act.

Enforcement Powers

The Time-Sharing Act (Section 11A-122) gives the Real Estate Commission the authority (1) to issue regulations and orders consistent with the Act, (2) to investigate possible violations of the Act, and subpoena witnesses and documents in connection with the investigations, (3) to bring suit against violators, (4) to order violators to correct conditions resulting from the violation, and (5) to revoke the registration of any developer who is convicted of violating the Act. In addition, the Secretary of State is authorized to adopt regulations necessary to implement and enforce the provisions of the Act pertaining to public offering statements. The Time-Sharing Act does not specifically provide for the suspension or revocation of a broker's or salesperson's license for violation of the Act. However, a violation of the Act could provide grounds for the suspension or revocation of a broker's or salesperson's license under Section 224 of Article 56, the License Law. This is discussed in Chapter 14.

Exemptions

Section 11A-123 of the Time-Sharing Act provides for certain exemptions from the requirements of registering with the Commission, preparing public offering statements, and delivering documents in the sale of timeshares. Exempt situations include (1) a gratuitous disposition; (2) a court-ordered disposition; (3) a disposition by the government; (4) a disposition by foreclosure for enforcement of a lien or security interest; (5) a disposition that may be cancelled by the purchaser at any time and for any reason without penalty; (6) a disposition of a timeshare situated outside this state and pursuant to a contract executed wholly outside this state; or (7) a disposition of a timeshare project or all timeshares to one purchaser.

Project Broker

A developer is required to designate a licensed real estate broker as project broker for each timeshare project. Each timeshare project is considered a separate real estate office for purposes of the real estate license law. Any person who sells, advertises, or offers for sale any timeshare must be a licensed broker, associate broker, or salesperson, or be exempt from licensure under the license law. An unlicensed person may be employed by a developer or project broker to contact, but not solicit, prospective buyers so long as the unlicensed person (1) performed only clerical tasks; (2) merely arranges appointments induced by others; or (3) only prepares or distributes promotional materials.

Penalties and Remedies

Remedies provided by the Time-Sharing Act are intended to fully compensate aggrieved parties. A court, upon finding that a sales contract or a clause in a contract is unconscionable, may refuse to enforce the contract. If a developer or any other person fails to comply with any provisions of the Act, punitive damages may be awarded, along with reasonable attorney's fees. Any purported conveyance, encumbrance, judicial sale, foreclosure sale, or other voluntary or involuntary transfer of a timeshare made without the use period which is part of that timeshare is void. Penalties and remedies provided by the Act are in addition to penalties and remedies available under any other law.

Conflicts of Law

In the event of any conflict with the Maryland Real Estate Time-Sharing Act and the Maryland Condominium Act, the provisions of the Time-Sharing Act prevail. This does not invalidate or otherwise affect rights or obligations vested under the Condominium Act before the effective date of the Time-Sharing Act or prior to the recording of a timeshare instrument.

QUESTIONS

1. All but which of the following forms of ownership are recognized in Maryland?

   a. tenancy-in-common
   b. community property
   c. trust
   d. ownership in severalty

2. In Maryland, a deed that conveys ownership to "Jean Tomaso and Philip Tomaso, husband and wife" but does not specify the form of ownership:

   a. automatically creates a tenancy-in-common.
   b. must be redrawn before the property is sold, specifying the form of ownership.
   c. creates a tenancy by the entirety.
   d. creates an ownership in severalty.

3. In Maryland, a tenancy by the entirety:

   a. may only be held by a husband and wife.
   b. continues after the death of one of the owners.
   c. gives an individual possession of the entire estate.
   d. may not be partitioned.

4. A timeshare developer is required to:

   a. register with the Real Estate Commission.
   b. register with the State Treasurer.
   c. register with the local board of Realtors® in the area where the timeshare units are located.
   d. be a licensed real estate broker.

5. Beverly Miller is the owner of a Baltimore condominium unit. Recently, she has become delinquent in the payment of her monthly assessments for common expenses. If she sells her unit without making these assessment payments current:

   a. she can be held liable jointly with a buyer if a lien statement is recorded prior to the sale.
   b. she can sell her unit without any possible liability.
   c. she will be guilty of a misdemeanor and will be subject to criminal prosecution.
   d. the buyer will become solely liable for the debt if the lien is recorded prior to the sale.

6. The bylaws of a condominium can be changed or altered by:

   a. the manager of property.
   b. a two-thirds vote of the unit owners.
   c. the council of unit owners by majority vote.
   d. a simple majority of unit owners.

7. A condominium declaration:

   a. must be recorded along with a copy of the project's bylaws and condominium plat in order to place the property under a condominium regime.
   b. cannot be rescinded once it is recorded.
   c. can be changed with the unanimous approval of the council of unit owners.
   d. must be printed in a daily newspaper before changes may be made.

8. Co-owners have the right to terminate their co-ownership of Maryland real estate by a suit for partition if they are:

   a. tenants-in-common.
   b. tenants by the entirety.
   c. joint tenants.
   d. a and c are correct

9. A developer selling a newly built condominium unit to an original purchaser:

   a. is liable for damages as a result of misleading statements for five years after the sale.
   b. is subject to the seller voiding the contract if the developer fails to deliver a Public Offering Statement.
   c. is protected by the doctrine of caveat emptor from liability for misleading statements.
   d. must file a Public Offering Statement with the Maryland Real Estate Commission.

10. Purchasers of timeshares:

   a. have a right to cancel the contract only if the seller has misrepresented material facts.
   b. have ten days in which to cancel the sale for any reason.
   c. must close the sale within ten days after signing the sale contract.
   d. must obtain a payment and performance bond to assure their compliance with the contract.

9

Legal Descriptions

In Maryland, land may be described by any of the following types of legal description, all of which are discussed in the text:

1 a metes and bounds description
2 a survey of the particular property, prepared by a licensed surveyor or engineer
3 a recorded plat of subdivision.

Note that, in Maryland, a street address or postal address alone is not normally an adequate legal description of real estate; a description which identifies land with "reasonable certainty" is required.

EXAMPLES OF LEGAL DESCRIPTIONS

Examples of the types of descriptions for use in contracts are as follows:

1 "That part of lot 8 of Block A of Honeysuckle Hills subdivision (recorded in FWH Liber 267, Folio 1769) beginning at the southwest corner of said lot 8, thence northerly along the westerly line of lot 8 a distance of 50 feet, thence southerly parallel with the westerly line of said lot 8 to Wolf Road, thence westerly along the northerly line of Wolf Road to the place of beginning." (See the plat on page 40).

2 "That certain parcel of real estate located in Worcester County, Maryland, being on the east side of Farm Lane, north of Jerry Road, being further known as the Arthur R. Jackson property, consisting of one acre, more or less, with the improvements thereon, previously conveyed by deed of Robert Allen, grantor, recorded in FWH Liber 29, Folio 1312, the exact boundaries and acreage to be determined by means of a survey, which has been ordered to be prepared by Johnson and Landsman, surveyors, Snow Hill."

3 "Lot #16, Block #3 of the Plat of Melvale Development Corporation as surveyed by John Walmer, Catonsville, Maryland, August 15, 1968, as recorded in FWH Liber 295, Folio 1720 in the County of Ridge, State of Maryland."

Plat of Honeysuckle Hills Subdivision

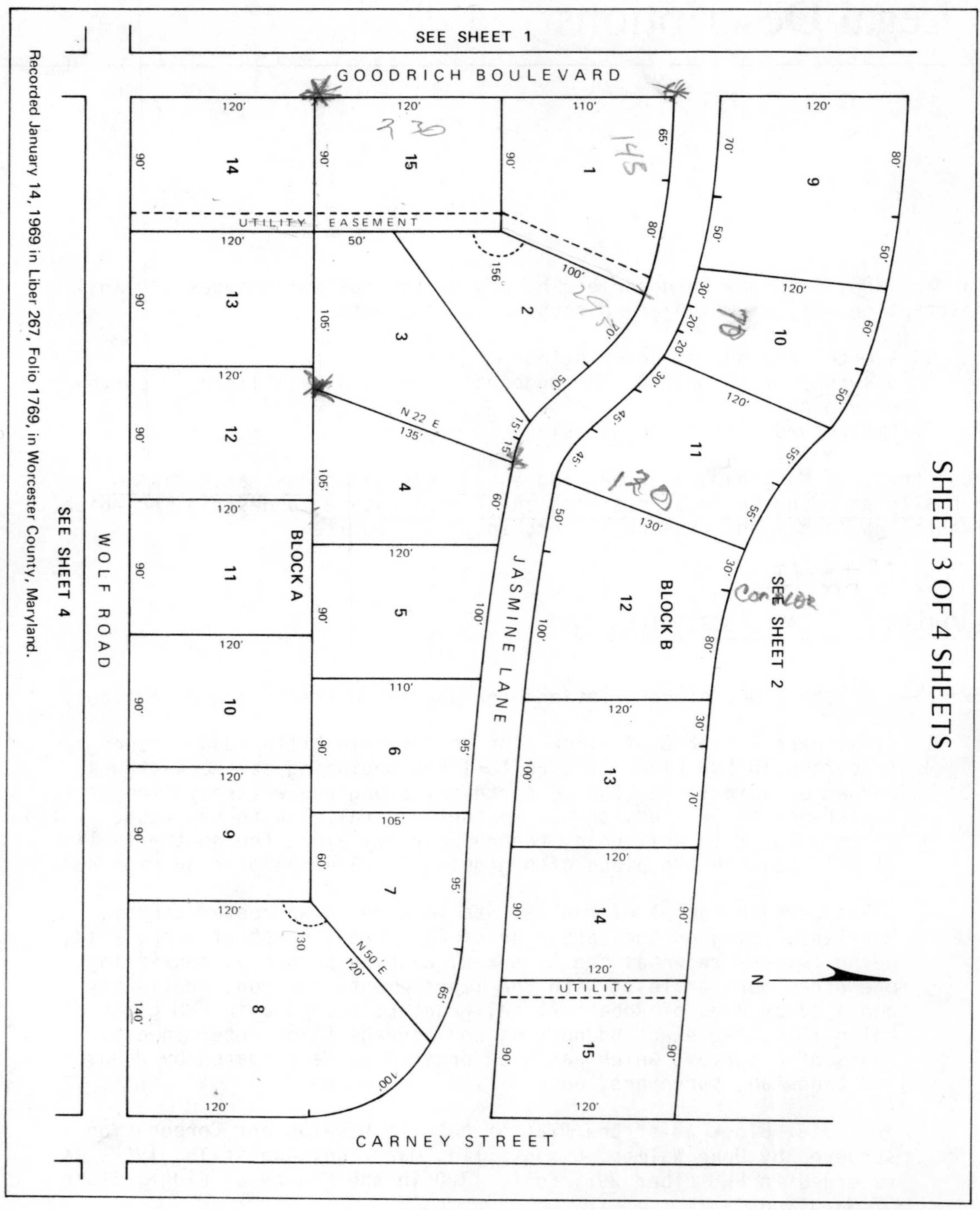

Grantor-Grantee Index

In Maryland, land is never indexed in the public records according to its legal description. The real estate records of each county (and Baltimore City) are indexed by the names of the grantor and grantee. All references to previously recorded conveyances should include not only the liber and folio (book and page) number, but also the name of the grantor and/or the grantee. This index is discussed in more detail in Chapter 13 of this supplement.

Survey Markers

Any person who willfully obliterates, damages, or removes any stake, marker, monument, or other landmark set in property by any civil engineer, surveyor, or real estate appraiser or assistant, except if the marker interferes with the proper use of the property, is guilty of a misdemeanor and on conviction can be fined not more than $500.

If there is a dispute over any boundary line or if the bounds mentioned in a document are lost, on the petition of any interested party, the circuit court of the county where the property is located may establish the boundary lines or the location of the missing bounds. Engineers, surveyors, or other experts may be appointed by the court to assist the court in its determination. The experts' fees are considered costs in the proceeding.

SUBDIVISION PLATS

Subdividers and developers of land must comply carefully with state and local laws regarding the approval of subdivisions. Subdivision plats must be prepared by licensed surveyors or engineers and must be submitted to local authorities, as well as to the planning commission, if requested, having jurisdiction. A subdivision plat cannot be recorded without being properly approved; failure to comply with the approval and recordation of subdivision plats not only may subject an offending subdivider to criminal penalties and punishment, but also to civil penalties, whereby a buyer may sue for damages or have the transaction set aside.

A plat of a subdivision of land may not be recorded without written approval of the planning commission or other appropriate official.

QUESTIONS

1. A legal description in Maryland:

   a. is written according to the rectangular survey system.
   b. consists of the street or mailing address of the property.
   c. consists of the lot and block number or metes and bounds.
   d. consists of the box number.

2. In Maryland, subdivision plats:

   a. are an adequate form of legal description if properly recorded.
   b. must be prepared by licensed surveyors or engineers.
   c. need not be recorded prior to sale of the lots.
   d. need not have planning and zoning approval prior to recording.

Answer questions 3-6 using the information given on the plat of Honeysuckle Hills on page 25.

3. Which of the following statements is true?

   a. Lot 9, Block A is larger than Lot 12 in the same block.
   b. The plat for the lots on the southerly side of Wolf Road between Goodrich Boulevard and Carney Street is found on Sheet 3.
   c. Lot 8, Block A has the most frontage on Wolf Road.
   d. Utility easements are located on eight lots.

4. Which of the following lots has the most frontage on Jasmine Lane?

   a. Lot 10, Block B
   b. Lot 11, Block B
   c. Lot 1, Block A
   d. Lot 2, Block A

5. "Beginning at the intersection of the east line of Goodrich Boulevard and the south line of Jasmine Lane and running south along the east line of Goodrich Boulevard a distance of 230 feet; thence easterly parallel to the north line of Wolf Road a distance of 195 feet; thence northeasterly on a course of N 22 E a distance of 135 feet; and thence northwesterly along the south line of Jasmine Lane to the point of beginning." Which lots are described here?

   a. Lots 13, 14, and 15, Block A
   b. Lots 9, 10, and 11, Block B
   c. Lots 1, 2, 3, and 15, Block A
   d. Lots 7, 8, and 9, Block A

6. On the plat, how many lots have easements?

   a. one
   b. two
   c. three
   d. four

10

Real Estate Taxes and Other Liens

GENERAL (AD VALOREM) TAX

Maryland property taxes are levied by and for the support of state, county, and city governments, as well as local special taxing districts. Taxes are levied for the taxable year from July 1 through June 30, and are paid in advance. Payment dates are set by each county, but taxes are generally due on or after July 1. Many counties allow specified discounts to taxpayers who make payment prior to October 1.

Real estate tax bills are issued by local county and municipal authorities; one bill is issued for each taxable parcel of real estate. The bill indicates the amount of state tax and also county or local tax, which includes taxes for schools, sanitary districts, and all other local taxing bodies. Tax rates are usually stated as so much per $100 of assessed value, such as "$3.10 per $100 of assessed valuation."

In some communities, special taxing districts have been authorized. For example, a small rural community located on a river or bay may receive permission to build a special bulkhead or retaining wall because of a serious erosion problem. After the wall is completed, this community may set up a special taxing district and levy an annual special tax for the maintenance of this bulkhead. A tax levied by such a special taxing district would be the third kind of tax that is assessed by a local taxing body and may appear on the real estate tax bill. The licensee should be aware of this third type of tax, since many times it is overlooked in a real estate transaction or omitted on the real estate tax bill. The property owner must be aware that he or she is responsible for all taxes.

Assessment

Real property is assessed for tax purposes by the state's Department of Assessments and Taxation. There are local offices of the department in each Maryland county, as well as in Baltimore City; each is under the control of a Supervisor of Assessments.

Method of assessment. The procedure for assessing property in Maryland, commonly called triennial assessment, is based on a three-year cycle in which one-third of all property is reviewed every year for tax purposes.

Each county has been organized into three principal assessing areas to coincide with each year of the assessment cycle. The areas generally have similar density and common characteristics, and they are reviewed on a rotating basis. By the end of a three-year period, all properties will have been physically reviewed and valued once, then a new cycle commences. An inspection of the exterior premises always accompanies a revaluation. Note that if changes in zoning or use occur, or if additions or extensive improvements to property have been made, the property can be revalued out of sequence.

Assessments are based upon estimates of the market value of property, which under Maryland law is known as the full cash value. Land is assessed separately from its improvements (for tax purposes, improvements refer only to buildings and structures permanently attached to the land, and not to recent alterations, modifications, or modernization of an existing structure). Estimating is completed each year by January 1, often referred to as the date of finality. Although assessments become final on this date, they can be adjusted through appeal (as will be discussed later in the chapter).

Growth factor. Although assessments are based on the full cash value of a property, in fact they are equal to only a fraction of it. Generally, this amounts to less than one-half of the full cash value. The assessment is reached by multiplying the property's full cash value by the year's growth factor.

The growth factor, which varies from year to year, was enacted to limit growth in the statewide assessable base to no more than six percent per year. Each year's growth factor is determined by dividing the year's updated statewide assessable base by the full cash value of all taxable real estate. For example, in 1984, the state growth factor equaled 43.5 percent. The State Department of Assessments and Taxation must determine the statewide growth rate while local governments are responsible for setting actual property tax rates. These vary among the counties.

Phase-in-provision. A real property assessment is further controlled by a phase-in-provision, designed to take some of the financial sting out of inflation. Of the one-third of all real properties reassessed in a particular year, one one-third of any increase in value is added in that year, with the balance being added in equal increments over the next two years in the three-year cycle. For example, a property increasing in value from $50,000 to $56,000 would have a value for tax purposes of $52,000 the first year, $54,000 the second year, and $56,000 the third year.

Notice of reassessment. If upon completion of the triennial review the value of a property is found to have increased, the owner is sent a notice of reassessment. When no increase occurs, no notice is sent. The assessment notice shows the property's assessment for the next three years; no other notice is sent until the new cycle begins three years later. The notice includes the following information:

1 the previous assessment and the previous full cash value
2 the phased-in amount and the assessment for the next taxable year
3 the new (proposed) full cash value
4 the full cash value for the second and third years of the cycle and the projected assessments for the next two years
5 the separate values assigned to the land and to the improvements on the land.

Assessment appeals. A taxpayer who feels that his or her assessment is improper must take the following actions in order to appeal it:

1 The taxpayer must reply to the taxing authority concerning the assessment within 45 days of the date of the notice. A hearing will then be scheduled, and the taxpayer will be required to appear at the local asssessment office.
2 The taxpayer must appear at the hearing, an informal meeting between the homeowner and the local assessment officials, to present his or her objections. By the same token, the local assessor will be given an opportunity to explain how the valuation in question was determined.
3 After reviewing the facts concerning the valuation, the assessor will send the taxpayer a final notice of assessment, which represents the official decision of the assessor's office in the matter.
4 If the homeowner is still dissatisfied, he or she may appeal the decision to the Property Tax Assessment Appeal Board within 30 days of the final notice of assessment.
5 A final hearing will then be held in which both the homeowner and the assessor will present relevant information to the appeals board. After considering the facts, the board will reach a final decision and inform the property owner.
6 If the homeowner is still dissatisfied at this point, he or she may appeal the matter further to the Maryland Tax Court and then, if necessary, through the state judicial system.

Constant Yield Tax Rate Provision

Although the setting of local property tax rates is the task of elected officials, Maryland's constant yield tax rate provision guarantees property owners a voice in the process. This is done through advance notification and the holding of public meetings in each taxing jurisdiction prior to rate-setting. Property tax rates are determined before every July 1 by each local taxing authority. Meetings are required if local officials propose a higher tax rate than the constant yield tax rate.

Under the constant yield concept, the tax rate diminishes as assessments rise, so the revenue derived from the property tax stays at a constant level from one year to the next. Prior to February 15 of each year, the Department of Assessments and Taxation notifies the counties, Baltimore City, and the other separate taxing authorities what the tax rate should be to maintain revenue from the property tax at last year's level. The new rates, referred to as the constant yield tax rates, are computed on the basis of the new, adjusted assessable base for each jurisdiction. The constant yield figures are subject to later adjustments through actions of appeals, etc. New property appearing on the roles for the first time is excluded in the calculation. Also, allowances for contingencies are deducted, giving local governments a built-in cushion.

Local taxing authorities cannot increase the tax rate to the point that it exceeds the constant yield tax rate until they advertise their intent to do so. The taxing authority may, at its option, mail a copy of the notice to each taxpayer instead of publishing an advertisement. Nothing prevents the local taxing authorities from reducing the tax rate or setting one that is lower than the constant yield tax rate.

Most counties have separate taxing jurisdictions, towns, and other special taxing authorities within them, which, if not taken into consideration, can lead to distorted interpretations. Caroline, for example, has ten towns within its boundary which levy an additional tax rate. Baltimore City and Baltimore County each have but one tax rate for their entire jurisdictions; while Frederick, Montgomery, and Prince George's Counties have numerous municipal and special taxing authorities within their boundaries.

Two counties, Anne Arundel and Harford, have two county tax rates. Anne Arundel has one for the county at large and another for property located within the city limits of Annapolis. Harford has one rate for the county at large and another for property located within Aberdeen, Bel Air, and Havre de Grace. When municipal and other local tax rates exist, they must be considered along with the county rate to make a fair comparison.

The following is a listing of the 1984/85 actual tax rates and the 1984/85 constant yield tax rates. The average local property tax for the state as a whole for 1984/85 remained at $2.38, the same as 1983/84. The state property tax rate for 1984/85, which is not subject to the constant yield tax rate provision, remained the same as 1983/84, at 21 cents per $100 of assessed valuation.

1984 PROPERTY TAX RATES

County	Constant Yield Tax Rate	Actual
Allegany	$2.36	$2.56
Anne Arundel	2.52	2.68
Baltimore	2.88	3.125
Baltimore City	5.67	6.00
Calvert	1.89	1.96
Caroline	1.98	2.31
Carroll	1.93	2.08
Cecil	2.50	2.65
Charles	2.13	2.30
Dorchester	2.14	2.24
Frederick	2.12	2.25
Garrett	2.69	2.68
Harford	2.60	2.73
Howard	2.43	2.54
Kent	1.90	2.00
Montgomery	2.10	2.06
Prince George's	2.42	2.43
Queen Anne's	1.91	2.00
St. Mary's	1.86	1.99
Somerset	1.82	1.90
Talbot	1.18	1.18
Washington	1.94	2.05
Wicomico	1.74	1.78
Worcester	1.44	1.51

PROPERTY TAX CREDITS

Homestead Tax Credit

A 15-percent homestead credit protects owner-occupied residences from inflation. It provides a credit if an assessment on a dwelling increases by more than 15 percent over the previous year. The credit equals the amount of the reassessment that exceeds 15 percent, and applies if the following conditions were met during the previous calendar year:

1 The property was not transferred.
2 The increase in value did not come about as a result of a change in zoning classification.
3 No substantial change occurred in the use of the property.
4 No extensive improvements were made.
5 The previous year's assessment was not clearly erroreous.

In addition, the dwelling must be the owner's principal residence for more than six months of a 12-month period (unless the dweller is ill or otherwise in need of special care).

Generally, the taxing authority will include the tax credit in calculating the property tax bill. If it has not been deducted, however, the owner may apply to the taxing authority and request that it either be credited or deducted from the tax bill.

"Circuit Breaker" Tax Credit

Since the 15 percent homestead credit discussed above does not help a homeowner on a fixed income with a rising assessment that is substantial but less than 15 percent, the state legislature devised what is popularly known as the "circuit breaker."

Credits for homeowners. The plan provides a property tax credit not to exceed $1,200 to any homeowner who applies, regardless of age. The tax credit is equal to the amount of the total real property taxes in excess of a percentage of the homeowner's gross income. The percentage is 0.75 percent of the first $4,000 of combined income, 3.5 percent of the next $4,000, 5.5 percent of the next $4,000, 7.5 percent of the next $4,000, and 9.0 percent of all combined income over $16,000.

To qualify for a tax credit, a homeowner's net worth cannot exceed $200,000, as of December 31 of the calendar year preceding the year in which the application is made. If the amount of the tax credit calculated is less than $1, no credit is allowed for that year.

Credits for renters. Effective June 1, 1983, a renter 60 years of age or disabled, upon application to the State Department of Assessments and Taxation, is eligible for property tax relief from rent paid, which consists of payment of a portion of the assumed real property tax included in the occupancy rent paid by the renter. The payment cannot exceed $450, and must be equal to the amount of assumed real property tax included in occupancy rent that is in excess of a percentage of the gross income, or combined income, of the renter. The percentages of income that cannot be exceeded are the same as those for homeowners, as is the maximum net worth of $200,000.

Application. Homeowners must apply for the tax credit no later than September 1 of the taxable year in which the tax credit is sought on a standard form provided by the Department of Taxation and Assessments. If the application has not been made on or before September 1, the tax credit may not be allowed.

Credit for dwellings and commercial property. Effective July 1, 1983, the owner of an unsold and unrented single dwelling unit or commercial property that is newly constructed or substantially rehabilitated may be entitled to a tax credit not exceeding the property taxes on the improvements. The credit applies to the unsold or unrented period immediately following construction or substantial rehabilitation. Tax credits are for one continuous period of time, but not exceeding one year.

Enterprise Zones

A state enterprise zone program offering tax breaks and low-interest loans to businesses that locate in designated high-unemployment areas was enacted by the 1982 General Assembly. Each year six such zones are to be established in pockets of poverty or joblessness throughout the state.

CORPORATION FRANCHISE TAX

Most corporations are taxed annually on their franchise or right to do business in the State of Maryland. The annual tax is $40; it becomes a general lien on the property or the corporation and can be enforced against it. When a broker files for a real estate license and the brokerage is a corporation, the Real Estate Commission requires that a copy of the brokerage's Articles of Incorporation be filed also.

PROPERTY TAX ASSESSMENT, AGRICULTURAL USE

Lands that are actively devoted to farm or agricultural use are assessed on the basis of such use and are not assessed as if subdivided. The State's Department of Assessments and Taxation establishes criteria for the purpose of determining whether land qualifies for assessment as agricultural use. These include:

1 zoning applicable to land;
2 present and past use of the land, including land under federal soil bank provisions;
3 productivity of the land, including timberlands and lands used for reforestation;
4 gross income derived from the agricultural activity.

In identifying bona fide farms, the Department may, in the instance of parcels of less than 20 acres, require the property owner to certify that agricultural activity results in an average annual gross income of $2,500, defined as the average of the two highest years of annual gross income during a three-year period. The income requirement may be waived under certain specific circumstances.

Agricultural Transfer Tax

Maryland adopted, effective July 1, 1981, the Agricultural Transfer Tax to replace the Agricultural Development Tax that had been in effective since July, 1979. The Agricultural Transfer Tax is calculated by the Assessments Office and is payable at the time the property transfer takes place. Details are discussed in Chapter 12.

DELINQUENCY

Taxes are due July 1 each year. Taxes that are not paid by October 1 are considered delinquent, bear interest as provided by law, and are subject to a real estate tax sale held by the county treasurer. The dates and rules regarding such sales are generally made by each county. Tax-delinquent properties that are sold at a tax sale are not conveyed immediately to the buyer. There is a one-year period of redemption during which the delinquent taxpayer may attempt to raise funds to redeem the property and pay the county treasurer the amount of the delinquent tax, plus the accumulated interest in penalty. If no redemption is made during the one-year period, the tax buyer may apply to the court for the issuance of a deed to the property.

Rate of Redemption for Tax Sales

The rate of redemption established by law for properties sold by the tax collector when certain taxes are in arrears is six percent per annum except as follows:

1 in Baltimore City, the rate is six percent per annum or as fixed by ordinance of the City Council;
2 in Calvert County, the rate is 10 percent per annum or as fixed by ordinance of the County Commissioners;
3 in Frederick and Kent Counties, the rate is six percent per annum or as fixed by the County Commissioners;
4 in Harford, Howard, Prince George's, Montgomery, Anne Arundel, and Baltimore Counties, the rate is six percent per annum or as fixed by resolution of the County Councils;
5 in Somerset, Wicomico, and Worcester Counties, the rate is six percent per annum or as fixed by the County Commissioners, or by resolution of the County Council.

LIENS

Mechanics' Liens

Mechanics' liens, as discussed in the text, are provided by state law to protect the rights of contractors, suppliers, and other persons engaged to improve real estate. After the completion of work, a contractor or supplier has six months in which to record a notice of his or her lien. The contractor or supplier then has one year from the date of recording in which to petition the courts to enforce the lien in the event the petition was not included when the lien was recorded.

Unperformed contracts (executory contracts) relating to construction, alteration, or repair of a building, structure, or improvement may not contain a provision that waives or requires the subcontractor to waive the right to claim a mechanic's lien or sue on a contractor's bond. A contract containing such a waiver provision in violation of the law is void.

Buyers purchasing properties that have been recently improved or constructed should seek protection against possible outstanding mechanics' liens. In the usual purchase of real estate, the attorney for the buyer will have the responsibility to see that the property being purchased is free from unpaid taxes, mechanics' liens, or other outstanding liens.

Release of Lien

When a lien on real property is satisfied, the lienholder is required to mail or deliver a release of the lien within seven days after receiving payment. The release may be in the form of the original note, marked paid or cancelled. If the lienholder fails to provide such a release after demand by the payor, the payor may bring action in the circuit court of the county where the property is located. In such an action, the lienholder or his or her agent may be liable for delivery of the release, as well as all costs and expenses of the action.

QUESTIONS

1. In Maryland, real estate tax bills are NOT issued by:

   a. cities.
   b. counties.
   c. special taxing districts.
   d. the state.

2. All real property in Maryland:

   a. is reassessed for tax purposes each year.
   b. is assessed for tax purposes based on the property's full cash value.
   c. is reassessed for tax purposes every three years.
   d. is reassessed at time of resale.

3. Which of the following statements about real property assessments is incorrect?

   a. The value of land is considered separately from the property's improvements.
   b. Assessments are reduced by the statewide growth factor.
   c. Assessments may be appealed within 45 days after receiving a notice of reassessment.
   d. The Maryland date of finality is October 1 of each year.

4. Peter and Ellen McCarver own a contracting firm in Maryland. On February 1, 1981, Sis Kelly hires the McCarver firm to construct a room addition to her two-bedroom house. The McCarvers finished work on the project on March 15; it is now April 15 and the McCarvers have not yet been paid. Based on this situation, which of the following is correct?

   a. The McCarvers have until August 1 to record a notice of lien.
   b. The McCarvers have until August 1 to enforce their mechanic's lien.
   c. The McCarvers have until September 15 to record their mechanic's lien.
   d. The McCarvers have until October 15 to enforce their mechanic's lien.

5. Taxes on real property:

   a. are levied by one taxing authority.
   b. are due July 1 of each year in Maryland.
   c. are due January 1 of each year in Maryland.
   d. are set every three years.

6. A house has an assessed value of $35,500. If the tax rate is $4.10 per $100 of assessed value, what is the amount of the tax?

   a. $1,455.50
   b. $ 145.55
   c. $865.85
   d. $ 86.58

7. The Martens' residence is assessed at $24,000. Last year they paid $840 in real estate taxes. This year the tax rate is being raised by $.25 per $100 of assessed value above the rate for the previous year. There is no change in the amount of the assessment. The Martens' tax bill for this year will be:

   a. $920.
   b. $900.
   c. $880.
   d. $850.

8. This year Carole Smothers paid $1,631 in real estate taxes. If the tax rate was $3.50 per $100 of assessed value, what is the assessed value of Carole's property?

   a. $30,000
   b. $32,500
   c. $42,500
   d. $46,600

9. How much tax will Fritz Howard pay this year if his house is valued at $22,500 and the tax rate is $2.40 per $100 of assessed value:

   a. $700.
   b. $680.
   c. $650.
   d. $540.

10. A general lien is a charge against:

   a. any and all property of the debtor, real and personal.
   b. only the parcel of property described in the tax bill, mortgage or other lien document.
   c. any and all real property of the debtor.
   d. any and all personal property of the debtor.

11

Real Estate Contracts

REQUIREMENTS FOR A VALID CONTRACT

The five essential elements of a valid contract described in the text are all applicable in Maryland.

Capacity to Contract

Under Maryland law, a person reaches majority and has the capacity to enter into a valid real estate contract at the age of 18. However, a minor who is married to a person who has reached the age of majority may enter into valid real estate contracts jointly with his or her spouse. As discussed in the text, a minor's contracts are generally voidable within a reasonable time after he or she reaches the age of majority. Note, however, that a contract not beneficial to a minor is considered by state law to be void.

Statute of Frauds

According to the Statute of Frauds, all contracts for the sale of real estate must be in writing and signed by the party sought to be charged, in order for the agreement to be enforceable. The Statute of Frauds is not applicable to a leasehold estate of one year or less. Written offers may be on the standard form of a sales contract used by the broker or on another type of purchase agreement.

Oral agreements. Note that, in Maryland, oral contracts (sometimes called parol agreements) are legal and valid as between the parties, but oral contracts for the sale of land are unenforceable in a court of law; sales for other than land may be enforced by the courts. State statutes hold that every corporeal estate or incorporeal interest in land created by parol (oral agreement) and not in writing will have only the force and effect of an estate at will. (This does not apply, however, in the case of a leasehold estate for three years or less.) Estates at will are discussed in Chapter 16 of the text and supplement.

Alterations to Contract

Any alterations or changes to a contract must be agreed to by buyers and sellers. Agreement may be shown by initialling and dating the alteration or change on the contract itself or by preparing an addendum or amendment to the contract and having the buyers and sellers sign. A sample amendment form is reproduced in this chapter.

In making changes or alterations to contracts, typewritten changes will prevail over printing, and handwritten changes will prevail over typewritten changes.

CONTRACTS FOR THE SALE OF REAL ESTATE

Contracts of Sale are made up of various clauses intended to protect the interests of the parties to the contract. The contract shown beginning on the facing page, a form recommended by the Maryland Association of Realtors®, consists of basic clauses that are a part of the contract itself; in addition, optional addendum clauses are shown separately. These may be inserted into a contract as they apply. Note: no responsibility is assumed for legal sufficiency or effect, either as to substance or form.

Required Clauses

Certain laws require that specific information be disclosed in contracts. These clauses are contained in the sample contract and discussed below.

Agricultural assessment. Sales contracts for agriculturally assessed land must, by law, contain a notice similar to Addendum clause 22.

Guaranty fund recovery. Real estate brokers must include a notice that the purchaser is protected by the Real Estate Guarantee Fund for not more than $25,000 (see Chapter 14). Clause 24 in the sample contract conforms to one suggested by the Attorney General's office.

Prohibited conditions of settlement. Article 56, Section 227C prohibits requiring that buyers of single family dwellings employ a particular title insurance, settlement, or escrow company or title attorney. Each contract must contain, in bold type, the notice in Contract clause 12.

The Real Estate Commission may revoke the license of any broker or salesperson who fails to inform the buyers of their rights.

Disclosure of water and sewer charges. In Maryland, all contracts for the sale of improved residential real property must disclose the estimated cost of any deferred water and sewer charges for which the purchaser may become liable. Addendum clause 18 is a version for first sale of new or owner-built construction.

Agent as seller. A real estate licensee may not act as a seller or purchaser of real estate without giving the other party notification of the licensee's professional status.

(Text continues on page 66.)

THIS IS A LEGALLY BINDING CONTRACT; IF NOT UNDERSTOOD, SEEK COMPETENT ADVICE.

AGREEMENT OF SALE

1. THIS AGREEMENT OF SALE, made this ______________ day of ______________, 19_____, by and between ______________________________________ (Seller) and ______________________________________ (Purchaser).

2. The seller sells and the Purchaser buys the following described property located in Tax Assessment/Election District ______________ County/City, being all/part of that property conveyed to Seller herein by deed recorded in Liber______, Folio______, among the land records of ______________ County, Maryland, and being further described as Lot____, Block______, Section______, in subdivision of ______________________/ (containing______________ acres more or less as shown on Tax Map Page__________, Parcel No.________), and being known as ______________________; together with all improvements thereon and all rights and appurtenances thereto. Included in the purchase price shall be all fuel oil, if any, stored on the property at time of settlement, all permanently attached fixtures and the number of installed operating smoke detectors required by law. The purchase price shall also include the following, as and if now installed in or on the premises: central heating, central air conditioning, plumbing, lighting fixtures, garbage disposal, built-in dishwasher, range and oven, refrigerator, screens, storm/insulated windows and doors, shades, curtain rods, TV antenna, wall-to-wall carpeting, portable outbuildings, awnings, trees, shrubbery and plants. Also included shall be the following: ______________ ______________________________________. The following shall be excluded from the purchase price and shall remain the personal property of Seller: ______________________________________.

3. PURCHASE PRICE is ______________________________________ Dollars ($__________) payable as follows: ______________________ Dollars ($__________) in the form of ______________________ on signing this Agreement and an additional deposit of ______________________ Dollars ($__________) in the form of ______________ on or before ______________ 19_____, said sum or sums to be deposited by Purchaser with ______________________, Broker, and to be held by the Broker in escrow until the time of final settlement and disbursed in accordance with the provisions of this Agreement at settlement or upon default. Failure of the Purchaser to pay the additional deposit as specified may, at the option of the Seller, render this Agreement null and void and of no further legal effect and cause forfeiture of any deposit paid.

The Balance of ______________________________________ Dollars ($__________) to be paid in cash or certified check at the time of settlement.

4. FINANCING CONTINGENCY. This Agreement is contingent upon the Purchaser's ability to place ( ), assume ( ), conventional ( ), VA ( ), FHA ( ), or ______________ First Mortgage or Deed of Trust in the amount of ______________________ Dollars ($__________) with interest at ______________ percent (________%) per annum, or, if VA financing, the maximum prevailing rate at the time of settlement, for a period of__________ years, amortized over a period of ______________ years.

5. MORTGAGE APPLICATION. Purchaser expressly agrees to make written application for the mortgage as herein described within ______________ ( ) banking days from the date hereof. Purchaser further agrees to execute such mortgage at settlement if the loan commitment therefor is granted by the mortgagee. Any action by the Purchaser concerning the execution of this Agreement of Sale resulting in the disqualification of the Purchaser for financing purposes as herein prescribed, including, without limitation, misrepresentation by the Purchaser in the Credit Application, failure to apply for such financing and pursue the same diligently, or application for a mortgage upon said terms in any respect different from those as to principal and interest set forth above shall constitute a default on the part of the Purchaser under the terms of this Agreement and the Seller may terminate the Agreement and declare the deposit hereinabove described forfeited. If such mortgage commitment is not obtained by the Purchaser, or by the Seller for the Purchaser, within ______________ ( ) days from the date of this Agreement, this Agreement of Sale may, at the option of the Purchaser, become null and void and of no further legal effect, and all monies on deposit shall be returned to the Purchaser and neither party shall have any liability to the other. Notice of such termination shall be given in writing by the Purchaser to the Seller, however, the Purchaser may elect to proceed with settlement notwithstanding the failure to obtain the mortgage commitment herein described.

6. ALTERNATE FINANCING. It is further understood and agreed that should the Purchaser make application for financing through a lending institution or other source whereby the interest, terms of payment, amount of loan, or any one of these differs from the financing conditions set forth above, upon notification to the Purchaser from the lending institution or party that the financing as requested has been approved and a loan commitment granted, the financing contingency of this Agreement shall be deemed to have been fully satisfied and of no further effect, provided the alternate mortgage does not increase costs to the Seller, or exceed the time allowed to secure the mortgage commitment as called for above.

7. LOAN FEES. If a new loan is to be placed pursuant to this Agreement, the Purchaser agrees to pay a loan origination fee of ____________ percent (_____%) of the principal sum of ANY CONVENTIONAL LOAN. The Seller agrees to pay a loan placement fee of ___________ percent (________%) of the principal sum of said loan. Lender's Fees, if any, shall be paid by the Purchaser, including mortgage insurance premiums as required by the lender. If the existing loan is to be assumed, the Purchaser agrees to pay any loan assumption fees, charges, or expenses required by the lender.

8. SETTLEMENT. Settlement shall be on ________________________________, 19_____, or sooner by mutual agreement of the parties.

9. TIME being of the essence of this Agreement.

10. AGENCY. The seller recognizes ____________________________________, Broker, as the listing broker negotiating this Agreement and agrees to pay said Broker a brokerage fee for services rendered in the amount provided for in the listing agreement.

The party making settlement is hereby authorized and directed to deduct the aforesaid brokerage fee from the proceeds of sale and pay the same to the Broker as a convenience to the Seller and not as a limitation upon Seller's liability to pay a commission. Settlement shall not be a condition precedent to Seller's liability for the brokerage fee.

11. ADDENDUMS. The attached addendums bearing the signatures of all parties concerned is hereby made a part of this Agreement and shall be construed to govern over any inconsistent portion of this printed form. ADDENDUM ATTACHED ________ YES ________ NO

12. SETTLEMENT COSTS. PURCHASER SHALL BE ENTITLED TO SELECT HIS/HER OWN TITLE COMPANY, SETTLEMENT COMPANY, ESCROW COMPANY OR TITLE ATTORNEY. The Purchaser will _____ will not _______ (strike one) select title insurance, settlement, or escrow company or employ his own title attorney. In either event, Purchaser authorizes the listing broker to order the examination of title and preparation of all necessary conveyancing papers and agree to pay all costs on account thereof including settlement charges subject to any statutory restrictions, conveyancing, notary fees, recordation taxes, tax certificate, survey where required, lender's fees and recording charges except those incident to clearing existing encumbrances.

Documentary stamps and transfer taxes required by law shall be paid by the Purchaser and Seller equally.

13. DEED AND TITLE. Upon payment as above provided of the unpaid purchase money, the Seller agrees to execute, at his expense, and deliver to the Purchaser a good and sufficient deed for the property, containing covenants of special warranty and further assurances. Title to the subject property is to be good and merchantable, free of liens and encumbrances except as provided herein and except: use and occupancy restrictions of public record which are generally applicable to properties in the immediate neighborhood or subdivision in which the property is located, and publicly recorded easements for public utilities and any other easements which may be observed by an inspection of the property. Purchaser hereby expressly assumes the risk that restrictive covenants, zoning laws or other recorded documents may restrict or prohibit the use of the property for the purpose(s) intended by the Purchaser.

In the event the Seller is unable to give good and merchantable title or such as can be insured by a Maryland licensed title company, with Purchaser paying not more than the regular rate; the seller, at its expense, shall have the option of curing any defect so as to enable Seller to give good and merchantable title or of paying any special premium on behalf of the Purchaser to obtain title insurance on the property to the benefit of the Purchaser. In the event the Seller elects to cure any defects in title, this Agreement shall continue to remain in full force and effect and the date of settlement shall be extended for a period not to exceed thirty (30) additional days. In the event Seller is unable to cure such title defects within thirty (30) days and is unable to obtain a policy of insurance on the property to the benefit of the Purchaser by a Maryland licensed title company, the Purchaser shall have the option of taking such title as the Seller can give without abatement of the price OR of being repaid all monies by Purchaser to Seller on account of the purchase price together with costs for searching title as may have been incurred, and in the latter event there shall be no further liability or obligation on either of the parties hereto and this Agreement shall become null and void and of no further legal effect.

14. TERMITE CLAUSE. Seller authorizes Purchaser or his agent to obtain, at Purchaser's expense, a certificate from a licensed pest control company that the property is free and clear of any visible termites and other wood boring insects. If any infestation or any damages is present, then the property shall be treated at Seller's expense to correct any such infestation and any damage caused by any present or prior infestation shall be treated at Seller's expense. In the event that the cost of the treatment and/or repair called for above exceed 2% of the purchase price of the Agreement, the Seller, at Seller's option, may declare this agreement null and void and of no further legal effect; however, if Purchaser, at his option and expense, should choose to pay the costs of the treatment and/or repairs exceeding 2% then this agreement shall remain in effect. All decisions regarding the above shall be made and communicated in writing to the other party within ten (10) days from the receipt of the inspection report. In the event this agreement is voided under this provision, then all deposits hereunder shall be returned immediately to Purchaser.

15. POSSESSION/OCCUPANCY. Seller agrees to give possession and occupancy at the time of settlement, and in the event Seller shall fail to do so, Seller shall be a tenant by sufferance of the Purchaser and liable for all damages. Seller hereby waives all notice to quit as provided by the laws effective in the State of Maryland.

16. COMPLIANCE WITH NOTICES. All notices of violations of orders or requirements noted or issued by any county or local authority, or actions in any court on account thereof, against or affecting the property at the date of settlement of this Agreement, shall be complied with by the Seller and the property conveyed free thereof.

17. PROPERTY CONDITION. At the time of settlement or occupancy (whichever occurs first) Seller will leave the premises free and clear of trash and debris and broom clean and have the electrical, well, septic, plumbing, heating, air conditioning, appliances, and any other mechanical systems and related equipment included in this Agreement in operating condition. The Seller will deliver the premises in substantially the same physical condition as of the date of final ratification. In addition to any other specific inspections provided for in this Agreement, the Purchaser, upon reasonable notice to the Seller, has the right of one (1) presettlement inspection of all the premises prior to settlement or occupancy (whichever occurs first). Except as expressly contained in this Agreement no other warranties have been made by the Seller, his agents, or relied upon by the Purchaser.

18. RISK OF LOSS & INSURANCE. The property is to be held at the risk of the Seller until legal title has passed or possession has been given to Purchaser. If prior to the time legal title has passed or possession has been given to Purchaser, all or a substantial part of the property is destroyed or damaged, without fault of the Purchaser, then this Agreement, at the option of the Purchaser, shall be null and void and of no further legal effect, and all monies paid shall be returned promptly by Seller to Purchaser. It is also understood and agreed that the Seller shall immediately have all of the insurance policies on the property so endorsed as to protect all parties hereto, as their interest may appear, and shall continue such insurance in force during the life of this Agreement of Sale. In the event it shall be determined by the Purchaser that the property is inadequately insured by the Seller, the Purchaser shall have the right at Purchaser's option and expense, to obtain such insurance, or additional insurance as shall be satisfactory to Purchaser. PURCHASER ACKNOWLEDGES THAT LENDER WILL REQUIRE HAZARD INSURANCE AND MAY REQUIRE FLOOD INSURANCE, AND PURCHASER AGREES TO PAY FOR SAME.

19. ADJUSTMENTS. Home Owners Association fees, rent and water rent, if any, shall be adjusted and apportioned as of the date of settlement. All taxes, general or special, and all other public or governmental charges or assessments against the premises which are or may be payable on an annual basis (including metropolitan District Sanitary Commission or other benefit charges, assessments, liens, or encumbrances for sewer, water, drainage, paving, or other public improvements completed or commenced on or prior to the date hereof, or subsequent thereto) are to be adjusted and apportioned as of the date of settlement and are to be assumed and paid thereafter by Purchaser, whether assessments have been levied or not as of the date of settlement if applicable by local law.

20. DEFAULT. Failure on the part of Purchaser to comply with the terms, covenants, and conditions of this Agreement of Sale, shall constitute a default and forfeiture of the deposit monies and shall entitle the Seller to retain the deposit paid by Purchaser, and to pursue such other rights and remedies as may be available, at law or in equity, including, without limitation, an action for specific performance on this Agreement of Sale and/or monetary damages. Notice of such default shall be given, in writing, by the Seller to the Purchaser within thirty (30) days after the default has occurred. In the event such notice of default is not given as provided in this section, Seller shall be deemed to have waived Seller's right to retain the deposit and the deposit shall be returned to the Purchaser.

In the event the deposit is retained as liquidated damages, Seller shall pay to Broker one-half (1/2) thereof as compensation for his/her services, but in no event to exceed an amount equal to the full fees due hereunder. In the event Seller obtains remedies other than liquidated damages, Broker shall be paid his/her full fees due hereunder from the escrowed funds or if such funds are insufficient the balance shall be paid by Seller.

21. AGENTS AGREEMENT. It is mutually and expressly understood and agreed between the parties that the listing broker, his salespeople and employees, or any officer or partner of the broker, and any cooperating broker and his salespeople and employees, or any officer or partner of the cooperating broker, are acting as agents only and will in no case whatsoever be held liable either jointly or severally to either party for the performance of any term or covenant of this Agreement of Sale, for damages for the non-performance thereof, nor be responsible for the soundness or condition of the property.

22. BROKER LIABILITY. Purchaser and Seller understand and acknowledge that Broker and any agents or employees of Broker are not, and were not at any time, authorized to make any representations respecting this Agreement or the property other than those expressly set forth herein. Broker and any agents or employees of Broker do not assume any responsibility for the condition of the property or for the performance of this Agreement by any or all parties hereto. By signing this Agreement, Purchaser acknowledges that Purchaser has not relied on any representations made by Broker and any agents or employees of Broker, except those representations expressly set forth herein. In the event of any litigation between Seller and Purchaser concerning return of the deposit monies, Broker's sole responsibility may be met, at Broker's

option, by paying the deposit monies into the court in which such litigation is pending, and Purchaser and Seller agree that upon payment of such deposit monies into court, neither Purchaser or Seller shall have any further right, claim, demand or action against Broker. In the event that any dispute arise under this Agreement between Seller and Purchaser resulting in Broker being made a party to any litigation, Seller and Purchaser, jointly and severally, agree to indemnify Broker for all costs, attorneys' fees and legal expenses incurred by Broker as a result thereof, provided that such litigation does not result in a judgment against Broker for acting improperly under this Agreement.

23. FINAL AGREEMENT. Seller and Purchaser mutually agree that this Agreement shall be binding upon them, theirs and each of their respective heirs, personal representatives, administrators, successors and assigns. This Agreement contains the final and entire agreement between the parties and neither they nor their agents shall be bound by any terms, conditions, statements, warranties or representations, oral or written, not contained in this Agreement of Sale.

24. GUARANTY FUND. NOTICE TO PURCHASERS AND ALL OTHER PARTIES HERETO. Any person aggrieved in accordance with Article 56, Section 217A of the Annotated Code of Maryland may be entitled to recover compensation from the Maryland Real Estate Guaranty Fund for his actual loss, as proven before the Maryland Real Estate Commission, in an amount not exceeding $25,000 in consideration of any claim. A Purchaser or other aggrieved person is not protected by the Guaranty Fund in an amount in excess of $25,000 for any claim.

______________________________ ______________________________ (SEAL) __________
Witness to Purchaser's Signature Purchaser's Signature Date

______________________________ ______________________________ (SEAL) __________
Witness to Purchaser's Signature Purchaser's Signature Date

25. APPROVAL BY SELLER. Seller hereby accepts the above Agreement this __________ day of ______________, 19____, at ____________ AM/PM, with the following changes:

____

____

______________________________ ______________________________ (SEAL) __________
Witness to Seller's Signature Seller's Signature Date

______________________________ ______________________________ (SEAL) __________
Witness to Seller's Signature Seller's Signature Date

26. ACCEPTANCE BY PURCHASER. Purchaser hereby accepts the above changes made by Seller and accepts the above Agreement this ________ day of ______________, 19____, at ______ AM/PM.

______________________________ ______________________________ (SEAL) __________
Witness to Purchaser's Signature Purchaser's Signature Date

______________________________ ______________________________ (SEAL) __________
Witness to Purchaser's Signature Purchaser's Signature Date

STANDARD SALES AGREEMENT ADDENDUM CLAUSES

1. SECOND TRUST BALLOON PAYMENT. Purchaser acknowledges that the second trust being taken back by Seller as a credit grantor pursuant to the provisions of Title 12, Subtitle 10 of the Commercial Law Article, Annotated Code of Maryland and provided for in paragraph will not payout in full by the expiration of the terms of the note and that they will be obligated to make a lump sum payment at the expiration of this note, and hereby consent to this provision. The parties to this Agreement acknowledge the second trust provides for a balloon payment due in __________ months after settlement and that the lender will grant a one-time postponement of not more than six (6) months from the due date for the balloon payment if a written request is made by the borrower of the lender prior to the due date of the balloon payment, provided the borrower continues to make the same monthly payments required by the original loan documents. It is understood that the lack of such request for a postponement or extension of the due date requires payment in full no later than the due date specified and no new closing costs, processing fees or similar fees may be imposed on the borrower as a result of the extension or postponement of payment.

2. SECOND TRUST. (Seller To Take Back) The balance of deferred purchase money amounting to $__________ is to be secured by a second deed of trust on said premises to be paid in monthly installments of $__________ or more, without penalty, at maker's option, including interest at the rate of__________% per annum, each installment when so paid to be applied, first, to the payment of interest on the amount of principal remaining at the balance credited to principal, which deed of trust the Seller agrees to accept as a part of the purchase price. In case of default in any payment, the entire amount then remaining unpaid, at the option of the noteholder, shall become due and payable. The entire unpaid principal balance shall be due and payable in full within______________, Trustees in all deeds of trust are to be named by the parties secured thereby.

3. FIRST TRUST. The deferred purchase money amounting to $______________ is to be secured by a first deed of trust on said premises to be paid in monthly installments of $____________ or more, without penalty, at maker's option, including interest at the rate of __________ percent per annum, each installment when so paid to be applied, first to the payment of interest on the amount of principal remaining and the balance credited to principal, which deed of trust the Seller agrees to accept as part of the purchase price. In case of default in any payment, the entire amount then remaining unpaid shall immediately become due and payable. Said trust and note may not be assumed or title taken subject to said trust and note without the prior written consent of the noteholder. Trustees in all deeds of trust are to be named by the parties secured thereby. The entire unpaid balance shall be due and payable in full within ______________________________.

4. PURCHASER SECOND TRUST. This Agreement is contingent on the ability of the Purchaser to obtain a second trust on subject property within____________ days of the date of this Agreement. Such second trust shall be upon the following terms and conditions: principal amount $__________, amortization $______________, interest rate_____________, principal and interest payments $______________, balloon payment $______________.

5. PURCHASER CONTINGENCY. The parties acknowledge and affirm that the Purchaser's obligation under this Agreement is conditional upon the sale and settlement of their existing home at ____, that no obligation of the Purchaser to make settlement shall arise under this Agreement until and unless these events have occurred, provided, however, should the sale of Purchaser's premises not be accomplished within__________ days of this date, the Seller may declare this Agreement null and void and of no further legal effect. The deposit shall be returned in full to Purchaser.

6. CONSUMER REPORT AUTHORIZATION. The Purchaser hereby authorizes the listing broker to disclose to the Seller or any lender the credit information provided to the listing broker by the Purchaser. In the event that terms of this Agreement require the Seller to take back financing from the Purchaser, and Seller desired to obtain a Consumer Report (credit report) regarding the Purchaser, Seller must notify listing broker within five (5) days of the date of ratification of this Agreement, in writing, that the listing broker is authorized and directed to order the report. In the event such a report is ordered within the stated time period, then this Agreement of Sale shall be contingent upon approval of a satisfactory Consumer Report (credit report) by the Seller within five (5) days after receipt of the report by Seller. If Seller does not approve the credit standing of the Purchaser, Seller shall notify the listing broker in writing within five (5) days after receipt of the report of Seller's rejection of the Purchaser's credit. In that event, this Agreement of Sale shall be null and void and of no further legal effect, and all deposits returned to the Purchaser. Failure to notify the listing broker of the rejection of the Purchaser's credit within the time provided shall constitute a waiver of the benefits of this provision and/or an approval of the Purchaser's credit. Additionally, if Seller shall fail to order the report within the five (5) days following the date of ratification of this Agreement, Seller shall be deemed to have waived the benefits provided in this paragraph. The Purchaser authorizes the listing broker to order and obtain a Credit Report from a credit reporting agency to be used in connection with this transaction whereby the Purchaser has applied for an extension of credit. Further, in the event the listing broker is acting on behalf of a creditor, Seller or other party directly or

indirectly affected by this transaction, the Purchaser authorizes the listing broker to forward all or any portion of the information contained in the report to the creditor, Seller or any other party directly involved. The cost of the report is to be paid by Purchaser.

7. SELLER CONTINGENCY. The parties acknowledge and affirm that the Seller's obligation under this Agreement of Sale is conditional upon the purchase and settlement of Seller's new home and that no obligation of the Seller to make settlement shall arise under this Agreement until and unless these events have occurred; provided, however, should the purchase of Seller's new home not be accomplished within ____________ days of this date, the Purchaser herein may declare this Agreement null and void and of no further legal effect, and all deposits shall be returned in full to Purchaser.

8. 72 HOUR WITHDRAWAL NOTICE. This Agreement may be cancelled upon 72 hours' written notice from the Seller or their agent to the Purchaser or their agent that a bona fide offer has been made on the property and will be accepted unless the Purchaser removes the contingency conditions set forth by the Purchaser within the 72 hour period and the Purchaser proceeds with the purchase as provided. The 72 hour period shall be exclusive of Saturdays, Sundays, and holidays.

9. CASH ABOVE APPRAISAL. Purchaser acknowledges (VA), (FHA), (CONVENTIONAL) appraisal is $________________, and hereby agrees to pay $________________ cash above the appraisal for a total sales price of $________________.

10. RE-WRITTEN AGREEMENT BETWEEN PURCHASER AND SELLER. This Agreement of Sale supercedes the prior agreement by and between the parties dated the ____________ day of ________________, 19______, and the Purchaser authorizes ________________________ to apply all deposits paid by Purchaser under the earlier Agreement to the present Agreement whether by cash, check, note, or other consideration.

11. DEPOSIT. It is understood that the amount of deposit reflected in this Agreement is currently held by ____ and that $____________ is the total amount of any and all deposits received from the Purchaser by ________________________ ________________________ who is authorized to transfer the deposit to this Agreement.

12. SUBJECT TO RELEASE. This Agreement is subject to Purchaser being released from the prior real estate agreement not later than the __________ day of ________________, 19______.

13. PRELIMINARY LENDER'S APPROVAL. This Agreement of Sale is subject to Purchaser obtaining written preliminary lenders' approval within ____________ banking days of the date of acceptance. If such approval is not obtained, Seller may declare this Agreement null and void and of no further legal effect, and all deposits made shall be returned to the Purchaser.

14. SECONDARY CONTRACT. The Purchaser recognizes and acknowledges and affirms that there is an existing Agreement of Sale on the subject premises. This Agreement shall be valid until the __________ day of ________________, 19______, at which time if the existing Agreement on the premises dated the ____________ day of ____________________, 19______, by and between ____ and ________________________ has not been cancelled, withdrawn or otherwise cancelled, this officer shall terminate.

15. PRE-SETTLEMENT OCCUPANCY AGREEMENT. Seller agrees to grant occupancy to Purchaser on ________________________________ at a rental basis of $__________ per day. Seller and Purchaser agree to the terms and conditions of the occupancy agreement which is attached and made part of this Agreement of Sale. Seller and Purchaser acknowledge that they have read the rental agreement and understand its terms and provisions.

16. POST-SETTLEMENT OCCUPANCY AGREEMENT. Purchaser agrees to grant occupancy to Seller from the date of Settlement at a rental basis of $__________ per day. Seller and Purchaser agree to the terms and conditions of the occupancy agreement which is attached and made part of this Agreement of Sale. Seller and Purchaser acknowledge that they have read the rental agreement and understand its terms and provisions.

17. PAYMENT OF CLOSING COSTS. Seller agrees to pay $__________ of Purchaser's closing costs at the time of settlement. Prepaid items to be paid by (Seller) (Purchaser) and (are) (are not) included in the above cost to Seller. For the purposes of this addendum, prepaid items shall be defined as: mortgage insurance premiums, fire and extended coverage premiums, real estate taxes, and advance escrows for these items.

18. NEW CONSTRUCTION OR OWNER BUILT FIRST SALE. (Select one or more of the applicable paragraphs.)

A. In the event of new construction or first sale of owner built premises, Seller informs Purchaser of the existence of deferred water and sewer charges for which Purchaser assumes liability in the approximate amount of $__________ and which may be paid monthly in the approximate amount of $__________ until satisfied.

B. Seller informs Purchaser that a schedule of deferred water and sewer charges has not been established by appropriate authority.

C. Seller informs Purchaser that the local jurisdiction has adopted a plan to benefit the property in the future.

19. TITLE SUBJECT TO AN EXISTING LEASE. Purchaser agrees to take title to the property subject to the existing lease. Purchaser has inspected the lease and is fully familiar with all of the covenants, terms and conditions of the lease.

20. STRUCTURAL SOUNDNESS AND ELECTRICAL, PLUMBING AND MECHANICAL EQUIPMENT. The Purchaser, at their expense, has the right to have the property inspected for structural soundness and to insure that all electrical, plumbing and mechanical equipment is in proper

operating condition. In the event there are any defects found, the Seller shall agree, by written acceptance, within ten (10) days of such discovery, to correct the defects, or this Agreement of Sale shall become null and void and of no further legal effect at the option of the Purchaser and any deposits shall be returned to the Purchaser. All such defects shall be corrected by Seller prior to settlement.

The Purchaser shall have the inspection completed and any defects found shall be submitted by written notice to the Seller within ten (10) days of acceptance of this Agreement or this Agreement shall continue in force and the right for the inspection shall be waived.

21. HOME INSPECTION OPTIONS. Purchaser hereby acknowledges having been given the opportunity to have qualified individuals and/or firms inspect the condition of the dwelling, the condition of its plumbing, electric and heating systems, appliances and water and sewerage systems (if applicable) and having been given the opportunity to have the property warranted and/or guaranteed by any home inspection and/or warranty firm for a fee. Purchaser declines these inspections (unless otherwise specified in the Special Conditions of this agreement) with the full knowledge and understanding that neither the Broker nor the agents are responsible for undisclosed defects in the property.

22. AGRICULTURAL LAND DEVELOPMENT TAX. Pursuant to Article xx, Section 278F of the Annotated Code of Maryland the Seller hereby notifies the Purchaser that the land being transferred may be subject to the Agricultural Transfer Tax. Agricultural Transfer Tax not to exceed__________ percent (_____%) is to be paid by (Seller) (Purchaser).

23. SUBDIVISION PLAT NOT RECORDED. The subdivision of land to be created by this Agreement has not been approved by the Maryland__________________________, the Department of Health, or any other agency of the State or county. The approval of one or more of these agencies may be necessary before any building permit is issued.

24. GROUND RENT. The Purchaser acknowledges that the property is subject to annual ground rent in the amount of Dollars ($__________) payable______________________________ Dollars ($__________) per ______________________________ and that failure to timely pay the ground rent when due may result in the reversionary owner of the ground rent bringing an ejectment action against the ground rent tenant under Section 8-402(c) under the Real Property Article, Section 14-117, Annotated Code of Maryland. As a result of such action, the reversionary owner of the ground rent may own the property in fee, discharged from the lease.

25. WELL AND/OR SEPTIC TANK. In the event that property is served by well and/or septic tank, Seller agrees to provide Purchaser with a certification that the well and/or septic tank is/are in proper operating condition prior to settlement.

26. SALE AND SETTLEMENT. The sale and settlement are NOT conditioned or contingent in any manner upon the sale or settlement of any other real estate NOR subject to any mortgaging or financing EXCEPT as herein provided.

27. NEGOTIATION. The Seller may not negotiate new leases without the Purchaser's written consent.

28. UNIMPROVED PARCEL OF LAND. If the property being purchased hereunder is an unimproved parcel of land, intended to be used for residential purposes, you should, before signing this Agreement, consult the appropriate public authorities to ascertain whether public sewerage and water facilities are available, or, if not, whether the property will be approved by such authorities for the installation of a well and/or private sewerage disposal system.

29. ADJUSTABLE RATE MORTGAGE (ARM). This contract is given subject to the Purchaser's ability to obtain a conventional loan or loans in the amount of__________________________ Dollars ($________) with a calculated monthly repayment term of not less than________ years, being interest at an initial rate of not more than__________ percent per annum, with provision for interest rate adjustments each______________ year(s), and on a basis which when made, variably applies amounts so paid to the payment of accrued interest and the reduction of principal, if any, with not more than a__________ percent variance in the rate for each adjustment period and with a limit of__________ points required to be paid by Purchaser. The Purchaser shall use reasonable diligence to obtain such loan and in the event Purchaser is unable to obtain such loan commitment within__________ day hereof, that this Agreement shall be null and void and of no further legal effect and the earnest money deposit shall be returned to the Purchaser.

NOTICE TO MEMBERS

These standard clauses have been developed as a convenience to members for use, at their option, in situations where additional clauses are necessary to a contract condition. It is suggested that any of the listed clauses may be selected and added to a particular agreement or placed on a standard addendum form and made a part of the Agreement.

FHA ADDENDUM

Special Provisions attached to and hereby made a part of the contract dated____________ on Lot__________ Block_______________ Subdivision__________________________ located at____
____________________________ County, Maryland by and between the undersigned Seller (hereinafter referred to as Seller) and____ (hereinafter referred to as Purchaser).

A. I. It is expressly agreed that, notwithstanding any other provisions of this contract, the Purchaser shall not be obligated to complete the purchase of the property described herein or to incur any penalty by forfeiture of earnest money deposit or otherwise unless the Seller has delivered to the Purchaser a written statement issued by the Federal Housing Commissioner setting forth the appraised value of the property (excluding closing costs) of not less than $________________________________ which statement the Seller hereby agrees to deliver to the Purchaser promptly after such appraised value statement is made available to the Seller. The Purchaser shall, however, have the privilege and option of proceeding with consummation of the contract without regard to the amount of the appraised valuation made by the Federal Housing Commissioner. The appraised valuation is arrived at to determine the maximum mortgage the Department of Housing and Urban Development will insure. HUD does not warrant the value or the condition of the property. The Purchaser should satisfy himself that the price and the condition of the property are acceptable.

II. Paragraph A.I. is applicable only in the event that Purchaser places a Federal Housing Administration (FHA) insured loan. Purchaser shall exercise the above-mentioned privilege and option to proceed at the contract price which is over and above the FHA appraisal by giving the Seller notice of his intention to do so by the method provided in Paragraph 28 hereof. Said Notice shall be given within FIVE days after Purchaser receives the FHA appraisal. This contract is subject to FHA and lender's approval. If the aforesaid approval is not obtained, it is expressly agreed that the Purchaser shall be refunded his deposit and the contract shall be null and void.

B. I. **FHA MORTGAGE & MORTGAGE INSURANCE PREMIUM.** Purchaser agrees to pay mortgage insurance premium as required by FHA regulations. Purchaser has the right to pay the entire premium at the time of settlement or the portion of the premium permitted by FHA regulations may be added to the loan amount and financed over the term of the loan. If the Purchaser elects to add the premium to the loan amount as aforesaid, the total loan amount shall consist of the loan amount of $__________________ specified in Paragraph 2a of the Contract plus the mortgage insurance premium of approximately $______________.

II. **FHA LOAN FEES.** The Purchaser agrees to pay a loan origination fee of one percent (1%) of the loan as permitted by FHA regulations. The Purchaser also agrees to pay a loan discount fee of____________ percent (______%) of the total loan amount. The Seller agrees to pay a loan discount fee of_____________ percent (______%) of the total loan amount. The above loan origination and discount fees are based on the present mortgage money market, and the Purchaser will comply with any reasonable change in said fees at the time of settlement, provided said change is permitted by FHA regulations and is due to a change in the mortgage money market. Any reduction in the loan origination fee and/or the discount fee shall be shared by the Seller and Purchaser on a basis equal to their respective proportionate obligation for the original total of said fees.

III. **LENDER'S FEES.** Lender's fees to the Seller, if any, shall be paid by the Seller.

C. **LOAN PROCESSING.** All parties acknowledge that the processing of a government loan is not subject to specific time limitations. Nevertheless, Purchaser agrees to diligently pursue such loan commitment in accordance with Paragraph 2d of this contract.

D. **FHA GRADUATED PAYMENT PLAN.** Purchaser understands that his monthly payments are estimated to increase as follows:

$____ PI Year 1
$____ PI Year 2
$____ PI Year 3
$____ PI Year 4
$____ PI Year 5
$____ PI Year 6

It is further understood that the outstanding loan balance will increase during the graduated time period. The highest outstanding loan balance will be approximately $________________________ which will occur during the___________________ year.

__________________________ ______________________________
DATE SELLER

__________________________ ______________________________
DATE PURCHASER

VA ADDENDUM

Special Provisions attached to and hereby made a part of the contract dated__________________
on Lot_______________ Block____________ Subdivision__________________________________
located at____
______________________ County, Maryland by and between the undersigned Seller (hereinafter referred to as Seller) and____
(hereinafter referred to as Purchaser).

A. **VA LOAN.** The Veteran Purchaser's deposit shall be placed in an escrow account as required by Title 38, US Code, Section 1808. It is expressly agreed that, notwithstanding any other provisions of this contract, the Purchaser shall not incur any penalty by forfeiture of earnest money or otherwise be obligated to complete the purchase of the property described herein, if the contract purchase price or cost exceeds the reasonable value of the property established by the Veterans Administration or the Purchaser is not approved by the Veterans Administration and the lending institution. In the event the Certificate of Reasonable Value is less than the amount of the contract price the Purchaser shall have the privilege and option for five (5) days after receipt of the VA appraisal to proceed with the consummation of this contract without regard to the amount of reasonable value established by the Veterans Administration by giving the Seller notice of his intention to do so by the method provided in Paragraph 28 hereof within said five (5) days. In the event that he shall not so elect, then the Seller shall have the privilege and option of reducing the contract price to the VA appraised value. This option must be exercised by the Seller, within seven (7) days after delivery to the Purchaser of the VA appaisal, by giving the Purchaser notice of his intention to do so by the method provided in Paragraph 28 hereof. If the Seller elects to reduce the contract price to the appraised valuation, the Purchaser covenants and agrees to be bound to proceed with consummation hereof at the appraised valuation price. If the Seller does not elect to reduce the price after the Purchaser's refusal to consummate this contract at its full price, then this contract shall be null and void. This contract is contingent on the approval of the house and the Purchaser by the Veterans Administration and the lending institution. If the aforesaid approval is not obtained, it is expressly agreed that the Purchaser shall be refunded his deposit and the contract shall be null and void.

B. **VA LOAN FEES.** The Purchaser agrees to pay a loan origination fee of one percent (1%) of the principal sum of the loan. The Seller agrees to pay a loan discount fee of______% of the principal sum of said loan. The above loan origination and discount fees are based upon current VA regulations or the present mortgage money market. It is further agreed that the parties will comply with any reasonable change in said fees at the time of settlement, provided said change is permitted by VA regulations or is due to a change in the mortgage money market. Lender's fees to the Seller, if any, shall be paid by the Seller. The Purchaser agrees to pay at settlement a VA funding fee equal to 1/2% of the principal sum of the loan unless the Purchaser is eligible for and obtains an exemption from the VA or elects to add the funding fee to the principal sum of the loan amount.

C. **LOAN PROCESSING.** All parties acknowledge that the processing of a government loan is not subject to specific time limitations. Nevertheless, Purchaser agrees to diligently pursue such loan commitment in accordance with Paragraph 2d of this contract.

D. **VA GRADUATED PAYMENT PLAN.** Purchaser understands that his monthly payments are estimated to increase as follows:

$____ PI Year 1
$____ PI Year 2
$____ PI Year 3
$____ PI Year 4
$____ PI Year 5
$____ PI Year 6

It is further understood that the outstanding loan balance will increase during the graduated time period. The highest outstanding loan balance will be approximately $____________________ which will occur during the____________________ year.

______________________________ ______________________________
DATE SELLER

______________________________ ______________________________
DATE PURCHASER

"NOTICE: This form should not be used for the initial sale of a condominium unit to a member of the public, since it does not contain the Notice required by Section 11-126 of the Real Property Article of the Annotated Code of Maryland."

CONDOMINIUM RESALE ADDENDUM

Special provisions, herein specified, are attached to and made a part of the Agreement dated__________________________ by and between____________________________________ ("Purchaser") and________________________________ ("Seller") relative to the sale and purchase of the condominium unit known as number___________ in building_________________ in____ subdivision.

1. SUBSTITUTION. Wherever, in the herein specified agreement, the words house, property, premises or residence appears, the words Condominium Unit shall be substituted, when appropriate and necessary.

2. DEED. The deed conveying the condominium unit and the undivided interest in the common elements shall be subject to the terms, conditions, limitations and restrictions set forth in the Declaration or Master Deed and Bylaws, including any amendments thereto, for the condominium project, including the rights of present co-owners in the common elements and the operation of the condominium project.

3. EXPENSES, COSTS, CHARGES AND RESERVE. Any interest in the common expenses, private charges, assessments and condominium assessments against the condominium unit shall be adjusted between the parties at and to the time of settlement, thereafter assumed by the Purchaser. All adjustments listed in paragraph number nineteen (19) of the agreement are to include any items paid by the Seller directly including all prepaid condominium fees, assessments or other charges excepting, if in existence, the savings or replacement reserve maintained by the condominium project, the value of which is included in the purchase price of the condominium unit.

4. HOMEOWNER ASSOCIATION MEMBERSHIP. If the Seller is a member of a Homeowner Association which is separate and apart from the Condominium Association, Seller warrants that such membership is current, that all assessments and charges have been, or will be paid at settlement by Seller and that Seller's membership is transferable to the Purchaser. Seller shall present, at settlement, certification of such from an authorized officer of the Homeowners Association as well as make available a copy of current rules or bylaws.

5. CONTINGENCIES. If this sale is subject to the approval or right of first refusal of the government body of the Condominium Project, then Seller agrees to immediately present this agreement to such proper authority for their action or consideration. In the event that such approval is not obtained in writing within thirty (30) days after the acceptance by the Seller of this offer, or this sale is disallowed by the appropriate Condominium authority, whichever shall first occur, then Agent shall promptly return any deposits and this agreement shall be null and void.

6. CONDOMINIUM REQUIREMENTS. Seller warrants that he will perform as required by the Declaration and Bylaws or any other rules and regulations promulgated by the Condominium Regime to facilitate the sale. The Seller further warrants that he will hold harmless the Purchaser for any failure on the Seller's part to perform such requirements or for failure to inform the Purchaser of any requirements that the Purchaser is obligated to perform to properly consummate the sale.

7. NOTICE Regarding Condominium Documents, Resale Certification and/or Unit Owner's Statement. (This notice is applicable only to the resale by a unit owner other than a developer of a residential unit in a condominium containing seven (7) or more units.)

NOTICE (A)

THE SELLER IS REQUIRED BY LAW TO FURNISH TO THE PURCHASER NOT LATER THAN 15 DAYS PRIOR TO CLOSING CERTAIN INFORMATION CONCERNING THE CONDOMINIUM WHICH IS DESCRIBED IN SECTION 11-135 OF THE MARYLAND CONDOMINIUM ACT. THIS INFORMATION MUST INCLUDE AT LEAST THE FOLLOWING:

1. A copy of the Declaration (other than the plats).
2. A copy of the bylaws.
3. A copy of the rules and regulations of the condominium.
4. A certificate containing:

i. A statement disclosing the effect on the proposed conveyance of any right of first refusal or other restraint on the free alienability of the unit, other than any restraint created by the unit owner;

ii. A statement of the amount of the monthly common expense assessment and any unpaid common expense or special assessment currently due and payable from the selling unit owner;

iii. A statement of any other fees payable by the unit owners to the council of unit owners;

iv. A statement of any capital expenditures approved by the council of unit owners or its authorized designee planned at the time of the conveyance which are not reflected in the current operating budget included in the certificate;

v. The most recently prepared balance sheet and income and expense statement, if any, of the condominium;

vi. The current operating budget of the condominium, including details concerning the amount of the reserve fund for repair and replacement and its intended use, or a statement that there is no reserve fund;

vii. A statement of any judgments against the condominium and the existence of any pending suits to which the council of unit owners is a party;

viii. A statement generally describing any insurance policies provided for the benefit of the unit owners; a notice that the policies are available for inspection stating the location at which they are available; and a notice that the terms of the policy prevail over the general description;

ix. A statement as to whether the council of unit owners has knowledge that any alteration or improvement to the unit or to the limited common elements assigned to the unit violates any provisions of the declaration, bylaws, or rules and regulations;

x. A statement as whether the council of unit owners has knowledge of any violation of the health or building codes with respect to the unit, the limited common elements assigned to the unit, or any other portion of the condominium;

xi. A statement of the remaining term of any leasehold estate affecting the condominium and the provisions governing any extension or renewal of it; and

xii. A description of any recreational or other facilities which are to be used by the unit owners or maintained by them or the council of unit owners, and a statement as to whether or not they are to be a part of the common elements; and

5. A statement by the unit owner as to whether the unit owner has knowledge:

i. That any alteration to the unit or to the limited common elements assigned to the unit violates any provision of the declaration, bylaws, or rules and regulations;

ii. Of any violation of the health or building codes with respect to the unit or the limited common elements assigned to the unit.

The Purchaser will have the right to cancel this Agreement without penalty, at any time within seven (7) days following delivery to the Purchaser of all of this information. However, once the sale is closed, the Purchaser's right to cancel the Agreement is terminated.

(This notice is applicable only to the resale by a unit owner other than a developer of a residential unit in a condominium containing less than seven (7) units.)

NOTICE (B)

THE SELLER IS REQUIRED BY LAW TO FURNISH TO THE PURCHASER NOT LATER THAN 15 DAYS PRIOR TO CLOSING CERTAIN INFORMATION COVERING THE CONDOMINIUM WHICH IS DESCRIBED IN SECTION 11-135 OF THE MARYLAND CONDOMINIUM ACT. THIS INFORMATION MUST INCLUDE AT LEAST THE FOLLOWING:

1. A copy of the declaration (other than the plats).
2. A copy of the bylaws.
3. A copy of the rules and regulations of the condominium.
4. A statement by the Seller of his expenses relating to the common elements during the preceding twelve (12) months.

The Purchaser will have the right to cancel this Agreement without penalty, at any time within seven (7) days following delivery to the Purchaser of all of this information. However, once the sale is closed, the Purchaser's right to cancel the Agreement is terminated.

______________________ Witness	______________________ Purchaser
______________________ Witness	______________________ Purchaser
______________________ Witness	______________________ Seller
______________________ Witness	______________________ Seller

Date of Acceptance ______________________, 19______.

____

Address of Purchaser Phone Phone

Ground rent or leasehold interest. A real estate sales contract should indicate whether there is a ground rent or leasehold interest involved in the sale. When the seller is proposing to convey only his or her leasehold interest, then the contract will require a clause such as Addendum clause 24. If the ground rent is irredeemable, this fact should be indicated. If the ground rent is to be redeemed so that the seller will convey a fee title to the buyer free of the lease, then it should be provided that the seller will give the required notification of redemption to the owner of the ground rent.

Multiple dwelling code. Contracts for the sale of multiple dwelling property in Baltimore City are required to contain a clause whereby the seller guarantees that the property being purchased complies with the Baltimore City Multiple Dwelling Code and that the license will be delivered to the buyer at time of settlement.

Sewerage and wells. Property in Maryland not served by public sewer and water is subject to the State Department of Health and Mental Hygiene laws and regulations pertaining to individual sewage disposal systems and wells. The agent must provide the buyer of unimproved land with a notice such as that in Addendum clause 28.

The VA, the FHA and many private lenders require an evaluation by the local health department of the sewerage disposal system and the water supply on residential property prior to settlement. A bacteriological sample must be collected from the well and analyzed by the health department laboratory. This requires considerable time and should be taken into consideration when setting up a settlement date.

Assistance and information is available from the Department of Health and Mental Hygiene, O'Connor Building, 201 West Preston Street, Baltimore, Maryland 21201. State of Maryland Department of Health and Mental Hygiene laws and regulations applicable to sewer and water are contained in Article 43 of the Annotated Code of Maryland. Local health boards are also available to provide any information needed.

Cease to show release clause. To assure compliance with the Fair Housing Laws and to avoid claims of steering, a number of brokers use a "Cease to Show Release...From Buyer." This is an equal opportunity agreement between the buyer and the broker. This clause, signed by the buyer(s), usually reads as follows:

> I (We) (insert names of buyer(s)) request (insert name of selling agent) , agent for (insert name of broker) to assist me/us in preparing this Contract offer. I (We) understand that I (We) do not have to make this Contract offer and I (We) understand that (insert name of broker) , is obligated, under Fair Housing Laws, to show me (us) housing anywhere I (We) wish to look, regardless of race, color, creed, national origin, sex, age, marital status or disability.
>
> This service has been performed to my (our) satisfaction, and I (We) understand that I (We) may, at this time, speak to the office manager if I (We) believe that I (We) have been denied the opportunity to see every home within my (our) price range, in any area that I (We) have requested.

> I (We) understand that my (our) refusal to sign this equal opportunity statement in no way affects my (our) ability to make this Contract offer.
>
> I (We) understand that (insert names of selling agent and broker) under all the conditions outlined above, is asking me (us) of my (our) own free will, to release them from the obligation of showing any more houses unless the Contract offer is rejected, and to indicate my (our) belief that I (We) have received equal housing opportunity and the (insert name of broker) has presented itself ready and willing to enforce equal housing laws.

Contingency Clauses

The Maryland Real Estate Commission requires that licensees see to it that financial obligations and commitments regarding real estate transactions are in writing, expressing the exact agreements of the parties. Licensees are also required to protect and promote the interests of their clients. A number of contingency clauses may be used.

Financing. A common clause in a contract of sale is some version of Contract clause 4.

Valuation. When the buyer's purchase is contingent on obtaining a Federal Housing Administration (FHA) insured loan or a Veterans Administration (VA) guaranteed loan, a contingency clause is required because FHA and VA loan approvals depend on the appraised value of the property. If the property does not appraise for the required amount, a contingency clause may give the buyer the choice of cancelling the purchase or proceeding by paying cash for the difference between the maximum FHA or VA loan available and the purchase price. FHA and VA Addendums are included with the sample contract.

Mortgage application. To assure the buyer makes mortgage application, the Contract of Sale may include Contract clause 5.

Home inspection services. There are a number of "inspection and approval contingency" clauses that may be used. These make the purchase of the property contingent upon the buyer receiving a satisfactory inspection report of the property. Usually the report states the condition of the property, including plumbing, electric, heating and air conditioning systems, appliances, and water and sewerage systems (when applicable). When the contract of sale is contingent upon the buyer receiving a satisfactory inspection report, it should state that the buyer will furnish the seller with a copy of the report. This assists the buyer in any court action if the buyer should fail to perform under the contract of sale after having received a favorable inspection report. Seller may also be given the opportunity to correct any defects.

Buyers who do not wish to avail themselves of a home inspection service often have something similar to Addendum clause 21 inserted.

Sale of buyers home. Another common contingency clause makes the buyer's offer contingent upon the sale of the buyer's property. Special safeguards are included, such as allowing the seller to continue to market the property. In the event an acceptable second offer is obtained, the first buyer is then given the choice of either removing the sale contingency or cancelling the offer. This is referred to as a 72-hour release clause or kickout clause since the buyer is usually given 72 hours to remove the contingency. Other protection makes sure the buyer's property is reasonably priced and listed for sale with a reputable broker, and that a reasonable time, such as 60 to 90 days be given to the buyer to sell the property.

Without these safeguards, the seller's house would be tied up without any assurance that the buyer would sell his home and remove the contingency.

GENERAL RELEASE

When the buyer is unable to consummate the contract of sale because of inability to obtain financing, underappraisal of property, or through mutual agreement with the seller, a release is prepared specifically releasing the buyer from any and all responsibilities in connection with the contract of sale and also authorizing the broker to release the deposit.

OPTION AGREEMENTS

In Maryland, a lease option agreement is defined as any lease agreement containing a clause that confers on the tenant some power, either qualified or unqualified, to purchase the landlord's interest in real property. No lease option purchase of improved residential property, with or without a ground rent, executed after July 1, 1971 is valid in Maryland unless it contains a statement in capital letters: THIS IS NOT A CONTRACT TO BUY, and a clear statement of its purpose and effect with respect to the ultimate purchase which is the subject of the option.

INSTALLMENT CONTRACTS

Maryland requirements concerning installment contracts for the sale of real estate will be detailed in Chapter 15 of this supplement. The main text covers general information on installment contracts.

ESCROW AGREEMENTS

The escrow procedure of closing a real estate transaction, as described in the text, is rarely used in Maryland--absolute delivery of the title to the purchaser is much more common. Closing will be discussed in Chapter 23.

CONTRACT OF SALE FORMS

The form shown in this chapter is a sales contract developed by the Maryland Association of Realtors®.

An important caveat (notice) is printed across the top of the contract of sale form. Licensees should be sure that buyers and sellers understand that an executed sales contract is legally binding. Since licensees cannot act as attorneys in their selling activities, the buyer and seller should obtain legal counsel to interpret and approve the provisions of contracts.

Disclosure Requirements on Condominium Sales

A contract for the initial sale of a condominium unit and also the resale of the unit requires the disclosure of certain information to the purchaser before the execution of the contract. The buyer of a condominium unit has 15 days (for initial sale) or seven days (for resale) within which the contract may be rescinded. A condominium resale addendum is included with the sample contract in this chapter.

RECEIPT OF EARNEST MONEY

As required by the state real estate license law, all earnest money deposits taken in connection with an offer to purchase, as well as any other deposits of money belonging to parties other than the broker, must be held by the broker in a separate bank account and deposited either the day they are received or the next banking day. By law, the broker must not commingle the funds of other parties with his or her own funds; such funds, in the absence of proper written instructions to the contrary, must be held in a noninterest-bearing account that is clearly identified as funds belonging to others. In addition, brokers must keep accurate records of all transactions, including bank account numbers, deposits, and withdrawals; these records must always be available during business hours for inspection by the state Real Estate Commission or its field representatives.

Furthermore, such funds must be kept in a financial institution in Maryland that is insured by either the Federal Deposit Insurance Corporation (FDIC), the Federal Savings and Loan Insurance Corporation (FSLIC), the National Credit Union Administration, the Maryland State Savings-Share Insurance Corporation, or the Maryland Credit Union Insurance Corporation. Such funds must be retained in this account, according to the state real estate license law, "until the transaction involved is consummated or terminated, or until proper written instructions have been received by the broker directing the withdrawal or other disposition of such funds, at which times all such funds shall be promptly and fully accounted for by the broker."

Deposits on New Homes

In connection with the sale and purchase of new single-family residential units, including condominiums that are not completed at the time of contracting the sale, if the vendor or builder obligates the purchaser to pay any sum of money before the unit has been completed and the realty has been granted to the purchaser, the builder or vendor is required to:

1 deposit or hold the sum in a neutral escrow account to assure the return of the sum to the purchaser who is entitled to it; or
2 obtain and maintain a corporate surety bond conditioned on the return of the sum to the purchaser who is entitled to it.

DUTIES AND OBLIGATIONS

The Code of Ethics of the Maryland Real Estate Commission sets forth a number of duties and obligations that the real estate licensee has toward clients, the public, and fellow licensees, as discussed in Chapter 21. Those pertaining to contracts of sale are summarized below, along with other guidelines:

1 Protect the rights of all parties.
2 Be sure your actions cannot be construed as negligent.
3 Always conduct yourself in an ethical manner.
4 Be sure the obligations and commitments of all parties are set forth in writing, particularly financing arrangements.
5 Be sure that the entire agreement in writing represents a true "meeting of the minds," showing the intent of buyers and sellers.
6 Disclose any personal interest that you have in the property, including any kinship to buyers or sellers.
7 Submit all formal written offers to your seller, regardless of your personal opinion, unless you have written instructions to the contrary.
8 Cooperate with other licensees when it is in the interest of your client.
9 Remember, commissions are paid to the broker and divided as previously agreed.
10 All negotiations with the owners pertaining to the sale are done through the listing broker.
11 Disclose all material facts, being truthful in your representations; engage in no form of fraud.
12 Assure that buyers and sellers understand the contract of sale.
13 When required, legal counsel should be recommended.
14 Never engage in the practice of law unless you are an attorney.
15 Specify in the contract of sale all inclusions and exclusions.
16 Ensure deposits are placed in escrow.
17 Never witness a signature unless you have actually seen the person sign.

QUESTIONS

1. Sam Billows, age 15, enters into an agreement to purchase Jane and Renee Peters' Maryland real estate with the proceeds of his late father's estate. The purchase is intended to be an investment for Billows' college education. The Peters' land, however, is a tract of virtually useless, swampy land, for which the sellers charged Billows top dollar. Based on the above information:

   a. this contract is void.
   b. the contract will become valid if not disaffirmed by Billows shortly after reaching his 18th birthday.
   c. the contract is voidable.
   d. the contract is valid.

2. In Maryland, contracts for the sale of real estate:

   a. must be in writing in order to be enforceable.
   b. must be on a standard printed form.
   c. must be signed by the seller only.
   d. must be signed by the buyer only.

3. Oral contracts for the sale of real estate:

   a. are void.
   b. are also called parol agreements.
   c. are enforceable in a court of law.
   d. are illegal.

4. Which of the following, if applicable, does <u>not</u> need to be disclosed in a Maryland real estate sales contract?

   a. leasehold interest involved in the sale
   b. the seller is a real estate licensee
   c. possible tax charges for agricultural land development
   d. the name of the title insurance company

5. By law, earnest money deposits:

   a. may be commingled with the broker's own funds.
   b. must be deposited in a financial institution in Maryland that is insured by the FDIC, the FSLIC, the Maryland State Savings-Share Insurance Corporation, or the Maryland Credit Union Insurance Corporation.
   c. may not be placed in an interest-bearing account.
   d. may be withdrawn at any time prior to settlement as long as a licensee's signature appears on the escrow check.

12

Transfer of Title

TRANSFER OF TITLE BY DESCENT

Maryland Law of Descent and Distribution

As discussed in Chapter 7, Maryland has eliminated the rights of dower and curtesy in favor of the Maryland Law of Descent and Distribution. This law names the classes of heirs who inherit real estate owned by a deceased owner who dies intestate, that is, without leaving a valid will. A surviving spouse is always an heir, as are children of the deceased. All distributions are made after payment of the decedent's debts and estate taxes.

TRANSFER OF TITLE BY WILL

Requirements for a Valid Will

A person aged 18 or over who is of sound mind and is legally competent may make a will. Wills should be carefully prepared by the testator's attorney and signed and witnessed as required by law.

Wills must be admitted to probate in the county or city in which the decedent resided. Probate is defined as the verification of the validity or authenticity of a will by a proper court of law. Probate includes the legal process of the payment of debts of the deceased and the distribution of the assets of the deceased's estate.

Rights of a surviving spouse. If the deceased property owner died testate, that is, leaving a will, the surviving spouse may accept the terms of the will or, if the will provisions deprive the surviving spouse of his or her share as allowed by the law of descent, then the surviving spouse is given the right to elect to renounce the will and take the share that would normally come to the spouse under the terms of the intestate law of descent and distribution, as if the deceased had died without a will.

TRANSFER OF TITLE BY ACTION OF LAW

Adverse Possession

In order to obtain title to real estate through adverse possession, as discussed in the text, an adverse user must be in actual possession of the property which for an unbroken, continuous, and uninterrupted period of 20 years has been in possession of claimant or combined with that of previous owners and must be or have been open, notorious, exclusive, and hostile (all of which are highly technical legal terms). Any questions about adverse possession should be considered only with the advice of legal counsel.

TRANSFER OF TITLE BY DEED

Requirements for a Valid Deed

A deed must be in writing, executed by a competent grantor 18 years of age or older, signed by the grantor, and acknowledged before a notary public or other authorized public officer. An acknowledgment is necesary to enable a deed to be recorded. In addition, a deed must state the actual consideration given for the property.

Maryland law specifies that no estate of inheritance or freehold, any declaration or limitation of use, or any estate extending beyond seven years shall pass or take effect unless the deed conveying the same is executed and recorded. Further explanations of recording, possession, and constructive notice are found in Chapter 13 of the text.

Documentary Stamp Taxes and Transfer Taxes on Deeds and Conveyances

The documentary stamp tax is a Maryland state tax levied at the rate of $.55 per $500 or fraction thereof of the full sale price of the property. Several cities and counties have added their own tax to the state stamp tax. There is a second tax in Maryland, called a state transfer tax, which is one-half of one percent (1/2 of 1%) of the full consideration paid for the property sold. Many counties have also levied an additional amount of transfer tax. The schedule of tax rates that are applicable to deeds and other real estate documents in the various counties follows:

MARYLAND TAXES ON REAL ESTATE
DEEDS AND CONVEYANCES

County	Documentary Stamps* Rate per $1,000 of Sale Price	Transfer Tax** on Sale Price
Allegany	$2.20	1/2%
Anne Arundel	7.00	1-1/2%
Baltimore City	4.40	2%

continued on next page

Maryland Taxes (cont.)

County	Documentary Stamps* Rate per $1,000 of Sale Price	Transfer Tax** on Sale Price
Baltimore	5.00	2%
Calvert	3.30	1/2%
Caroline	3.30	1/2%
Carroll	6.60	1/2%
Cecil	4.40	1/2% plus $3 flat fee
Charles	6.60	1/2%
Dorchester	3.30	1/2%
Frederick	6.60	1/2%
Garrett	2.20	1/2%
Harford	5.50	1/2%
Howard	4.40	1-1/2%
Kent	3.30	1%
Montgomery	4.40	1-1/2%
Prince George's	$4.40	1-1/2%
Queen Anne's	4.40	1/2%
St. Mary's	6.60	1/2%
Somerset	3.30	1/2%
Talbot	3.30	1/2%
Washington	4.40	1/2%
Wicomico	3.30	1/2%
Worcester	3.30	1/2%

*The state recordation tax is $1.10 per $1,000 or fraction thereof of sale price. The figures shown in the chart are the total of state and county county taxes per $1,000 or fraction thereof.

**The state tax is one-half percent of the total consideration. The figures shown in the chart are the total of the state and county taxes. In those counties that have not levied a county tax, the only tax due is the one-half percent state tax.

Agricultural Transfer Tax

In 1981, Maryland adopted the Agricultural Transfer Tax to replace the Agricultural Development Tax that had been in effect since 1979. Any development tax levied under Article 81, Section 19 (b)(2) and due in 1981 remains in effect. Any land transferred after July 1, 1981, not still subject to the provisions of the Development Tax, is subject to the Agricultural Transfer Tax, which is calculated by the Assessments Office and is payable at the time of property transfer.

The Agricultural Transfer Tax will be levied when these conditions in transactions involving land transfers occur:

1 whenever the property sold represents land only, the tax shall be applied to the total consideration if the property has been assessed solely on the basis of agricultural use, or the net consideration if the property has been assessed on the basis of a combined agricultural

and nonagricultural use. The net consideration is the total price paid less the most recent full cash value on the nonagriculturally assessed portion;

2 whenever the property has been assessed on the basis of an agricultural use and a nonagricultural use assessment including structures, the tax shall be applied to the net consideration;

3 whenever the transaction comprises individual building lots of less than 20 acres that did not receive the combined agricultural use and the nonagricultural use assessment, the tax shall be imposed on the total consideration.

Tax rate. The rate of tax to be imposed is:

1 five percent when the land being transferred is a parcel of 20 acres or more;

2 four percent when the land is a parcel of less than 20 acres and is assessed on the basis of its agricultural use or on the basis of unimproved land;

3 three percent when the land is a parcel of less than 20 acres and is assessed as improved land or land with the site improvements;

4 the full tax imposed is reduced by 25 percent for each consecutive full taxable year in which real property taxes were paid on the basis of a nonagricultural use assessment.

Declaration of intent. When a buyer files a Declaration of Intent to keep the land being transferred in agricultural use for at least five full consecutive, taxable years, and provided the property otherwise meets the qualifications for an agricultural use assessment, the tax is deferred until the next sale of the property occurs.

If the buyer fails to adhere to the stipulations contained in the Declaration of Intent, the rate of the tax does not decrease until taxes based on nonagricultural use have been paid for five years.

State Transfer Tax Exemptions

The state transfer tax does not apply to the recordation of any instrument that transfers an interest in property to an organization that:

1 is exempt from federal income taxation;

2 is incorporated in Maryland or, if not, is registered to do business in Maryland;

3 has as its principal purpose the preservation of agricultural land, including temporary ownership of interests in land for the purpose of preservation of its character as agricultural land;

4 has been certified by the Department of Assessments and Taxation that it meets all of the above requirements.

Recordation Tax and State Property Transfer Tax on Leases

In the case of a lease creating a perpetually renewable ground rent, the tax is based upon the capitalization of the annual ground rent, plus the actual consideration, other than the ground rent, paid or to be paid.

QUESTIONS

1. To be valid, a will must be:

    a. in writing and signed by the grantor.
    b. signed and witnessed as required by law.
    c. acknowledged and recorded.
    d. prepared by an attorney at law.

2. John, a bachelor, died testate and left his real estate to his married brother. The brother's ownership actually took effect:

    a. when the will was signed and witnessed.
    b. when the will was probated and the estate distributed.
    c. as of the date of death.
    d. as of the date the will was recorded.

3. When the documentary stamp tax is at the rate of $1.10 per $500 or fraction thereof of sale price and the sale price is $34,350, then the amount of the required stamp tax is:

    a. $75.90.
    b. $74.80.
    c. $76.95.
    d. $74.90.

4. The transfer tax on a sale of real estate for $27,800 at the rate of one-half percent of the total consideration is:

    a. $ 13.93.
    b. $139.
    c. $ 138.30.
    d. $1,390.

13

Title Records

RECORDING DOCUMENTS

According to Maryland state law, deeds, mortgages, contracts, and other documents creating an estate in real estate that will exist for longer than seven years, as well as similar documents affecting title to real property, must be recorded to be enforceable. In the purchase of real property, the grantee is responsible for seeing that the deed is recorded and for paying the necessary recording fees.

Subdivision plats, after being approved by state and local authorities, are recorded in order to comply with the law. Then the recorded plat data (liber and folio) can be used in later documents as a reference source to locate the exact boundaries of the lots within the subdivision.

Consideration. In order to be eligible for recordation, a deed must recite the full, actual consideration paid for the property; if the information is not in the deed, it must be stated in an affidavit attached to the deed.

Place of recording. Deeds and mortgages of real estate are recorded by the circuit court clerk of each county and Baltimore City. Recording must take place in the county or city in which the subject land is located; if the property is located in two counties, it must be recorded in both, and each county will charge a recording fee proportionate to the amount of land located in the county, as shown by the tax assessment. It should be noted that Maryland has only one system of recording; the Torrens system, as described in the text, does not exist in Maryland.

Grantor-grantee index. Real estate records are indexed by the names of the grantor and the grantee. All reference to previously recorded conveyances should not only give the liber and folio number, but also the name of the grantor and the grantee. The attorney for the buyer of a parcel of real estate should be concerned with checking the grantee index to be sure that the proposed seller is still the property owner of record. If the purchaser was financing the purchase by a mortgage to a financial institution, then the buyer who will be the grantee in the new deed will become a grantor when the mortgage is executed to the financial institution.

Payment of real estate taxes required. No deed conveying real estate may be recorded in any county of Maryland until all taxes and other public assessments or charges on the property have been paid and the record of ownership has been transferred on the tax assessment books to the grantee who is named in the deed to be recorded. If the deed transfers all of the real estate owned by the grantor in the county, then, in many counties, all of the grantor's personal property tax must also be paid prior to recording.

Payment of water bill required. In Baltimore City, a deed conveying real estate may not be recorded if there is an unpaid water bill over $50. In Harford County, no deed conveying real estate may be recorded unless the water bill is paid. Requirements should be checked in the county or municipality involved.

Recording Fees

The amount of fees to be charged for the recording of deeds and other documents is set by state law. In many counties it is $3 per page, or portion thereof, of the document plus $1 for each name to be indexed in the grantor-grantee index. When a document is recorded, it is taken to the court clerk's office, the proper amount of documentary stamps and transfer tax stamps are paid for, the proper recording fee is paid, and the document is left with the clerk. By microfilm or other photographic process, the contents of the document are reproduced in the public record. The document is stamped to indicate both the book or liber number and the folio or page number where the contents have been recorded. Then the document is imprinted with a notice that it has been recorded and is returned to the person to whom it belongs.

Real Estate Brokers and Subdivision Laws Regarding Recording

Recordation and development of individual lots in a subdivision are regulated on a local level by the county in which the property is located. A licensee should always be sure that the deeds to the individual lots for sale in a subdivision have been properly recorded and that all local laws regarding recordation have been met before advertising the lots for sale. Failure to do so could result in a judicial injunction, which would halt the licensee from marketing the property further. In addition, depending on the situation, the licensee may also be in violation of the state license law and subject to suspension or revocation of his or her real estate license.

TITLE EVIDENCE

In Maryland, it is the buyer's responsibility in a real estate transaction to obtain and pay for title evidence. Generally, the purchaser will hire an attorney, who will examine the title records. After examining the records, the attorney will usually adopt one of two possible courses of action. The attorney might have an abstract of title prepared and then, from the study of this abstract, prepare a certificate of title indicating his or her personal opinion of the present condition of the title. Or, if the attorney happens to be a licensed representative of a title insurance company, he or she might personally issue a title insurance policy based on an examination of the abstract. The attorney will either deliver this to the purchaser or forward the abstract to the title insurance company so that the company may issue a title policy.

Note that Maryland law requires that the following notice be given to buyers, printed in bold type in the body of each sales contract presented by licensees: YOU ARE ENTITLED TO SELECT YOUR OWN TITLE INSURANCE COMPANY, SETTLEMENT COMPANY, ESCROW COMPANY, OR TITLE ATTORNEY.

Uniform Commercial Code

The Uniform Commercial Code is in effect in Maryland. Two sections of this code might affect real estate practices: (1) chattel mortgages on fixtures or contents have been replaced with security agreements and financing statements; and (2) the article covering bulk sales applies when a person sells all of the stock in trade in the sale of a business. See Chapter 13 of the text for further comments regarding the code.

QUESTIONS

1. A buyer purchased a parcel of real estate that is in both Montgomery and Frederick Counties, and one deed was received from the seller. The buyer has properly protected his or her interest when the deed is recorded with the clerk of the court:

    a. in Montgomery County.
    b. in Frederick County.
    c. in the state capitol.
    d. in both counties.

2. When a parcel of Maryland real estate is sold, the responsibility for having the title searched falls on the:

    a. seller.
    b. buyer.
    c. broker.
    d. seller and broker together.

3. In order to be eligible for recordation, a deed need not:

    a. recite the full consideration paid for the property.
    b. have an affidavit attached to the deed which includes information pertaining to the full consideration when the full consideration is recited in the deed.
    c. be recorded in two counties when the majority of the land is located in one county.
    d. have all property taxes paid on the property being transferred.

4. Deeds and mortgages may be recorded in each county with the:

    a. circuit court clerk.
    b. Torrens system.
    c. tax office.
    d. office of planning and zoning.

5. In Maryland, county real estate records are not:

   a. indexed under the name of the grantor.
   b. indexed under the name of the grantee.
   c. indexed under the name of selling broker.
   d. referenced to previously recorded conveyances.

14

Real Estate License Law

The Maryland Real Estate License Law was enacted on June 1, 1939, by the State Legislature as part of Article 56 of the Annotated Code of Maryland. A copy of this law may be picked up at the Real Estate Commission of Maryland, 501 St. Paul Place, 8th floor South, Baltimore, Maryland or from one of the local boards.

There are four parts to the Maryland Real Estate License Law:

1 The basic law (code), Sections 212-232A, sets general guidelines and provides for the Real Estate Commission of Maryland to administer the license law. This also includes the establishment and operation of the Real Estate Guaranty Fund provided to compensate persons who have suffered a monetary loss resulting from the unlawful action of a broker or salesman.
2 The regulations issued by the Commission state specific requirements and have the same importance as the basic law.
3 The Code of Ethics for brokers and salespeople has the same importance as the basic law.
4 The section of the law entitled "Hearing Rules" includes the general rules of procedure governing judicial hearings conducted by the Real Estate Commission, as well as claims for reimbursement from the Real Estate Guaranty Fund. Hearings are required when the Commission is considering the denial, suspension, or revocation of a license.

The summary of the license law contained in this lesson is intended only to acquaint you with its general provisions. Under the COMAR (Code of Maryland) codification system, every regulation is assigned a unique four-part identification number. All regulations found in COMAR are arranged by title. Each title is divided into numbered subtitle, which is divided into numbered chapters, which are divided into numbered regulations. A regulation may be divided into letter sections, a section divided into number paragraphs, and a paragraph into number subparagraphs.

For example, components of the citation 09.11.01.25 B(2) are as follows:

09 - Title - Department of Licensing and Regulation
11 - Subtitle - Real Estate Commission
01 - Chapter - General regulations of the Commission (02 refers to Hearing Rules, 03 refers to the Code of Ethics)
25 - Regulation - Use of Trade Names
B - Section - Definitions
(2) - Subsection - Meaning of "Trade Name."

Regulations are recodified periodically. For simplification, only the regulation instead of the complete citation is referred to in this supplement. Due to recodification between printings, the actual regulation number and the number shown in the supplement could differ.

WHO MUST BE LICENSED

Definitions (Section 212)

Broker A real estate broker is any person, association, copartnership, or corporation (foreign or domestic) who performs or attempts to perform one of the following acts for another person for a fee, commission, or other valuable consideration, or promises thereof:

1 sells, purchases, exchanges, leases, or rents real estate
2 collects rents for the use of real estate
3 offers verbally, through advertisement, telephone solicitation, or any other means, to perform any of these acts
4 aids or tries to aid any person, for a fee, in locating or obtaining any residential real estate for purchase or lease
5 regularly engages in the business of dealing and trading in real estate, leases, or options
6 engages in the business of charging and collecting a fee in connection with any contract by which he or she promises to promote the sale of real estate by listing in a publication that is primarily issued for such purposes, or refers information about such real estate to brokers, or both
7 engages in the business of subdividing and selling land in building lots or sites, no matter where in the United States such real estate is located
8 builds or sells condominium properties.

Associate broker Any person, including an independent contractor, must be licensed as an associate broker if he or she is licensed as a real estate broker and engages in brokerage acts for a firm but also continues to work for a licensed broker.

Real estate salesperson Any person, including an independent contractor, who performs any of the specified brokerage acts on the behalf of a licensed real estate broker must be licensed as a salesperson.

Commission The Real Estate Commission of Maryland.

Real estate This includes any interest or estate in real property located in or outside of Maryland. It also includes a timeshare estate.

Real property This includes a condominium.

Timeshare estate The ownership during separated time periods, over a period of at least five years, including renewal options, of a timeshare unit or any of several timeshare units, whether the ownership is a freehold estate or an estate for years.

Timeshare developers Any person in the business of creating or disposing of that person's timeshares in timeshare projects as provided under Title 11A of the Real Property Article.

Timeshare developers were required in 1983 under Article 56 of the Annotated Code of Maryland to register with the Commission and to open their books to state auditors. Developers were also required to maintain a surety bond to cover the deposits of purchase money, a provision aimed at keeping under-capitalized developers out of the business. A more comprehensive Time-Share Model Act was studied for the 1984 legislative session, resulting in the enactment of Title 11A Real Estate Time-Sharing Act of the Real Property Article of the Annotated Code of Maryland. This is explained in Chapter 8. Under Title 11A, developers are still required to register with the Commission. Title 11A also describes the Real Estate Commission's powers regarding timeshares.

Acts of brokerage Any person, partnership, association or corporation who, for a fee, directly or indirectly, performs or offers or attempts to perform any single act or transaction described in the definition of broker, associate broker, or salesperson, whether the act is an incidental part of a transaction or the entire transaction, is considered to be a real estate broker or salesperson as defined in Section 212 of the Code. However, a secretary or receptionist in a broker's office does not require a license to answer telephone inquiries regarding listed real estate. The State Attorney General has indicated that a license is not needed merely to quote a listed price. However, if the receptionist or secretary goes into details about the price, value, or financing arrangements, then this is the kind of information or advice that "requires the training and discretion of a real estate salesperson or broker."

Exceptions

The definitions of real estate broker and real estate salesperson stated above do not include the following persons:

1 receivers, trustees, administrators, executors, guardians, and other persons appointed by or acting under the judgment or order of any court.
2 public officers who are performing their official duty.
3 any bank, trust company, or mortgage loan institution organized under the laws of Maryland or the United States that is acting in the management or sale of property acquired through or in connection with mortgage foreclosures.
4 owners or lessors of property acting in the management or sale of that property, except when their principal and regular business is purchasing, selling, exchanging, or trading real estate, options, or leases.
5 investment home builders who are selling or renting homes they have built.
6 attorneys-at-law who are not regularly engaged in the real estate business and who do not offer to the public in any way the services listed in the definition of a real estate broker.
7 any person acting in good faith under a valid power of attorney from a real estate owner that authorizes the sale, conveyance, or leasing of the owner's real estate, providing only one such transaction is involved.
8 any duly-licensed auctioneer acting in the sale of real estate at a public auction.

9 owner of property selling fewer than seven lots per year, subdividing or selling property owned for 10 years or more. This exemption from licensure for an owner continues with respect to the heirs inheriting the property and, if the owner remains personally liable, with respect to any corporation wholly owned by the owner or heirs to which the property may have been conveyed.

REAL ESTATE COMMISSION OF MARYLAND

Creation and Membership (Section 213)

The Real Estate Commission of Maryland is a part of the Department of Licensing and Regulation, created for the purpose of administering the Real Estate License Law. There are eight members on the Commission, each appointed by the governor for a four-year term. Five of the members must be licensed real estate brokers or salespeople and must have been citizens and residents for at least five years of the particular areas from which they were appointed. One commissioner is appointed from each of the five districts into which the state is divided for this purpose. The other three commissioners are appointed from the public at large and specifically shall not be engaged in the real estate business. From its members, the Commission annually elects a chairman and a vice-chairman who serve one year and are eligible for reelection.

The Commission has the authority to adopt, fix, and establish reasonable rules and regulations to conduct its business, hold hearings, and generally carry out the provisions of the license law. (Section 214)

Real estate brokers are required to post a preprinted "Notice to Public" to inform the general public of the existence and purpose of the Commission. The notice must be displayed in a conspicuous manner in all offices where real estate business is conducted. Copies of this notice may be obtained through the Real Estate Commission.

Executive Director and Employees (Section 214)

The Commission, subject to the approval of the Secretary of Licensing and Regulations, may employ an executive director and any assistants necessary to aid in performing its duties. Such persons serve at the Commission's pleasure and can be removed at any time by the Commission or the Secretary of Licensing and Regulation. The Commission also has the power to employ field inspectors to investigate violations of the Real Estate License Law.

To avoid any conflicts of interest, the executive director, the field inspectors, and any other persons employed by the Commission, may not be licen$ed as real estate brokers or salesmen in Maryland while employed by the Commission.

Article 56, Section 214(a) was amended, effective July 1, 1983, to authorize the Secretary of the Department of Licensing and Regulation to select the Executive Director of the Real Estate Commission. The selection must be one of three nominees recommended by the Real Estate Commission. The Executive Director prior to this served at the pleasure of the Secretary.

Office, Records, Meetings, Authority, and Funds (Sections 215 and 216)

The Commission must maintain its own office. Copies of some of the Commission's records are available for public inspection. The Maryland Public Information Act applies to records, and, therefore, some information, such as unresolved formal chages, may be withheld from public inspection. The Commission is required to hold public meetings at least once a month and public notice must be given of every regular meeting. The public also has the right to appear before the Commission and be heard on subjects that fall within the Commission's jurisdiction.

All powers, authority, duties, and functions of the Commission are subject to the power and authority of the Secretary of Licensing and Regulation.

All fees collected by the Commission are deposited with the State Treasurer. The executive director of the Commission must maintain books of account that must be audited regularly by the State Auditor.

ISSUANCE OF LICENSES

Any person, copartnership, association, or corporation who engages in the business of, or acts in the capacity of, a real estate broker or salesperson must first obtain a license.

Applications (Section 217)

An applicant for a real estate broker's or salesperson's license must meet these requirements:

1 must be at least 18 years of age.
2 must apply in writing on the blank forms prepared by the Commission.
3 must be trustworthy and qualified to perform the authorized functions of a broker or salesperson.
4 must complete a required real estate principles and practices course that is approved by the Commission.
5 must pass a written examination required by the Commission to test the applicant's qualifications and knowledge of Maryland law and general real estate principles.
6 must submit a credit report from an approved credit agency, including a statement regarding the applicant's involvement in any personal lawsuits (Regulation .07).
7 must file the proper application form for licensure, accompanied by documentation supporting the successful completion of the educational requirements, and the "pass" notice issued by the real estate exam testing service.
8 must pay the proper fees.

Broker's Application

Applicants for a broker's license must present evidence of having satisfactorily completed 135 clock hours or semester credit hours of the prescribed Broker's Real Estate Principles and Practices course at a degree-granting college or university. Details of the requirements are included in Regulation 16. These requirements are under review and possibly will be upgraded in the near future. An applicant must have at least three years' experience in selling real estate as a licensed real estate salesperson, or related experience.

Note, however, that a member of the Maryland Bar may apply for a broker's license without having to meet the educational requirements. However, all applicants must take the exam. (He or she, however, must establish an escrow account and furnish the information regarding such account to the commission.)

Salesperson's Application

An application for a salesperson's license must be signed by the applicant and also by the licensed broker through whom the salesperson will be licensed or by whom he or she will be employed. Applicants must present evidence of having satisfactorily completed the required salesperson's course in Real Estate Principles and Practices as approved by the Commission. Details of this course are set out in Regulations 13 and 22.

Corporations, Copartnerships, and Associations (Section 218)

A copartnership, association, or corporation may apply for a real estate broker's license and authorize one of its members or officers to represent the organization as its real estate broker of record. The broker of record's name is entered on the license and he or she performs all the functions of the real estate broker in the name of the applicant. All other members or officers who will actively engage in the real estate business of the firm must apply for and obtain associate brokers' or salespersons' licenses in their own names. Such associate brokers and salespeople can only function as such on behalf of their partnership, association, or corporation and not on their own behalf, unless permitted by the broker of record.

The law was amended to permit members or officers of copartnerships, associations, and corporations to be licensed as salespeople, as well as associate brokers. However, the law limits the cumulative amount of ownership that salespeople may hold in the firm to 49 percent of the outstanding ownership interests.

With the consent of a broker, an individual salesperson, or two or more salespeople licensed to act on behalf of the broker, may form a professional service corporation wholly owned by the salesperson(s). Those salespeople who have incorporated may direct that their commissions be paid to the corporation, with the consent of the broker.

Examinations (Section 217)

Every applicant for a real estate salesperson's or broker's license must take and pass the appropriate qualifying examination required by the Commission. The written examination is prepared and administered for the State of Maryland by Assessments Systems Incorporated (ASI) of Philadelphia, Pennsylvania.

Applicants must receive a passing grade on the exam to be eligible to receive a license. An applicant for the broker's or salesperson's license who fails the examination may take another exam. Arrangements for taking or retaking the license exams are handled by ASI.

Nonresident Licensing and Reciprocity (Section 219)

A nonresident of Maryland who is licensed as a real estate broker or salesperson in another state may become a broker or salesperson in Maryland by conforming to all of the conditions of the Maryland Code. A nonresident applicant must furnish a certified copy of his or her real estate license along with the application, instead of the various statements that usually accompany an application from a Maryland resident. An applicant who is already a broker in another state is required to maintain an active place of business in that state.

Irrevocable consent. Every nonresident applicant must file an irrevocable consent document, which provides that suits and actions may be properly commenced in any county in Maryland where there is cause for such a suit or where the plaintiff resides. By the consent document, the nonresident also agrees that any such suit and its outcome will be valid and binding on him.

Such a suit is commenced when a process or pleading is served upon the Secretary of the Commission. At this time, a duplicate copy must be forwarded by registered mail to the main office of the person against whom the process or pleading is directed.

Splitting fees. Maryland resident broker licensees are permitted to split fees with nonresident brokers, providing that the arrangement is compatible with the laws of the state where the other broker is licensed. By splitting a fee, holding deposits, or participating in any real estate transaction in Maryland, a nonresident broker or salesperson has created an irrevocable consent that has the same effect in legal actions arising out of the transactions as the consent form required of nonresidents.

Maryland residents. A Maryland licensee may obtain a license to practice real estate in several other states without being required to meet their educational prerequisites. Salespeople as well as brokers must be licensed by a state in order to engage in transactions in that state. Presently, reciprocal licensing for Maryland brokers and salespeople is possible in Delaware, the District of Columbia, North Carolina, Pennsylvania, Virginia, and West Virginia.

License Fees (Section 223)

The following real estate license fees are charged to residents of Maryland when licenses are issued and when they are renewed every two years (biennially).

	Original	Renewal
Broker	$70.00	$80.00
Associate Broker	$20.00	$30.00
Salesperson	$20.00	$30.00
For each additional office or place of business	$ 5.00	$ 5.00

In addition, the following fees are also charged.

For taking broker's examination	$10.00
For taking a salesperson's examination	$ 5.00
Each change of office or place of business; each change of name on licensee's records	$ 5.00
Transfer of salesperson's license to new broker or certification of licensure	$10.00
Each duplicate license (where original is lost or destroyed)	$ 2.50
Each duplicate pocket registration card (where original is lost or destroyed and an affidavit is made to give the facts)	$ 1.00
Returned checks for lack of funds	$ 5.00
Certification of licensure	$10.00

The proper amount of fees must accompany an application. Total fees payable to the Commission are:

For	License fee		Processing fee		Guaranty Fund		Total
Broker	$70	+	$10	+	$20	=	$100
Associate Broker	$20	+	$10	+	$20	=	$ 50
Salesperson	$20	+	$ 5	+	$20	=	$ 45

Note that if the licensee has already paid into the guaranty fund as a salesperson and is upgrading his or her license to broker or associate broker, this fee will be waived.

Also, applicants taking an examination are required to pay to the testing service, Assessment Systems, Inc., which has been selected by the Commission to administer the examinations, an additional fee that covers the actual cost of giving the exam (presently $15.45, or $25.45 for applicants who have not preregistered) and walk into the testing center on the day of the examination.

Issuing a License (Section 221)

A license and pocket identification card are issued to each new licensee by the Commission. The Commission must issue licenses to all applicants who are qualified under the provisions of the law and who prove their intention to actively engage in the real estate business. If the Commission wishes to refuse to issue a license to an applicant who has filed a proper application, the Commission must hold a hearing on the matter before refusing the license.

The Commission may refuse to issue or renew a license to any person who has been convicted in any court in the United States of any crime that constitutes a violation of the Maryland Code and for which a license might be revoked (Section 217(d)).

On application, the Commission will issue a nonresident license to a Maryland licensee who moves from the state but continues to do business regularly in Maryland.

Maryland Securities Act

The Maryland Securities Act, Maryland Corporations and Associations Article, Sections 11-101 through 11-805 requires licensing of persons engaged in the offer and sale of real estate-related securities, including limited partnership interests. In addition, the Act may require registration of the actual limited partnership interest or other securities. Failure to obtain the proper license or registration may result in the imposition of civil, administrative, or criminal penalties.

Whenever it appears to the Maryland Securities Commissioner that any person has engaged or is about to engage in any act or practice constituting a violation of any provision of the state's Security Act, the Commissioner may bring an action to enjoin the acts or practices and to enforce compliance. A permanent or temporary injunction or restraining order may be granted and a receiver or conservator appointed for the defendant or the defendant's assets.

REAL ESTATE GUARANTY FUND (Section 217A)

The Commission has established, maintains and administers a real estate guaranty fund, as required by law. Any person who has suffered loss from a real estate transaction through any of the following illegal actions by any broker or salesperson licensed in Maryland or any unlicensed employee of the broker may apply to recover compensation in an amount not exceeding $25,000.

1 embezzlement or theft of money or property
2 the unlawful obtaining of money from any person by false pretenses, artifice, trickery, or forgery
3 any fraud, misrepresentation, or deceit by or on the part of a broker, salesperson, or unlicensed employee of a broker
4 any violation of the Maryland Real Estate License Law by a broker, salesperson, or unlicensed employee of a broker

Licenses are required to give written disclosure in the sales contract that the purchaser is not protected by the fund in an amount in excess of $25,000.

Establishing and Maintaining the Fund

Since the establishment of the fund in July, 1971, every applicant who applies for and receives a real estate broker's or salesperson's license has been required to pay a one-time fee of $20 to the guaranty fund. Brokers and salespeople licensed prior to July, 1971, paid their $20 fees the first time they renewed their licenses thereafter.

The Commission must maintain a minimum of $250,000 in the fund. All monies in the fund may be invested and reinvested, and the income will be credited to the fund. If the fund falls below $250,000, the Commission will assess each Maryland licensee a sum sufficient to meet the minimum.

Claims Against the Fund

Any person commencing a claim against the fund must immediately notify the Commission in writing of that action. The aggrieved person who has suffered a monetary loss must also file a verified claim with the Commission. The Commission will then hold a hearing on the claim and the aggrieved person must show the following:

1 that he or she is not the spouse of the debtor or a personal representative of the debtor's spouse
2 that the claim arose from a real estate transaction not including the purchase of any interest in a limited partnership whose purpose is to invest in real estate, a joint venture promoted by a licensee for the purpose of investment in real estate by two or more people, or the purchase of commercial paper secured by real estate
3 that he or she is not a spouse of the licensee or unlicensed employee alleged to be responsible for the claim, or the personal representative of such spouse
4 that the broker or salesperson violated provisions of Section 217A or any other provision of the real estate broker subtitle (Art. 56.212 et Seq.).

A copy of the claim is forwarded by the Commission to the licensee(s) alleged to be responsible for the loss of the claimant. The licensee(s) must furnish the Commission with a written response to the allegations set forth in the claim within 10 days. After review of the claim and the response and any investigation, the Commission sets the hearing date or dismisses the claim if frivolous, made in bad faith, or legally insufficient.

When the claim is caused by misconduct of a currently licensed broker or salesperson, the Commission joins the proceedings against the licensee on charges of violating the license law. The claimant is a party to the hearing and may participate to the extent necessary to establish the claim. Before the Commission can direct any payment from the guaranty fund, the Commission must conclude that the action of the licensee causing the monetary loss to the claimant constitutes violation of the provisions of the license law for which the licensee was charged.

When the Commission is satisfied that the claim is valid, it can direct payment from the guaranty fund of whatever sum it finds to be fair compensation for the claim. If, at any time, there is not enough money in the fund to pay a claim authorized by the Commission, payment shall be delayed until there are sufficient funds in the guaranty fund to cover the claim, plus ten percent interest on the unpaid balance. Such claims are limited to actual cash damages incurred in the transaction, not including any commissions paid or owed to a licensee acting in the capacity of either a principal or agent in the transaction, or attorney's fees perfecting the claim. Claims against the guaranty fund are valid only on real property located within the state of Maryland. Any person whose claim is denied or a licensee on whose account a claim is paid may appeal.

A three-year time limit has been placed upon the filing of a claim against the Real Estate Guarantee Fund after the grounds for recovery have been discovered (or by the exercise of ordinary diligence should have been discovered). This applies only to claims accruing after July 1, 1981.

Reimbursement to the Fund

The amount paid from the guaranty fund, plus interest of not less than 10% per year, is to be repaid by the licensee on whose account a claim was paid in full within 30 days after the order becomes final. If payment is not made, the Commission or the Commission's assignee, the State Central Collection Unit, may bring suit for judgment against the licensee for the unpaid amount. The Commission or its assignee is entitled to a judgment in the amount remaining unpaid upon showing that:

1 a claim was paid out of the guaranty fund on account of the defendant;
2 the Commission's order was final, in accordance with the Administrative Procedure Act, and no appeal is pending; and
3 the fund has not been reimbursed in whole or part.

If the guaranty fund has insufficient money to satisfy current claims, the Commission pays them in the order that the claims were originally filed when sufficient funds have been deposited, plus accumulated interest at the rate of 10 percent a year.

Subrogation

When the Commission has authorized and paid a claim to an aggrieved person, it shall be subrogated by operation of the law to take over all rights of the aggrieved person (up to the amount paid) against the broker, salesperson, or unlicensed employee whose actions caused the claim. The Commission forwards claims paid on the behalf of licensees to the Central Collection Unit of the Department of Budgets which attempts to recover the amount of funds paid. Any money and interest that the Commission recovers on the claim is to be deposited in the guaranty fund.

In addition, the Commission is deemed a creditor with respect to the amount paid for the purpose of exempting to any discharge of a licensee under the Bankruptcy Act (11 U.S.C.A.).

Disciplinary Actions Against Registrants

False statements. Any person who knowingly files with the Commission any notice, statement, or other document required by the guaranty fund provisions that is untrue or contains important misstatements of fact is subject to a fine of not less than $200.

Revocation. If the Commission pays from the fund any amount in settlement of a claim against a licensed real estate broker or real estate salesperson, the license of the broker or salesperson shall be automatically revoked. No such broker or salesperson will be eligible to receive a new license until he or she has repaid in full the amount paid from the guaranty fund on his or her account plus interest at the rate of 10 percent a year. Until the fund is repaid, the broker or salesperson is barred from any association, in any capacity whatsoever, including as a stockholder, investor, or through ownership of any other interest, with any real estate broker or firm doing business in this state.

The repayment in full by a licensee of the amount paid from the fund on the licensee's behalf does not prevent the Commission from taking disciplinary action against the licensee. There is nothing to limit the authority of the Commission to take disciplinary action against any licensee for violation of the law.

LICENSE TRANSFERS AND RENEWALS

License Renewal (Section 230(f))

Licenses are renewed on April 30 every two years, and the Commission assesses penalties for late renewals. Regulation .05 provides that a licensee who fails to renew his or her license during the calendar year following its date of expiration must fulfill the educational requirement again and retake the exam before another license will be issued. There are, however, individual cases where the Commission may have cause to waive this requirement. Section 230 also provides that any licensee who fails to pay the renewal fee and penalties after 30 days' written notice from the Commission shall be deemed to be operating without a license and be subject to the penalties provided in Section 231 of the Act. Anyone receiving a license any time prior to April 30 of the renewal year is subject to renewal of license.

Computerized licenses. Effective with the 1982 renewal, all licenses are printed by computer. The licenses are no longer color-coded. Because of limited space on the computer, some longer trade names have been abbreviated.

Processing delays. Due to the large volume of mail received during renewal time, processing delays are inevitable. In the past, the Commission has experienced difficulty in two areas: repeated phone calls from licensees, and licensees arriving personally at the Commission's office to fill out applications. With the cooperation of licensees, delays can be minimized if licensees handle their renewals strictly by mail.

Continuing education (Section 217). Licensees are required to complete a continuing education requirement within every two-year license renewal period after May 1, 1984. However, a licensee obtaining a license during the second year of a license renewal period will not have to fulfill the educational requirement until his or her second renewal period.

In order to fulfill this requirement, a licensee must complete 12 clock hours of approved continuing education. The Commission has discretion in requiring subjects for continuing education instruction.

Every educational institution approved by the Commission to teach continuing education courses is required to issue a standard certificate attesting to the licensee's completion of the indicated number of classroom hours. The Commission will accept only the original copy of this certificate.

In 1983, when the continuing education requirement was changed from every other two-year license renewal period to every two-year license renewal period effective May 1, 1984, the law was revised in such a way that it was no longer clear that the completion of continuing education clock hours prior to the effective date met the continuing education requirement. Because of this, the general assembly clarified the law so that for the real estate license renewal period of May 1, 1984 through April 30, 1986, the Real Estate Commission will accept clock hours of approved continuing education completed by the licensee between July 1, 1983 and April 30, 1986, to meet the continuing education requirements.

Armed services (Section 217(c)(1)). Any licensed broker entering the armed services may designate an attorney, an adult member of his or her immediate family, or any licensed salesperson-employee to supervise and carry on the business during the broker's military service. The broker's license may be regularly renewed during this period by the designated person.

Death of broker (Section 217(c)(1). Any adult member of a deceased broker's family has the right to carry on the broker's business for the remainder of the license year or six months, whichever is longer. Any member of the immediate family who has been licensed as a salesperson for at least three continuous years may make proper application, take the examination, and be licensed as a broker without fulfilling the educational requirement. Such a license will be valid for four years, during which time the broker must complete the educational requirement. If it is not completed during this time, the Commission will not renew the license.

Inactive Status (Section 217(e))

A broker or salesperson holding a current and unrevoked license may return his or her license to the Commission and have it placed on inactive status. The license may remain inactive for four years, during which time the licensee may not engage in the activities of a broker or salesperson. The licensee must, however, still pay the regular license fee. An inactive license will be reinstated to active status 30 days after the licensee submits a request for reinstatement to the Commission and pays all fees due. If the license has been inactive for more than four years, the licensee must meet the current educational requirements before the license will be reinstated to active status. The Commission recommends that anyone planning to go on inactive status during the renewal period should wait until the license is renewed, then forward the application with a written request that the license be held on inactive status. Prior to 1983, inactive status was limited to two years.

Transfer of Salesperson's License

In 1973, the Commission introduced new transfer forms to simplify the procedure for a transfer of employer or change of name or address. However, according to Regulation .10, a salesperson may not transfer a license from one broker to another (change employers) during the 30 days preceding the expiration date on the license. This regulation was created to avoid transfers during the renewal period when the Commission is busy with license renewal applications. In addition, the Real Estate Commission will not process any office transfer request made by a salesperson unless the request includes the signature of the new broker. Any request submitted without this signature will be returned to the salesperson.

Termination of Salesperson's Employment (Section 222(b))

When a salesperson's employment is terminated, either by the employing broker or the salesperson, it is the broker's duty, as the person responsible for all salespeople licensed under him or her, to immediately notify the Commission of the termination and the reasons therefore, and to surrender the salesperson's license. At the same time, the broker must send a signed notice of termination to the salesperson's last known address. The Commission's notice should include a copy of the notice sent to the salesperson.

A salesperson whose employment has been terminated must not directly or indirectly engage in any of the activities of a real estate salesperson. The salesperson, upon acquiring a new employer, must apply for a license transfer and resume activities only when the Commission, at its discretion, issues a license with the new employer's name on it.

Regulation .03 states that a broker must surrender to the Commission the license of any salesperson who has not performed any of the acts listed in the definition of a broker given in Article 56, Section 212(a) of the Maryland Code for a period of one year. Brokers can comply with this regulation by mailing to the Commission the license and pocket card of inactive licensees together with a letter of explanation. This reduces possible requests for transfer from one broker to another and also enables the Commission to annotate the files of the inactive salespeople for future reference.

In addition, the Commission can demand that a broker surrender an employee's license. Regulation .09 requires a broker to comply with such a demand. Willful refusal or failure to comply can be cause for the revocation or suspension of the broker's license by the Commission.

Every license returned to the Commission should arrive with a separate letter signed by the broker. A copy of this letter should also be mailed to the agent's last known address. In addition, an attempt should be made to retrieve the agent's identification card.

REFUSAL, SUSPENSION, OR REVOCATION OF LICENSES

The Commission may refuse to issue or renew, or may suspend or revoke, a real estate license for any one of the reasons listed in Section 224 and other sections of Article 56 of the Annotated Code of Maryland. The Commission may take such action on its own or must act upon the written complaint of another person. The complaint must be substantiated by sufficient evidence (documentary or otherwise) to make a prima facie case against the accused licensee.

In addition to suspending or revoking a license, the Commission also has the power to seek a court-imposed penalty of up to $2,000 per violation upon any licensee who has obtained a license by false or fraudulent representation or who, in performing or attempting to perform any of the acts covered by this law, is deemed to be guilty of any of the following acts (Section 224(a)):

1 willful misrepresentation or knowingly making false promises directly or through agents or salespeople (Section 224(b))
2 using for the listing of property, or for the sale, rent or exchange of property, any form or advertising matter that includes the name of any association or organization of which the licensee is not a member (Section 224(c))

3 retaining the services of any person as a salesperson on a purely temporary or single-deal basis as a means of evading the law regarding payment of commissions to a nonlicensed person on some contemplated transaction (Section 224(d))

4 acting for more than one party in a transaction without the knowledge of all parties involved in the transaction (Section 224(e))

5 accepting a commission or valuable consideration as a real estate salesperson for the performance of any of the acts specified in the law from any person except the real estate broker named in his or her license (Section 224(f))

6 representing or attempting to represent any other real estate broker as a salesperson without the express knowledge and consent of the broker named in his or her license (Section 224(g))

7 failing to account for and remit as soon as possible any monies coming into his or her possession which belong to others; or failing to promptly furnish a duplicate copy of all listing contracts to sell or rent property, leases, or contracts of sale, when prepared by the licensee, to all parties to the contracts or leases; or failure to retain a copy of such contracts. However, nothing in the law shall be construed to authorize any broker or salesperson to personally prepare any such legal papers (Section 224(h))

8 disregard or violation of any provisions of this law (Section 224(i))

9 any misleading or untruthful advertising, including advertising property for sale or rent or offering to buy property as an agent or broker without disclosing in such advertisement the name of the advertiser or the fact that the advertiser is an agent or broker. Where any such advertising is published over the name of a licensed real estate salesperson, failure to disclose in the advertisement the name of the broker whom the salesperson is licensed to represent is in violation of this law (Section 224(j))

10 paying or receiving any rebate, profit, compensation, or commission in violation of this law (Section 224(k))

11 knowingly soliciting any party to an exclusive listing contract that exists with another licensee or soliciting any party to an existing sales contract, lease, or agreement to break such contract negotiated by another licensee for the purpose of substituting in lieu thereof a new contract, lease, or agreement where such soliciting or inducing is motivated by anticipated personal gain on the part of the licensee (Section 224(l))

12 conviction of the licensee in a court of competent jurisdiction of this or any other state for forgery, embezzlement, obtaining money under false pretenses, larceny, extortion, conspiracy to defraud, or other like offense (Section 224(m))

13 guaranteeing, or having authorized or permitted any person to guarantee, future profits resulting from the resale of real property (Section 224(n))

14 soliciting, selling, or offering for sale real property by offering "free lots," by conducting lotteries or contests, or by offering prizes for the purpose of influencing a purchaser or prospective purchaser of real property; advertising "free appraisals," unless the advertiser is equipped and stands ready to appraise real estate for any person requesting such an appraisal free of charge, regardless of the purpose for which the appraisal is requested; accepting a listing contract to sell property, unless such contract provides for a definite termination date without notice from either party; or accepting any listing contract

that provides for a "net" return to the seller or vendor, leaving the licensee free to sell the property at any price obtainable in excess of the "net" price named by the vendor (Section 224(o))

15 a nonresident licensee whose license in his or her home state has been revoked by the local real estate commission may have a Maryland license revoked without a hearing by the Maryland Real Estate Commission (Section 224(p))

16 conviction by a court of competent jurisdiction of any act which constitutes a violation of the law; upon such final conviction and expiration of the period for appeal, the Commission has the right to revoke the license without hearing (Section 224(q))

17 negligence or failure to disclose, or to ascertain and disclose, to any person with whom the licensee is dealing, any material fact, data, or information concerning or relating to the property with which the licensee is dealing, which the licensee knew or should have known (Section 224(r))

18 any act or conduct, whether of the same or a different character than those already specified, which constitutes or demonstrates bad faith, incompetency or untrustworthiness, or dishonest, fraudulent, or improper dealings; or a conviction for a crime involving an act of moral turpitude (Section 224(s))

19 any unlawful act or violation of any of the provisions of the law by any licensee shall not also be cause for suspension or revocation of a license of any other licensee with whom the offender is associated in any manner whatsoever, unless it appears to the satisfaction of the Commission that the licensee or licensees with whom the offender is associated had actual knowledge of the violation (Section 224(t))

20 violating any provision of a regulation or of the Code of Ethics adopted by the Commission (Section 224(u))

21 knowingly inducing or attempting to induce another person to transfer an interest in real property located in developed or high-density areas, as defined by the Commission, whether or not acting for monetary gain, or discouraging another person from purchasing real property by representations regarding the existing or potential proximity of real property owned, used, or occupied by persons of any particular race, color, religion, or national origin, or by representations that the existing or potential proximity will or may result in (1) the lowering of property values; (2) a change in the racial, religious, or ethnic character of the block, neighborhood, or area in which the property is located; (3) an increase in criminal or antisocial behavior in the area; or (4) a decline in the quality of the schools serving the area (Section 224(v))

When the Commission suspends or revokes the license of any person, and no appeal to the courts has been filed within the time specified for those appeals, the Commission must notify both the Maryland Association of Realtors® and the local board of Realtors® having jurisdiction over the geographic area in which the person maintained an office. In the case of a nonresident whose license is suspended or revoked, the Commission reports such action to the Real Estate Commission of the licensee's home state.

Guidelines and standards have been established for the Real Estate Commission to consider when levying a monetary fine. The Commission may impose a penalty of up to $2,000 per violation upon any licensee at any time where the licensee has by false or fraudulent representation performed or attempted to perform any of the acts set forth in Section 224. In determining the amount of financial penalty to be imposed, the Commission considers the seriousness of the violation, the deleterious effect of the violation on the complainant, the good faith of the licensee, and the licensee's history of previous violations.

Authority to Reprimand

Article 56, Section 224(a) gives the Commission the authority to issue reprimands to any licensee for violations. If the Commission issues a second or any further official notice of reprimand to a licensee, the licensee must show cause why his or her license should not be suspended or revoked.

Injunctions (Section 231A)

The Commission has the power to seek a permanent or temporary injunction against violators of the real estate law. When seeking an injunction against a nonlicensee, the Commission is not required to file a bond.

HEARING REVIEW (Section 225)

Before denying an application for a real estate license or suspending or revoking the license of any resident licensee, the matter must be reviewed at a hearing before the Commission or a real estate hearing board.

Hearing Board

The Commission may appoint hearing officers or three of its members to act as a real estate hearing board or panel to hear complaints. One member will be designated to chair the board or panel (Section 224A), the other will be vice-chairperson serving as the head of the second panel. There are two panels--one hears, and the other reviews. Each panel consists of three members: two industry representatives and one lay member. There are two alternates for each member. Most of the cases are heard by hearing officers. The two panels, besides reviewing charges, spend considerable time hearing appeals from the hearing officer.

The executive director and assistant director of the Commission are authorized to administer oaths and issue subpoenas in conjunction with hearing proceedings before the Commission.

The applicant or licensee who is charged must be given written notice of the hearing at least ten days prior to the date set. Such notice may be served personally or sent by registered mail. The applicant or licensee must be given an opportunity to be heard in person or by counsel. If the person is a licensed salesperson, the Commission must also notify by registered mail the broker named in the salesperson's application of license (Section 225(a)).

The Commission sets the time and place of the hearing. Any member of the Commission, its secretary-treasurer, or any member of a real estate hearing board has the power to administer oaths, subpoena any person in Maryland, or take testimony by deposition from any person, as prescribed by state law for judicial procedure in civil cases. At such a hearing, the person charged has the right to call or subpoena witnesses for the defense (Section 225(a)). The Commission suggests that licensees or applicants obtain legal counsel.

Regulation .18 requires a licensee to reply in writing to inquiries made by the Commission within ten days of receipt.

If, upon hearing a case, the Commission refuses to issue or renew a license, or suspends or revokes a license, the applicant or license holder may have the case reviewed by the Superior Court of Baltimore City or the Circuit Court of the county involved, the choice of location being up to the licensee (Section 225(c)).

If the court grants a stay of suspension or revocation, then while waiting for the court to review the case, a licensee in such a situation may continue to perform the duties of a broker or salesperson provided that the licensee posts a corporate bond not exceeding $25,000, as determined by a judge. This bond will benefit any member of the public who suffers a loss due to the actions of such licensee (Section 225(c)).

Section 224(a-1) requires each real estate board to advise the Commission of any action taken against a licensee as a result of monetary losses, misappropriation of funds, or fraud.

Hearing Rules

The Commission has created a list of hearing rules which are part of the Maryland Real Estate License Law. The rules are in four sections, titled as follows: (1) Judicial Hearings; (2) Applications for Licensure; (3) Revocation or Suspension of Licenses; and (4) Claims Against the Guaranty Fund. The procedures prescribed in these hearing rules follow the provisions of the Administrative Procedures Act.

The licensee or applicant may be represented by counsel. The Commission or hearing board is usually represented by an assistant attorney general of Maryland. Hearings are open to the public.

PENALTIES FOR ACTING WITHOUT A LICENSE (Section 231)

Any person acting for him- or herself, or on behalf of any partnership or corporation, who commits any of the following acts is deemed guilty of a misdemeanor:

1 acting as a real estate broker or salesperson without a license when a license is required by this law
2 acting as a real estate broker or salesperson after his or her license has been suspended, revoked, or refused renewal
3 retaining anyone as a real estate salesperson who is not licensed or whose license has been suspended or revoked.

Upon conviction, such a person shall be sentenced, at the discretion of the court, to pay a fine of not more than $2,000 or undergo imprisonment for a period of not more than one year, or both.

GENERAL OPERATING REQUIREMENTS

Place of Business (Section 222)

Every resident real estate broker must maintain a definite place of business in Maryland and must display a sign reading "Real Estate" or, when authorized and applicable, "Realtor®," or "Realtist." This sign must be visible from a public highway or hallway. Also, the broker must "conspicuously display" the licenses of all persons licensed to act as brokers or salespeople in such place of business.

Regulation .15 specifies that the place of business must be an office or headquarters where the broker and his or her employees regularly transact real estate business. Records of the brokerage's transactions, including the records of the broker's escrow account, must be kept at this office. A commercial answering service office does not meet the requirements set by Regulation .15.

A real estate broker must notify the Commission in writing within ten days of any change in his or her principal business location. The Commission will issue a new license for the rest of the unexpired period. Failure to so notify will automatically cancel the broker's license (Section 222 and Regulation .12).

In the normal course of business, the broker must designate to the Commission the name of the person authorized to act on his or her behalf when the broker is aware of an upcoming absenteeism. The broker's specific appointment of an authorized representative must be notarized, and must designate the person authorized to sign applications, renewals, transfer requests, and other such duties, for a temporary period during the broker's absence. In cases of emergencies, the Commission may authorize the appropriate party designated to act on behalf of the broker to enable the broker's business to continue while he or she is incapacitated.

Branch Offices (Section 222(c))

In addition to a regular place of business, a resident real estate broker may operate one or more branch offices (each of which must comply with the code and regulations). The broker must obtain a separate license for every branch office operated in Maryland. A nonresident broker may not establish a branch office in Maryland.

A broker cannot be the manager of a branch office. The broker must designate as manager either an associate broker or a salesperson holding an active license for at least three years. One individual may not manage more than one branch office. The manager's status as sales manager must be properly registered with the Commission.

Supervisory Duties

The independent contractor status of associate brokers and salespersons has been recognized with regard to the supervisory responsibility of a broker.

Listings

Listing contracts. Regulation .14 requires that all exclusive or open listing contracts for the sale, rental, lease, or exchange of residential real estate must be in writing and signed. In addition, Regulation .01 requires that all listing contracts, as well as sale contracts, must state the amount of brokerage commission agreed upon--either a specific amount or a specific percentage. A copy of the listing contract must be given to the seller or owner before the licensee begins to advertise, show, or offer the property involved.

Out-of-state listings. A Maryland licensee is not authorized to show out-of-state property that is listed and properly advertised in Maryland, unless that licensee also has a valid license issued in the state where the property is located, and complies with all laws of that state.

Solicitation of listings. Section 230B of the code prohibits licensees from soliciting listings of residential property when one purpose of such solicitation is to change the racial composition of a neighborhood. (This practice is termed blockbusting and is covered later in this chapter.)

Maintaining Records and Handling Money

Records. Regulation .08 requires both broker and salesperson licensees to maintain adequate records of all their real estate transactions. These records must include bank accounts and deposits, and must be available during business hours for inspection by the Commission, its field inspectors, or other Commission employees.

Section 224C requires that all records, books, and accounts of funds held in trust by a licensee be maintained within a secure area in the licensee's place of business, as designated in writing to the Commission. If the licensee fails to promptly account for such funds or to produce the records and books for examination by the Commission, the Commission may temporarily suspend the broker's license until he or she is able to comply with the Commission's order.

Handling of funds (Section 227A). When a licensee receives and is entrusted with monies belonging to other persons and no definite written instructions to the contrary have been received, such funds must be deposited in a special noninterest-bearing bank account. This account must be maintained in a financial institution within the State of Maryland whose deposits are insured by either the Federal Deposit Insurance Corporation, the Federal Savings and Loan Insurance Corporation, the National Credit Union Administration, the Maryland State Savings-Share Insurance Corporation, or the Maryland Credit Union Insurance Corporation. The funds should remain in this account until the transaction is closed or terminated, or until the broker has received written disbursement instructions. In all cases, the broker must promptly and fully account for the funds, depositing them either the same day they are received, or on the next banking day.

Regulation .27 provides that in any transaction in which a licensee has custody or possession of funds that belong to others, in the absence of a provision in the contract of sale, rental lease, option agreement, or other similar type of document to the contrary, and a dispute arises as to the disposition of these funds by and between the parties to the transaction, the licensee shall:

1 hold these funds until he or she has releases signed by all parties to the transaction authorizing disposition of the funds;
2 file a bill of interpleader in the proper court in the county or Baltimore City, thereby causing these funds to be deposited in the registry of the court; or
3 hold these funds until one of the parties to the transaction files suit and the court in which this suit is filed orders the disbursement of these funds.

Regulation .11 also stipulates the necessity for a broker to maintain an "escrow or special account." The name of the bank and the account number must be reported to the Commission as soon as the account is established. The Commission must be notified within ten days of any changes including bank name, account number, or establishment of another account. In addition, Regulation .26 stipulates that no funds may be drawn out of a broker's escrow account without the signature of the principal broker. The broker may, however, designate other licensees within the office to serve as alternate signors for such accounts. A nonlicensee may only sign escrow account checks that are cosigned by a designated licensee.

Other Provisions

Advertising ground rents (Section 227B). When a licensee posts an outdoor sign or other advertisement on a piece of real property offering that property for sale or exchange, the cost and capitalization of any ground rent on the property must be written on the sign in lettering as large as that which states the price. Ground rents are discussed in Chapter 16 of this supplement.

Sign display. Article .03C of the Code of Ethics of the Real Estate Commission (listed later in this chapter) requires the prior consent of the owner before placing "for sale" signs and other signs on a property. Local zoning ordinances control the number of signs that can be posted by the licensee on any one property.

Use of trade names (Regulation .25). Brokers operating under a trade name, trademark, or service mark other than their own (such as that of a real estate franchise) must prominently include their personal or registered business names on all advertisements, signs, business cards, contracts, or documents used in connection with real estate activities. Furthermore, in oral communication with members of the general public, licensees must state the broker's own personal or registered business name as well as the trade name under which the broker operates. Thus, a broker's personal or registered trade name must be meaningfully and conspicuously displayed to the general public at all times.

Acting as principal and broker. Regulation .02 prohibits a broker from acting as both principal and agent in the same transaction without the consent of all parties concerned.

Prohibited settlement conditions (Section 227C). It is unlawful for a broker, salesperson, or a lawyer acting as a broker to require as a condition of settlement that the buyer of a single-family residence employ a particular title insurance, settlement or escrow company, or title attorney. Every contract for the sale of such dwellings must contain, in boldface type, the buyer's right to select his or her own title or escrow company, or title attorney. While failure to include this offer will not make the sale contract invalid, it is sufficient cause for the Commission to suspend or revoke the licensee's license.

Lending license (Section 224B). A licensed broker may not lend his or her license to any salesperson or permit any salesperson to operate as a broker. Brokers must exercise reasonable and adequate supervision over all the activities of their salespeople. Note, however, that Section 8224A-1 stipulates that a broker have actual knowledge of an agent's wrongdoing in order to be held liable.

Splitting fees (Section 227). A real estate broker or salesperson can only pay compensation for performance of any of the functions of a real estate licensee to licensed real estate brokers, licensed real estate salespeople, or a corporation formed and wholly owned by real estate salesperson(s), or those exempted under the provisions of Section 212(b) attorneys or Section 219(e) nonresidents.

Contracts void (Section 228). No person, copartnership, association, or corporation can file such a suit unless that person or firm was licensed as a broker or salesperson prior to offering to perform the function or service involved.

Notice of legal action. Section 224A-1 requires that every real estate board must advise the Commission of any action taken against a licensee as a result of monetary loss, misappropriation of funds, or fraud.

ADDITIONAL PROHIBITED ACTIVITIES

The Maryland Real Estate Law places great importance on the area of human relations. The Commission requires that this subject be included in the educational requirement for both brokers and salespeople. In addition, the Maryland legislature has enacted several laws prohibiting certain practices.

Blockbusting (Section 230A)

The unlawful practice of blockbusting is defined as knowingly inducing or trying to induce another person to transfer an interest in real estate or sell or rent any dwelling, or discouraging that person from purchasing an interest in real estate by referring to persons of any particular race, color, sex, religion or national origin who may live in the area or by referring to the prospective entry of such persons into the area, or by representing that the presence of such persons will (1) lower property values; (2) change the racial, religious, or ethnic character of the block, neighborhood, or area where the property is located; (3) increase criminal and antisocial behavior in the area; or (4) cause a decline in the quality of local schools.

The Commission has declared that blockbusting "cheats homeowners, increases inter-group tensions, promotes neighborhood instability, and creates ghettos, which do harm to the citizens of Maryland," and that it "...utilizes and promotes panic, fear, and hate, usually for purposes of financial profit...." Blockbusting is always illegal, whether or not the blockbuster is acting for monetary gain.

Violations of this section of the Code are misdemeanors, punishable upon conviction by a fine of not more than $500 and/or imprisonment for one year.

Upheld by court. In an opinion dated June 1, 1972, the Maryland Court of Special Appeals held that Article 56, Section 230A of the Maryland Annotated Code is constitutional, since nothing in the section was intended to hinder free speech.

Solicitation of listings (Section 230B). Solicitation of listings door-to-door, by telephone, or by circulars, is prohibited when one purpose is to change the racial composition of the neighborhood. Upon conviction, violators of this section are subject to a maximum fine of $5,000 and imprisonment of up to one year.

Real Estate Conservation Areas (Section 230C)

In an effort to maintain economic and racial stability in Maryland's urban areas, the legislature has provided for the creation of conservation areas. To create such an area, the Commission must first hold a public hearing to determine (1) if the racial or economic stability of the neighborhood is threatened by the number of real estate transactions taking place; (2) if excessive sales offerings in the area are causing an abnormal real estate market with depressed values; or (3) if certain advertising or solicitation methods could damage the public or the dignity and integrity of the real estate profession or be in violation of any part of the Maryland Real Estate License Law.

If the Commission, under Regulation .23, finds any of these conditions, the area may be designated a conservation area. In such a case, the Commission will suspend certain methods of real estate advertisement and solicitation of listings of houses for resale or rental in the area for not more than 24 months (unless the Commission finds it necessary to extend the period for an additional 24 months). This suspension does not include advertising in regularly distributed newspapers, magazines, radio, television, or telephone directories.

The Commission has designated 16 areas of northeast and western Baltimore as conservation areas, and "for sale" signs on residential properties have been banned in these areas. To date, no area outside of Baltimore City has been so designated.

Persons who feel that such suspensions infringe on their legal rights may seek a review by the Circuit Court of Baltimore City or of the appropriate county. Any person or company who violates a suspension issued by the Commission is guilty of a misdemeanor and, upon conviction, is subject to a fine of not more than $1,000 and/or imprisonment for one year.

In considering an action to remove, renew, or modify a real estate conservation area designation, the Commission is required to provide the affected community with the following information: (1) the racial and economic composition of the community; (2) the number of real estate transactions in the community; and (3) the fair market values of properties affected by the real estate transactions in the community.

On November 1, 1984, a federal judge issued a preliminary injunction preventing enforcement of the For-Sale sign ban. As of this writing, no trial date had been set, and the injunction remained in effect.

Steering and Similar Practices in Baltimore City (Section 230D)

Section 230D of the Code was enacted to provide fair and equal housing practices and opportunities for all citizens of Baltimore City, regardless of their race, color, sex, religion, or national origin, by prohibiting steering and other discriminatory practices in the residential real estate business. It applies only in Baltimore City.

The Commission has established price categories for residential real estate in Baltimore City. All brokers doing business in Baltimore are required to keep separate registries of all residential properties they personally list for sale and to divide the listings into current and complete price categories. Any prospective buyer is entitled to see, upon request, the registry for the price range he or she is interested in.

Several important terms as they apply to Section 230D are specifically defined in that section as follows:

Dwelling Dwelling refers to any building, structure, or portion of a structure that is occupied or designed to be occupied as a residence. This includes vacant land that is offered for sale or lease for the construction or location of a dwelling.

Person Person can refer to one or more individuals, corporations, partnerships, associations, labor organizations, legal representatives, mutual companies, joint stock companies, trusts, unincorporated organizations, trustees, receivers, or fiduciaries.

To rent The definition of "to rent" also includes to lease, sublease, let, or otherwise grant for a consideration, the right to occupy premises not owned by the occupant.

Steering This practice includes any of the following acts of a real estate broker, salesperson, or agent:

1 refusing to or refraining from showing property for rent or sale to any person because of race, color, sex, religion, or national origin, or because of the racial composition or character of the neighborhood in which the property is located. (This is prohibited unless a client or prospective client requests it.);
2 refusing to show or refraining from showing all available listed properties in a certain price range to a client or prospective client who has requested to be shown all such properties in the area;
3 representing to any person that a dwelling is not available, or that listings other than the ones already shown in the price range requested by the client are not available, when this is not the truth, which is prohibited when it is done because of the client's race, color, sex, religion, or national origin, or the racial composition or character of the neighborhood in which the property is located.

The Commission enforces this section of the real estate law by receiving complaints, conducting investigations, issuing subpoenas, and holding hearings. If the Commission determines that the law has been broken, it will refer the case to the courts. A conviction in a court of law for a violation of this section of the Code is punishable by a fine of not more than $5,000 and/or imprisonment for one year. Convicted licensees are referred to the Maryland Real Estate Commission.

Discriminatory Real Estate Practices in Montgomery County (Section 230E)

The provisions of Section 230E, which apply only in Montgomery County, became effective July 1, 1974, and are similar in purpose to those of Section 230D, with three differences: they prohibit discrimination based on marital status and physical and mental handicaps in addition to race, color, sex, religion, and national origin; they allow the broker to belong to a multiple-listing service (and disclose the availability of all self-registered and multiple-listed properties to any prospect); and they stipulate a maximum fine of $1,000 for violations.

CODE OF ETHICS OF THE REAL ESTATE COMMISSION OF MARYLAND

The Real Estate Commission requires each applicant for a real estate license to agree to abide by the Code of Ethics, which is a part of the license law. The applicant's agreement is included in the state application form as follows:

> Further, I hereby certify that I have read and understand the Law including the Code of Ethics and will abide by and comply with and operate under the same.

The main points of the Code of Ethics are reproduced on the following pages. (Underlining denotes emphasis.)

CODE OF ETHICS
REAL ESTATE COMMISSION
STATE OF MARYLAND
(.09.11.02)

Accepting this standard as his or her own, every licensee pledges to observe its spirit in all his or her activities and to conduct business in accordance with the following Code of Ethics as adopted by the Real Estate Commission, State of Maryland:

.01 RELATIONS TO THE PUBLIC

Article A

The licensee shall keep informed as to matters affecting real estate in his or her community, the state, and the nation.

Article B

The licensee shall be informed on current market conditions in order to be in a position to advise clients as to the fair market price.

Article C

The licensee shall protect the public against fraud, misrepresentation, or unethical practices in the real estate field. He or she shall endeavor to eliminate in the community any practices which could be damaging to the public or to the dignity and integrity of the real estate profession. The licensee shall assist the commission charged with regulating the practices of brokers and salespeople in this state.

Article D

The licensee shall make a reasonable effort to ascertain all material facts concerning every property for which the licensee accepts the agency, so that he or she may fulfill an obligation to avoid error, exaggeration, misrepresentation, or concealment of material facts.

Article E

The licensee may not, acting as agent, discriminate in the sale, rental, leasing, trading, or transferring of property to or against any person or group because of race, color, creed, religion, national origin, or sex.

Article F

The licensee may not be a party to the naming of a false consideration in any document.

Article G

The licensee in his or her advertising shall be especially careful to present a true picture. A broker may not advertise without disclosing his or her name or the company name as it appears on the license. A broker may not permit salespeople to use individual names or telephone numbers, unless the salesperson's connection with the broker is obvious in the advertisement.

Article H

For the protection of all parties with whom he or she deals, the licensee shall see that financial obligations and commitments regarding real estate transactions are in writing, expressing the exact agreement of the parties and place copies of these agreements in the hands of all parties involved within a reasonable time after the agreements are executed.

.02 RELATIONS TO THE CLIENT

Article A

In accepting employment as an agent, the licensee shall protect and promote the interests of the client. This obligation of absolute fidelity to the client's interest is primary, but it does not relieve the licensee from statutory obligations towards the other parties to the transaction.

Article B

In justice to those who place their interests in his or her care, the licensee shall endeavor always to be informed regarding laws, proposed legislation, governmental orders, and other essential information and public policies which affect those interests.

Article C

A licensee may not accept compensation from more than one party to a transaction without the full knowledge of all the parties.

Article D

The licensee may not acquire an interest in or purchase from him- or herself, any member of his or her immediate family, firm or any member thereof, or any entity in which the licensee has any ownership interest, property listed with the agent's firm without making his or her true position known to the listing owner. In selling or leasing property in which the licensee, the licensee's firm, or any member of the licensee's immediate family or firm has an ownership interest, he or she shall reveal that interest in writing to all parties to the transaction.

Article E

When acting as agent in the management of property, the licensee may not accept any commission, rebate, or profit on expenditures made for an owner without the owner's acknowledgement and consent.

Article F

The licensee may not undertake to make an appraisal that is outside the field of his or her experience, without obtaining the assistance of an expert on such types of property, or disclosing a lack of experience to the client. If an expert is engaged, the licensee shall identify the expert to the client and inform the client of the expert's contribution to the assignment.

Article G

When asked to make a formal appraisal of real property, the licensee may not render an opinion without a careful physical inspection of the property and a thorough analysis of all factors affecting the value of the property. The licensee may not undertake to make an appraisal or render an opinion of value on any property where he or she has a present or contemplated interest. The licensee may not make a formal appraisal when the licensee's employment or fee is contingent upon the amount of the appraisal.

Article H

The licensee may not submit or advertise property without authority. In any offering, the price quoted may not be other than that agreed upon with the owners as the offering price.

Article I

If more than one formal written offer on a specific property is made before the owner has accepted an offer, all formal written offers presented to the licensee, whether by a prospective purchaser or another broker, shall be transmitted to the owner for his or her decision.

.03 RELATIONS TO FELLOW LICENSEES

Article A

The agency of a licensee who holds an exclusive listing shall be respected.

Article B

The licensee shall cooperate with other brokers on property listed by him or her exclusively whenever it is in the interest of the client, and share commissions on a previously agreed basis. Negotiations concerning property listed exclusively with one broker shall be carried on solely with the listing broker.

Article C

Signs giving notice of property for sale, rent, lease, or exchange may not be placed on any property without the owner's prior consent.

Limitations on Filing Complaints

Regulation .28 stipulates that a complaint against any real estate licensee subject to the jurisdiction of the Real Estate Commission will not be entertained after the expiration of three years from the date of the written listing contract, contract of sale, lease agreement, or option on which such complaint is based, except that if a complainant is kept in ignorance of a cause of action by the fraud of the licensee, the complaint shall accrue at the time when the complainant discovered, or by the exercise of ordinary diligence should have discovered the fraud.

CHANGES IN THE LICENSE LAW AND REGULATIONS

The real estate industry is an active and growing business, and frequent changes in the license law and the regulations are required and made by the state legislature and the Real Estate Commission. The material included in this chapter is current as of the date of publication. However, readers are cautioned to ascertain whether recent proposed changes have been made since publication of this supplement.

Article 56 is being reviewed by the Governor's Commission on the Annotated Code. It is expected that Article 56 will become part of a new Business Occupation article during the 1986 legislative session, and become effective in Fall, 1986.

There are a number of ways that regulations can be changed, including a petition to the Commission or the circuit court; the procedures for doing so are described in Article 41 of the Annotated Code. Proposed changes and notification of meetings are published in the Maryland Register, an official state publication issued biweekly, with an index published quarterly. Anyone interested may subscribe to the publication at an annual rate of $50 per subscription. For information, contact:

Circulation Manager
Maryland Register
Division of State Documents
P.O. Box 802
Annapolis, Maryland 21024

Adoption, Amendment, and Repeal of Regulations

Before the Real Estate Commission can adopt, amend, or repeal regulations, it must first publish in the *Maryland Register* a notice of the proposed action, an estimate of its economic impact, a notice giving the public an opportunity to comment on the proposal, and the text of the proposed regulations.

Following publication, 45 days must elapse before the Commission may take action, at which time a notice is published in the *Register*. This final action takes effect 10 days after the notice is published, unless the Commission specifies a later date. Occasionally, changes in the text are made; if the changes are not substantial, they are simply included in the notice of final action. If the changes are substantial, the entire process must be repeated.

Proposed action on regulations may be withdrawn any time before the final action is taken; once the proposal has been withdrawn, however, final action may not be taken unless the entire process is repeated. When the Commission proposes action on regulations but does not take final action within one year, the proposal is withdrawn by operation of law.

Emergency Regulations

Under Article 40, Title 40A of the Annotated Code, the Commission may petition the Joint Standing Committee on Administrative, Executive, and Legislative Review (AELR), asking that the usual procedures for adopting regulations be set aside because emergency conditions exist. If the request is approved, the regulations are given emergency status, and they become effective either immediately or at some other specified time.

Real Estate Practices in Baltimore City

Although Baltimore City does not issue or require a separate real estate license to perform real estate activities in the city, local law does regulate the activities of licensees who practice there. Many of the prohibited acts are similar, if not identical, to state law. The Baltimore City real estate license law is found in Section 132 of Article 19 of the Baltimore City Code under the title "Real Estate Practices."

QUESTIONS

This examination measures the student's understanding of the real estate laws, rules, regulations and other aspects of real estate practice in the State of Maryland as administered and enforced by the Maryland Real Estate Commission.

1. Which activity requires you to be a licensed real estate broker?

   a. Performing one act of brokerage for which you receive a commission.
   b. Acting as a buyer for a friend, without receiving any commission or compensation.
   c. Selling your own property at a profit.
   d. Selling real estate as a personal representative under a will.

2. A broker wishes to appoint his sales manager vice-president of the company. The sales manager:

   a. may continue to operate under a salesperson's license.
   b. needs no license if he does not directly show or sell real estate.
   c. must be licensed as an associate broker.
   d. must own at least 5% of the stock in the corporation.

3. You, a licensed salesperson, receive a lead from a friend who is not licensed as a real estate broker or salesperson. You want to split your commission with your friend.

   a. This is a violation of the license law.
   b. This is not a violation of the license law.
   c. This is a violation of the license law only if the seller is not informed of the arrangement.
   d. This is a violation of the license law only if your broker has not given written permission.

4. A broker is appointed to sell a property through an exclusive-right-to-sell listing contract. The broker will be entitled to a commission:

   a. only if the broker or one of her salespeople sells the property.
   b. if the property is sold during the listing period.
   c. only if the property is sold by the broker or the owner.
   d. whether or not a sale results.

5. Which of the following fees are paid biennially?

   a. guaranty fund fee
   b. broker's or salesperson's original license fee
   c. broker's or salesperson's license renewal fee
   d. guaranty fund reassessment

6. The act of "blockbusting" is:

   a. unethical, but <u>not</u> prohibited by law.
   b. a felony.
   c. a misdemeanor.
   d. a legitimate sales technique.

7. Individuals found guilty of operating in the real estate business without a license may be fined by:

   a. the district attorney.
   b. a court of law.
   c. the Real Estate Commission.
   d. the Attorney General.

8. An unlicensed person collecting a real estate commission is guilty of:

   a. duress.
   b. a felony.
   c. a misdemeanor.
   d. negligence.

9. The Real Estate Commission may revoke the license of a broker and/or salesperson who is found guilty of:

   a. slandering his or her competitors.
   b. intemperance.
   c. misrepresentation.
   d. violations of the motor vehicle code.

10. The penalty for filing a false claim with the Commission in reference to the guaranty fund is:

   a. <u>not</u> less than two hundred dollars.
   b. <u>not</u> more than two hundred dollars.
   c. $10,000 and up to 2 years' imprisonment.
   d. $10,000 and up to 1 year imprisonment.

11. Members of the Real Estate Commission of Maryland are appointed by:

   a. the state senate.
   b. the Governor.
   c. the House of Delegates.
   d. the Secretary of the Department of Licensing and Regulations.

12. A license issued by the Real Estate Commission to a licensee on November 1st will expire:

   a. one year from the date of issue.
   b. two years from the date of issue.
   c. at the end of the license year fixed by law.
   d. on the birthdate of the licensee.

13. The Executive Director of the Real Estate Commission is:

    a. appointed by the Governor.
    b. confirmed by the State Senate.
    c. appointed by the Secretary of the Department of Licensing and Regulation from three nominees submitted by the Real Estate Commission.
    d. selected from the Maryland State Employees Classified System.

14. Who of the following may act as real estate broker for a corporation?

    a. all members of the corporation
    b. one officer of the corporation
    c. the senior salesperson
    d. all officers of the corporation

15. A salesperson's license certificate must always be:

    a. carried by the salesperson.
    b. kept in the salesperson's kit.
    c. displayed in the broker's office.
    d. held by the Real Estate Commission.

16. The real estate license law was passed:

    a. to raise revenue.
    b. to protect the public.
    c. for political reasons.
    d. to restrict competition.

17. Real estate ads must include the name of:

    a. the seller.
    b. the listing salesperson.
    c. the listing broker.
    d. the salesperson attempting to sell the property.

18. The Guaranty Fund protects a buyer for amounts up to:

    a. $250,000.
    b. $ 25,000.
    c. $2,500.
    d. unlimited

19. A person who is authorized to perform acts for another under a power of attorney is called:

    a. an attorney-at-law.
    b. an attorney-in-fact.
    c. a corporation.
    d. a partnership.

20. The Maryland Real Estate License Law includes:

a. Article 56 of the state law, known as the Maryland Annotated Code.
b. the Code of Ethics prescribed by the Real Estate Commission of Maryland.
c. the General Regulations and Hearing Rules adopted by the Real Estate Commission.
d. all of the above

21. The Real Estate Commission of Maryland is composed of:

a. five members.
b. three persons who are <u>not</u> engaged in the real estate business, as well as five licensed brokers and salespersons.
c. four licensed and four unlicensed persons.
d. members of the real estate boards.

22. Applicants for licensing pay a fee to:

a. the Real Estate Commission of Maryland.
b. The Assessment Systems, Inc.
c. the Real Estate Board.
d. the Comptroller of the State of Maryland.

23. Which of the following is acting as a broker, according to the legal definition?

a. a mortgage loan institution that is selling real estate acquired through foreclosure
b. a person offering to sell, purchase, exchange, lease, or rent real estate on behalf of another person for a valuable consideration
c. attorneys-at-law who are <u>not</u> regularly engaged in the real estate business
d. an owner of property selling fewer than seven lots during any calendar year

24. Employees of the Commission:

a. include an executive director and field inspectors, who investigate license law violations.
b. must be licensed as brokers or salespeople while employed by the Commission.
c. must have been licensed before being employed by the Commission.
d. are permitted to perform acts of brokerage for which a license is required.

25. License fees are established by:

a. the Real Estate Commission.
b. the Real Estate Board.
c. the Secretary of the Department of Licensing and Regulation.
d. the General Assembly.

26. The Commission may refuse to issue a license to a Maryland resident who has filed a proper application:

    a. after holding a hearing on the matter.
    b. if the applicant has been convicted of a traffic violation within the past year.
    c. without holding a hearing on the matter.
    d. if the applicant has not reached the age of 21 years.

27. In Maryland, the person primarily responsible for the real estate activities of corporations licensed to engage in the real estate business is the:

    a. president of the corporation.
    b. real estate broker of record.
    c. chairman of the board.
    d. corporate attorney.

28. The real estate guaranty fund:

    a. guarantees pensions for retired brokers and salespersons who meet the requirements set by the fund.
    b. is available to compensate an aggrieved person who has suffered actual loss due to a licensee's actions.
    c. is available to compensate a broker for commissions on transactions where the seller has defaulted.
    d. guarantees that attorneys representing aggrieved persons to recover their legal fees.

29. A broker's "definite place of business" can refer to:

    a. an office where real estate business is regularly transacted.
    b. a post office box address.
    c. a telephone answering service.
    d. the place where the broker maintains records of transactions and escrow accounts in a safety deposit box.

30. The guaranty fund will <u>not</u> pay the claims of:

    a. the spouse of the person against whom the claim is brought.
    b. persons who misrepresent facts to the Commission.
    c. an attorney for legal fees.
    d. any of the above

31. In order to operate one or more branch offices, a broker:

    a. must appoint an associate broker or a salesperson with three years' experience to manage each branch office.
    b. need <u>not</u> obtain a branch office license in each branch.
    c. must directly supervise the operation of each branch.
    d. all of the above

32. A broker must notify the Commission:

    a. when any salesperson resigns.
    b. when there is a change in the location of the broker's office.
    c. when there is a change in the broker's address.
    d. all of the above

33. All licensees should:

    a. carry their pocket card as professional identification.
    b. renew their licenses every two years on January 1, or face possible reexamination by the Commission.
    c. pay a small compensation to all persons providing leads as a means of showing their gratitude.
    d. not include their broker's name in advertisements since this only increases the cost of advertising.

34. A real estate conservation area is created:

    a. to preserve endangered plant species.
    b. to maintain an area's economic and racial stability.
    c. to release funds for government aid in attaining energy efficiency.
    d. to prevent the destruction of historical landmarks.

35. A broker must surrender to the Commission the license of any salesperson:

    a. if the salesperson has not engaged in any activities of a real estate salesperson for a period of at least one year.
    b. if the salesperson has not earned at least $10,000 in commissions for the broker.
    c. if the salesperson has not earned at least $5,000 in commissions for the broker.
    d. only upon demand by the Commission.

36. Brokers and salespeople may solicit listings:

    a. freely in all areas of the state.
    b. by telling prospective sellers property values will fall because of the race or religion of new purchasers in the neighborhood.
    c. by telling prospective sellers that property values will fall because of the change in the racial, religious or ethnic character of the block, neighborhood or areas in which the property is located.
    d. none of the above

37. Residential listing contracts:

    a. may be oral.
    b. need not state the amount of brokerage agreed upon between the broker and the principal.
    c. must be in writing and a copy given to the seller.
    d. need not have a definite termination date.

38. An escrow or special account:

    a. must be opened by a broker to hold money that belongs to another party.
    b. may contain the broker's personal funds if the broker wishes to earn interest on such funds.
    c. must be placed in an interest-bearing account.
    d. may be placed in an interest-bearing account without the permission of the buyer in writing.

39. The irrevocable consent required by the real estate license law:

    a. provides that legal suits may be brought in Maryland against a nonresident licensee who is also licensed in Maryland.
    b. gives a broker who has only a Maryland license the right to show and sell out-of-state property that is listed in Maryland.
    c. permits salespersons in Maryland to share commissions with unlicensed salespersons.
    d. provides assurance that buyers will not default on real estate transactions.

40. Jones is not licensed as a real estate broker or salesperson in Maryland, and is not exempted from the Maryland Real Estate License Law. Jones may, under the law:

    a. refer his cousin, who is looking for a new home, to his friend, who is selling a home, without expecting any compensation.
    b. file suit for compensation after helping find a buyer for a friend's home.
    c. share in the commission if his friend purchases a home through a licensed salesperson.
    d. is only entitled to a 10% referral.

41. A licensee who induces a homeowner to sell his home by convincing the homeowner that the presence of persons of certain racial or religious background in the neighborhood will increase criminal behavior and lower property values is guilty of:

    a. a felony, and may be fined not more than five thousand dollars or imprisonment for one year, or both.
    b. a felony, and may be fined not more than five hundred dollars or imprisonment for one year, or both.
    c. a misdemeanor, and may be fined not more than five hundred dollars or imprisonment for one year or both.
    d. a misdemeanor, and may be fined not more than five thousand dollars or imprisonment for one year or both.

42. Real estate conservation areas:

    a. are designated areas in which all real estate sales are prohibited for up to 24 months.
    b. can be set up only in Baltimore City.
    c. may only be established or modified following a public hearing.
    d. are designated areas in which advertising in regularly distributed newspapers, magazines, radio, television, or telephone directories is prohibited.

43. The Commission may revoke the license of a salesperson who is found guilty of:

    a. accepting compensation from anyone except the broker named in the salesperson's license for performing the functions of a real estate salesperson.
    b. failing to disclose to any buyer or prospective buyer important facts that the salesperson knew, or should have known, about a parcel of real estate.
    c. willful misrepresentation or knowingly making a false promise.
    d. all of the above

44. Cases against licensees who are accused of violating the license law are:

    a. heard by a three-member hearing review panel or board.
    b. required to be originated in a court of law.
    c. settled in the small claims court.
    d. heard by a four-member panel.

45. A licensee who is charged with a violation of the license law:

    a. is entitled by law to a hearing.
    b. must be given 30 days' notice of the forthcoming hearing by the Commission.
    c. must post a $25,000 bond in order to continue in business.
    d. none of the above

46. A licensee who has been found guilty of violating the license law:

    a. may appeal the case to the Circuit Court.
    b. may not appeal except with the permission of the Real Estate Commission.
    c. may continue to perform the duties of a broker or salesperson upon filing a bond not to exceed $25,000 at the discretion of the court.
    d. may appeal to the local Real Estate Board in the county in which the licensee resides.

47. A licensee with a current active license may:

    a. place the license in inactive status for up to two years.
    b. place the license in inactive status for up to four years.
    c. place the license in inactive status for an indefinite period of time.
    d. not place the license in inactive status.

48. Broker R has been named agent for owner O by an exclusive-right-to-sell listing. Broker R, by his statement in his license application, has agreed to abide by and comply with the Code of Ethics adopted by the Real Estate Commission. Therefore, Broker R:

    a. owes absolute fidelity to protect and promote O's interest.
    b. must deal fairly with all prospective buyers.
    c. is legally bound to obey the Code.
    d. all of the above

49. Salesperson S, who is working for Broker R, when showing or discussing a listed property with a prospective buyer:

    a. is required to know all material facts concerning the listed property.
    b. is obligated under the license law to avoid error, exaggeration, misrepresentation or concealment of important facts.
    c. may rely on statements made by the seller.
    d. need only answer the specific questions asked by the buyer.

50. A licensee who has been found guilty of violating the license law:

    a. may appeal the case to the county circuit court.
    b. may under no circumstances engage in real estate activities while waiting for the final decision of the appeals court.
    c. should immediately transfer to another broker.
    d. may be required by the court to post a bond <u>not</u> exceeding $25,000 when appealing a decision of the Commission.

15

Real Estate Financing

MORTGAGE AND TRUST DEED LOANS

With regard to mortgage and trust deed financing, Maryland is considered to be a title theory state, as defined in the text. This means that by signing, delivering, and recording a mortgage or trust deed, a borrower, in effect, gives the lender lawful title to the real estate. (Note, however, in the areas of mortgage and trust deed foreclosure and sale, Maryland's laws operate much like those of a lien theory state. This will be discussed later in the chapter.) All banks, savings and loan associations, savings banks, or building and loan associations, making loans secured by real property in Maryland, by law, must use the direct reduction method of payment, as described in the text.

Deeds of Trust

Deeds of trust are widely used throughout the state as financing devices for real estate. The standard FHLMC/FNMA loan forms are used to facilitate the packaging and selling of such loans in the secondary market, as discussed in the text. A deed of trust note, which is not recorded, and deed of trust agreement appear on the following four pages.

Under the deed of trust forms used in Maryland, the trustee is usually given a power of sale in case of default. The lender notifies the trustee that there is a default by the borrower in the payment of the mortgage note, and the lender institutes a court action to authorize the trustee to sell the property. The money the trustee obtains from the sale would then be applied to the principal of the mortgage debt plus the accrued interest and legal costs incidental to the sale. Any excess over and above what is due any lienholder would be returned to the defaulted borrower.

In Maryland, only a natural person (as opposed to a corporation or partnership) may serve under a deed of trust and sell the property in the case of a default under the provisions of the document's power of sale clause. Note, however, that any person may generally serve as trustee under a deed of trust.

This form is used in connection with deeds of trust insured under the one-to four-family provisions of the National Hosuing Act.

DEED OF TRUST NOTE

FHA CASE NO.

$, Maryland , 19

FOR VALUE RECEIVED, the undersigned promise(s) to pay to

or order, the principal sum c
Dollars ($

with interest from date at the rate of per centum (%
per annum on the unpaid balance until paid. The said principal and interest shall be payable at the office of

, in

or at such other place as the holder hereof may designate in writing, in monthly installments of

Dollars ($

commencing on the first day of , 19 , and on the first day of eac month thereafter until the principal and interest are fully paid, except that the final payment of principal and interes if not sooner paid, shall be due and payable on the first day of

If default be made in the payment of any installments under this Note, and if the default is not made goo prior to the due date of the next such installment, the entire principal sum and accrued interest shall at once becom due and payable without notice at the option of the holder of this Note. Failure to exercise this option shall not cor stitute a waiver of the right to exercise the same in the event of any subsequent default.

Presentment, protest, and notice are hereby waiver.

Replaces Form FHA-9127, which is Obsolete

HUD-99127 (10-78
(24 CFR 200.15C

This form is used in connection with deeds of trust insured under the one- to four-family provisions of the National Housing Act.

DEED OF TRUST

THIS DEED, made this day of , 19 , by and between

party of the first part and , Trustee, as hereinafter set forth, party of the second part:

WHEREAS, the party of the first part is justly indebted unto

, a corporation organized and existing under the laws of , in the principal sum of Dollars ($),

with interest from date at the rate of per centum (%) per annum on the unpaid balance until paid, for which amount the said party has signed and delivered a certain promissory note bearing even date herewith and payable in monthly installments of Dollars ($), commencing on the first day of , 19 , and on the first day of each month thereafter until the principal and interest are fully paid, except that the final payment of principal and interest, if not sooner paid, shall be due and payable on the first day of

AND WHEREAS, the party of the first part desires to secure the prompt payment of said debt, and interest thereon, when and as the same shall become due and payable, and all costs and expenses incurred in respect thereto, including reasonable counsel fees incurred or paid by the said party of the second part or substituted Trustee, or by any person hereby secured, on account of any litigation at law or in equity which may arise in respect to this trust or the property hereinafter mentioned, and of all money which may be advanced as provided herein, with interest on all such costs and advances from the date thereof.

NOW, THEREFORE, THIS INDENTURE WITNESSETH, that the party of the first part, in consideration of the premises, and of one dollar, lawful money of the United States of America, to in hand paid by the party of the second part, the receipt of which, before the sealing and delivery of these presents, is hereby acknowledged, has granted and conveyed, and does hereby grant and convey unto the party of the second part, as Trustee, its successors and assigns, the following-described land and premises, situated in the County of and State of Maryland, known and distinguished as

together with all the improvements in anywise appertaining, and all the estate, right, title, interest, and claim, either at law or in equity, or otherwise however, of the party of the first part, of, in, to, or out of the said land and premises.

By the execution of this instrument, Mortgagors, Grantors or parties of the first part (whichever applies) certify and acknowledge that prior thereto they have received both a fully executed agreement as to the contractural rate of interest and a loan disclosure statement in connection with the actual sum of money advanced at the closing transaction by the secured party both as required by Md. [Com. Law] Code Ann. Title 12.

TO HAVE AND TO HOLD the said property and improvements unto the party of the second part, its successors and assigns

IN AND UPON THE TRUSTS, NEVERTHELESS, hereinafter declared; that is to say: IN TRUST to permit said party of the first part, or assigns, to use and occupy the said described land and premises, and the rents, issues, and profits thereof, to take, have, and apply to and for sole use and benefit, until default be made in the payment of any manner of indebtedness hereby secured or in the performance of any of the covenants as hereinafter provided.

AND upon the full payment of all of said note and the interest thereon, and all moneys advanced or expended as herein provided, and all other proper costs, charges, commissions, half-commissions, and expenses, at any time before the sale hereinafter provided for to release and reconvey the said described premises unto the said party of the first part or assigns, at cost. Prior to the execution and delivery of any partial or complete release, each trustee shall be entitled to charge and receive a fee of $5.00, plus 50 cents for Notary's fee, for each release. The right to charge and receive said fee shall be limited to two Trustees.

STATE OF MARYLAND
HUD-92127M (8-82)
(24 CFR 203.17(a) et al.)

Replaces Form FHA-2127M, which may be used until Supply is exhausted

AND UPON THIS FURTHER TRUST, upon any default made in the payment of the said note or of any monthly installment of principal and interest as therein provided, or in the payment of any of the monthly sums for ground rents, if any, taxes, special assessments, mortgage insurance, fire and other hazard insurance, all as hereinafter provided, or upon any default in payment on demand of any money advanced by the holder of said note on account of any proper cost, charge, commission, or expense in and about the same, or on account of any tax or assessment or insurance, or expense of litigation, with interest thereon at the rate set forth in the note secured hereby from date of such advance (it being hereby agreed that on default in the payment of any ground rent, tax, or assessment, or insurance premium or any payment on account thereof, or in the payment of any of said cost, expense of litigation, as aforesaid, the holder of said note may pay the same and all sums so advanced with interest as aforesaid, shall immediately attach as a lien hereunder, and be payable on demand), or upon failure or neglect faithfully and fully to keep and perform any of the other conditions or covenants herein provided: then upon any and every such default being so made as aforesaid, the said party of the second part, or the Trustee acting in the execution of this trust, shall have power and it shall be   duty to sell, and in case of any default of any purchaser, to resell, at public auction, for cash, in one parcel at such time and place, and after such previous public advertisement as the party of the second part, or the Trustee acting in the execution of this trust, shall deem advantageous and proper; and to convey the same in fee simple, upon compliance with the terms of sale, to, and at the cost of, the purchaser or purchasers thereof, who shall not be required to see to the application of the purchase money; and shall apply the proceeds of said sale or sales: Firstly, to pay all proper costs, charges, and expenses, including all attorneys' and other fees and costs herein provided for, and all moneys advanced for costs or expenses, or expense of litigation as aforesaid, or taxes or assessments, or insurance with interest thereon as aforesaid, and all taxes, general and special, and assessments, due upon said land and premises at time of sale and to retain as compensation a commission of one per centum (1%) on the amount of the said sale or sales; Secondly, to pay whatever may then remain unpaid of said note, whether the same shall be due or not, and the interest thereon to date of payment, it being agreed that said note shall, upon such sale being made before the maturity of said note, be and become immediately due and payable at the election of the holder thereof; and, Lastly, to pay the remainder of said proceeds, if any there be, to the party of the first part,   heirs, executors, administrators, or assigns, upon the delivery and surrender to the purchaser, his, her, or their heirs or assigns of possession of the premises so, as aforesaid, sold and conveyed, less the expense, if any, of obtaining possession.

AND in the event of the resignation, death, incapacity, disability, removal, or absence from the State of any Trustee or Trustees, or should either refuse to act or fail to execute this Trust when requested, then any other Trustee shall have all the rights, powers, and authority and be charged with the duties that are hereby conferred or charged upon both; and in such event, or at the option of the holder of the note and with or without cause, the holder of the note is hereby authorized and empowered to appoint, and to substitute and appoint, by an instrument recorded wherever this Deed of Trust is recorded, a Trustee in the place and stead of any Trustee herein named or any succeeding or substitute Trustee, which appointed and Substitute Trustee or Trustees shall have all the rights, powers, and authority and be charged with all the duties that are conferred or charged upon any Trustee or Trustees herein named.

AND the party of the first part, in order more fully to protect the security of this Deed of Trust, covenants and agrees as follows:

1. That he will pay the indebtedness, as hereinbefore provided. Privilege is reserved to pay the debt in whole, or in an amount equal to one or more monthly payments on the principal that are next due on the note, on the first day of any month prior to maturity; *Provided, however,* That written notice of an intention to exercise such privilege is given at least thirty (30) days prior to prepayment.

2. That, together with, and in addition to, the monthly payments of principal and interest, payable under the terms of the note secured hereby, he will pay to the holder of the said note, on the first day of each month until the said note is fully paid, the following sums:

(a) An amount sufficient to provide the holder hereof with funds to pay the next mortgage insurance premium if this instrument and the note secured hereby are insured, or a monthly charge (in lieu of a mortgage insurance premium) if they are held by the Secretary of Housing and Urban Development as follows:

(I) If and so long as said note of even date and this instrument are insured or are reinsured under the provisions of the National Housing Act, an amount sufficient to accumulate in the hands of the holder one (1) month prior to its due date the annual mortgage insurance premium, in order to provide such holder with funds to pay such premium to the Secretary of Housing and Urban Development pursuant to the National Housing Act, as amended, and applicable Regulations thereunder; or

(II) If and so long as said note of even date and this instrument are held by the Secretary of Housing and Urban Development, a monthly charge (in lieu of a mortgage insurance premium) which shall be in an amount equal to one-twelfth (1/12) of one-half (½) per centum of the average outstanding balance due on the note computed without taking into account delinquencies or prepayments;

(b) A sum equal to the ground rents, if any, and the taxes and special assessments next due on the premises covered by this Deed of Trust, plus the premiums that will next become due and payable on policies of fire and other hazard insurance on the premises covered hereby (all as estimated by the holder of the note) less all sums already paid therefor, divided by the number of months to elapse before 1 month prior to the date when such ground rents, premiums, taxes, and assessments will become delinquent, such sums to be held by Mortgagee in trust to pay said ground rents, premiums, taxes, and special assessments, before the same become delinquent; and

(c) All payments mentioned in the two preceding subsections of this paragraph and all payments to be made under the note secured hereby shall be added together and the aggregate amount thereof shall be paid by the party of the first part each month in a single payment to be applied by the holder of the note to the following items in the order set forth:

(I) premium charges under the contract of insurance with the Secretary of Housing and Urban Development, or monthly charge (in lieu of mortgage insurance premium), as the case may be;

(II) ground rents, if any, taxes special assessments, fire and other hazard insurance premiums;

(III) interest on the note secured hereby; and

(IV) amortization of the principal of the said note.

Any deficiency in the amount of any such aggregate monthly payment shall, unless made good by the party of the first part prior to the due date of the next such payment, constitute an event of default under this Deed of Trust. The holder of the note may collect a "late charge" not to exceed four cents (4¢) for each dollar ($1) of each payment more than fifteen (15) days in arrears to cover the extra expense involved in handling delinquent payments, but in no event shall such "late charge" exceed the limitations imposed by Md. [Com. Law] Code Ann. Title 12 as of the date hereof.

3. That if the total of the payments made by the party of the first part under (b) paragraph 2 preceding shall exceed the amount of payments actually made by the holder of the note for ground rents, taxes or assessments or insurance premiums, as the case may be, such excess, if the loan is current, at the option of the party of the first part, shall be credited on subsequent payments to be made by the party of the first part, or refunded to the party of the first part. If, however, the monthly payments made by the party of the first part under (b) of paragraph 2 preceding shall not be sufficient to pay ground rents, taxes, and

assessments, and insurance premiums, as the case may be, when the same shall become due and payable, then the party of the first part shall pay to the holder of said note any amount necessary to make up the deficiency, on or before the date when payment of such ground rents, taxes, assessments, or insurance premiums shall be due. If at any time the party of the first part shall tender to the holder of said note, in accordance with the provisions thereof, full payment of the entire indebtedness represented thereby, the said holder shall, in computing the amount of such indebtedness, credit to the account of the party of the first part all payments made under the provisions of *(a)* of paragraph 2 hereof, which the holder of said note has not become obligated to pay to the Secretary of Housing and Urban Development, and any balance remaining in the funds accumulated under the provisions of *(b)* of paragraph 2 hereof. If there shall be a default under any of the provisions of this Deed of Trust resulting in a public sale of the premises covered hereby, or if the holder of the note acquires the property otherwise after default, the holder of the note shall apply, at the time of the commencement of such proceedings, or at the time the property is otherwise acquired, the balance then remaining in the funds accumulated under *(b)* of paragraph 2 preceding, as a credit against the amount of principal then remaining unpaid under said note, and shall properly adjust any payments which shall have been made under *(a)* of paragraph 2.

4. That he will pay all taxes, assessments, water rates and other governmental or municipal charges, fines or impositions, and costs, expenses and charges of attorneys for services in any legal proceeding wherein Trustee shall be made a party by reason of this Deed of Trust, and ground rents, for which provision has not been made hereinbefore and will promptly deliver the official receipts therefore to the holder of the note; and in default of such payment by the party of the first part, the holder of the note may pay the same, and any sum or sums so paid by the holder of the note shall be added to the debt hereby secured, shall be payable on demand, shall bear interest at the rate set forth in the note secured hereby and shall be secured by this Deed of Trust.

5. That he will keep the said premises in as good order and condition as they are now and will not commit or permit any waste thereof, reasonable wear and tear excepted.

6. That he will keep the improvements now existing or hereafter erected on the said premises insured as may be required from time to time by the holder of the note against loss by fire and other hazards, casualties and contingencies in such amounts and for such periods as may be required by the holder of the note and will pay promptly, when due, any premiums on such insurance provision for payment of which has not been made hereinbefore. All insurance shall be carried in companies approved by the holder of the note and the policies and renewals thereof shall be held by the holder of the note and have attached thereto loss payable clauses in favor of and in form acceptable to the holder of the note. In event of loss he will give immediate notice by mail to the holder of the note, who may make proof of loss if not made promptly by the party of the first part, and each insurance company concerned is hereby authorized and directed to make payment for such loss directly to the holder of the note instead of to the party of the first part and the holder of the note jointly, and the insurance proceeds, or any part thereof, may be applied by the holder of the note at its option either to the reduction of the indebtedness hereby secured or to the restoration or repair of the property damaged. In event of foreclosure of this Deed of Trust or other transfer of title to the said premises in extinguishment of the indebtedness secured hereby, all right, title, and interest of the party of the first part in and to any insurance policies then in force shall pass to the purchaser or grantee.

7. The party of the first part further agrees that should this Deed of Trust and the note secured hereby not be eligible for insurance under the National Housing Act within from the date hereof (written statement of any officer of the Department of Housing and Urban Development or authorized agent of the Secretary of Housing and Urban Development dated subsequent to the time from the date of this Deed of Trust, declining to insure said note and this Deed of Trust, being deemed conclusive proof of such ineligibility), the party of the second part or the holder of the note may, at its option, declare all sums secured hereby immediately due and payable.

8. That if the said property shall be advertised for sale, as herein provided, and not sold the Trustee or Trustees acting shall be entitled to one-half (½) the commission above provided, to be computed on the amount of the debt hereby secured, and the same is hereby secured in like manner as other charges and expenses attending the execution of this trust, and shall bear full legal interest.

9. That if the premises, or any part thereof, be condemned under any power of eminent domain, or acquired for a public use, the damages, proceeds, and the consideration for such acquisition to the extent of the full amount of indebtedness upon this Deed of Trust, and the note secured hereby remaining unpaid, are hereby assigned by the party of the first part to the holder of the note secured hereby and shall be paid forthwith to said holder to be applied by it on account of the indebtedness secured hereby, whether due or not.

10. That if any suit, action, or proceeding whatsoever shall be commenced or prosecuted for the collection of the note, or any part of the note, or for the enforcement of any endorsement or endorsements thereof, or any other matters hereby secured, or in reference to the execution of the trust hereby created, or any of the trust or property of funds which may become part thereof, he will pay all costs and charges and expenses of the same, including all counsel and attorney's fees and charges, which shall also be deemed a charge attending the execution of this trust, be secured hereby as such and bear interest at the rate set forth in the note secured hereby.

11. That he specially warrants the property herein conveyed and that he will execute such further assurances thereof as may be required.

The covenants herein contained shall bind, and the benefits and advantages shall inure to, the respective heirs, executors, administrators, successors, and assigns of the parties hereto. Whenever used the singular number shall include the plural, the plural the singular, and the use of any gender shall be applicable to all genders.

WITNESS the signature(s) and seal(s) of the part of the first part on the day and year first above written.

Witness: ______________________ [SEAL]

______________________ ______________________ [SEAL]

______________________ ______________________ [SEAL]

______________________ ______________________ [SEAL]

STATE OF MARYLAND, to wit:

I HEREBY CERTIFY, that on this the day of , 19 , before me, a Notary Public of the State of Maryland, the undersigned officer, personally appeared known to me (or satisfactorily proven) to be the person(s) whose name(s) is (are) subscribed to the within instrument and acknowledged that executed the same for the purpose therein contained.

At the same time, also personally appeared , the of the party secured by the aforegoing deed of trust, and made oath in due form of law that the consideration of said deed of trust is true and bona fide as therein set forth; that the actual sum of money advanced at the closing transaction by the secured party has been paid over and disbursed by the party secured hereby unto the within named party of the first part or the person responsible for disbursement of funds in the closing transaction or their respective agent at a time no later than the execution and delivery of this deed of trust by the party of the first part; and he further made oath that he is the agent of the party secured by the aforegoing deed of trust and as such is duly authorized to make this affidavit.

IN WITNESS WHEREOF, I hereunto set my hand and official seal.

____
Notary Public

My commission expires:

RECEIVED FOR RECORD on the day of A.D. 19 , at o'clock M., and recorded in Liber No. at Folio one of the Land Records. Examined by

____
Recorder

GPO 899-243

HUD-92127M (8-82)

Lender's Affidavit

State law requires the lender in a residential mortgage loan to execute and attach an affidavit to each mortgage. This document must state that the mortgage funds are correctly stated in the mortgage and that they were disbursed when the mortgage was executed or delivered to the lender by the borrower.

Recording

As discussed in the text, recording a mortgage or deed of trust gives constructive notice to the world that there is a lien on the property given as security for the loan. Also, a mortgage or trust deed (but not the note) must have been recorded before a lender may initiate foreclosure proceedings against a borrower in default.

Usury

In Maryland, there is no limit on the rate of interest a lender may charge a borrower in first mortgage loans. The rate of interest, however, must be specified in a written agreement between mortgagor and mortgagee, and there can be no prepayment penalty. An exception, however, allows a prepayment penalty of no more than two months' interest when the interest rate is eight percent or less and the mortgage is paid off during the first three years of the loan. In addition, there is no interest ceiling on loans for the purchase of corporate or commercial real estate over $5,000.

The state interest ceiling on second mortgage loans is 24 percent, as set forth in the Commercial Law Article of the Maryland Annotated Code. There is no interest ceiling on loans secured by stocks and similar collateral; the maximum interest rate a lender may charge on loans secured by collateral other than stocks and similar securities is 10 percent. The maximum interest rate allowable on a land installment contract is 24 percent.

Violators of the state usury law are subject to penalties requiring the lender to forfeit an amount equal to three times the interest charges collected in excess of the permissible amount, or $500, whichever is greater.

Mortgage Expense Accounts

In Maryland, mortgage and deed of trust lenders (savings institutions, not mortgage brokers and bankers) who require borrowers to maintain an expense or escrow account to assure payment of such expenses as taxes and insurance must pay the borrower interest on such funds. The rate of interest, by law, must be the rate regularly paid by the lending institution on normal passbook savings accounts but may be no less than three percent. Such interest is computed on the average monthly balance accrued in the escrow account and is paid annually to the borrower by crediting the account with the amount of interest due.

Loans sold to agencies in the secondary mortgage market, as explained in the text, are exempt from this requirement.

Mortgage Brokers and Mortgage Bankers

Mortgage brokers and bankers are required to register with the State Banking Commissioner. A mortgage broker may not charge a finder's fee in any transaction in which he or she is the lender, a partner of the lender, or a part owner of the lender. The Bank Commissioner is authorized to receive and investigate written complaints received regarding a mortgage broker or mortgage banker.

Discrimination

Under Maryland law, a lender may not refuse loans to any person solely on the basis of geographic area, neighborhood, race, creed, color, age, sex, handicap, marital status, or national origin. However, a lender may refuse loans based on higher-than-normal risks connected with the loan.

Ground Rents--FHA/VA Loans

The Veterans' Administration will guarantee loans on leasehold properties located only in Anne Arundel County, Baltimore City, Baltimore County, and the Joppatowne subdivision in Harford County. If a veteran purchases leasehold property located in another part of the state using VA financing, the ground rent must be redeemed on or prior to the date of closing.

For FHA loans on Maryland property held subject to a ground rent, the FHA residential mortgage limit of $74,700 must be reduced by the capitalized value of the annual ground rent. For example, in the case of a residential leasehold property sold for $70,500 and subject to an annual ground rent of $180, the $74,700 limit must be reduced by $3,000 ($180 ÷ 6%), leaving the maximum amount the FHA will insure at $71,700. The limit for FHA-insured loans in Anne Arundel and Howard Counties is $82,300; in other counties the limit varies.

With current rates of interest greatly exceeding the maximum six percent annual ground rent, the owner of the ground rent may opt to redeem the ground rent for an amount less than the capitalized value of the land. This is known as discounting the ground rent and it effectively increases the percentage return to the purchaser of the ground rent. Ground rents will be discussed in Chapter 16 of the supplement.

Release of Mortgage Lien

When the mortgage note has been fully repaid by the borrower, the lender must release the lien of the mortgage. This may be done by a separate form referred to as a satisfaction of mortgage or a deed of release. If a trust deed or deed of trust form is used, there may be a separate form of release recorded in order to clear the borrower's title.

In some instances, the mortgagee simply enters the form of release directly upon the original recorded mortgage; then the mortgage form is rerecorded so that the public record will indicate the release. Recording of the release after the debt has been repaid is the only "notice to the public" that the original mortgage lien has been cancelled.

The receipt and recording of an original mortgage which is marked "paid" or "cancelled" by the mortgagee or the mortgagee's agent has the same effect as if a release has been executed by the mortgagee, provided that the mortgage is accompanied by an affidavit of the mortgagee, or his or her agent declaring that the mortgage has been paid or otherwise satisfied.

Presumption of Payment

A mortgage or deed of trust is presumed to have been paid if 12 years have elapsed since the last payment date called for in the instrument or the maturity date as set forth in the instrument. Previously, the law required a period of 20 years.

Foreclosure

Foreclosure of a mortgage that does not contain a provision giving the mortgagee the power of sale is normally undertaken by the lender after default by the borrower. This requires a court action, and the property is ultimately sold as the result of a court order. An equitable right of redemption is allowed in every Maryland mortgage loan transaction. However, as no statutory period is provided, a defaulted borrower has to make redemption by paying the necessary funds to the mortgagee before the foreclosure sale has been completed--that is, before the court officer delivers the sale deed to the purchaser. Holders of subordinate interests in real property may record a request for a notice of sale, requiring holders of superior interests in property to give notice of an impending foreclosure sale.

A foreclosure made under a power of sale clause contained in a deed of trust or mortgage has the same effect as a foreclosure sale made under court decree. The mortgagee or trustee may opt to purchase the property in default personally, rather than sell it to satisfy the debt, provided he or she has attempted to obtain the best possible price for the property on the market.

Annual crops planted or cultivated by the mortgagor do not pass with property sold under a foreclosure sale unless so stated in the mortgage or deed of trust; such crops remain the property of the debtor. After the sale, an agreement may be reached on a reasonable rental of that part of the property occupied by the crops. This rental becomes a lien on the crops and continues until paid. If the parties cannot agree on such rental, it may be determined by the courts.

Note that a foreclosure sale under a deed of trust in default will cancel any tenancy of the property, such as a lease that began after the deed of trust was executed and recorded.

Strict foreclosure, as described in the text, is not recognized in Maryland.

LAND INSTALLMENT CONTRACTS

The state law regarding land installment contract sales of real estate may be found in the Annotated Code of Maryland, Real Property Article, Title 10. Note that this law applies only to the sale of improved properties, occupied or to be occupied by the purchaser as a dwelling, or of an unimproved, subdivided lot or lots intended to be improved for residential purposes.

All land installment contracts must be in writing and signed by all parties to the document, according to the state statute.

The vendor (seller) must give a completed, signed copy to the vendee (buyer), who in turn must give the vendor a receipt for this completely executed copy. The law allows the vendee the right to terminate or cancel the contract if he or she is not provided with the completely executed copy from the vendor.

Within 15 days after the contract has been signed by both vendor and vendee, the vendor must file the installment contract for record with the land records of the county in which the property is located. The vendor is required to mail the receipt for the recording of the document to the vendee. These conditions must be written as part of the contract terms, and a vendor's failure to comply with them allows the vendee the unconditional right to terminate and cancel the contract.

The contract must contain all terms of the transaction, including any special charges or fees for service, the cost of any insurance coverage charged to the vendee, and full details of the purchase price, due date, the total number of installment payments, and all interest charges. Provisions of the contract must include the vendee's right to pay any and all installment payments in advance. A statement must be included as to whether or not the vendor has received written notice from any municipal authority requiring that repairs or improvements be made to the property under the contract of sale.

Under a land installment contract, the vendor retains title to the property until the vendee has fully performed all of his or her obligations and has paid the purchase price in full. The vendor retains the right to mortgage the property, although a vendor may not place or continue on the sold property any outstanding mortgage lien greater than the unpaid purchase price due under the installment contract. Also, no such outstanding mortgage may require payments in excess of the periodic payments due from the buyer under the installment contract.

A provision must be made in the contract to give the vendee the right, when he or she has paid 40 percent or more of the original purchase price under the installment contract, to demand that the vendor convey title to the vendee in exchange for a purchase money mortgage executed by the vendee and delivered to the vendor. Or, upon obtaining a mortgage loan from another mortgage lender, the vendee has the right to demand title from the vendor. The vendee is to pay the cost of drawing the deed and mortgage and a negotiated share of the cost of state revenue and transfer tax stamps, recording fees, and other such expenses.

In the event that the vendor serves notice on the vendee of default on any terms of the contract, the vendee has the right to correct the default by proper compliance within the time limit designated in any default notice received from the vendor. If the default is corrected within the time allowed, the contract will continue in full force and effect.

Periodically, the vendor is required to provide the vendee with a statement showing the total amount paid to date, the ground rent (if any), the insurance coverage in effect, taxes and other charges, and the unpaid balance due. This notice must be made annually within 30 days of the first of each calendar year, or not more than twice a year upon demand of the vendee, and also whenever 40 percent of the original purchase price under the installment contract has been paid in full.

All of the vendee's rights are enforceable in court. Upon determination by the court that the vendor has failed to comply with the legal requirements, the court will appropriate relief to the vendee, including reasonable attorney's fees.

JUNIOR FINANCING

The maximum interest rate a lender may charge in Maryland for a second mortgage is 24 percent; the maximum loan origination fee that may be charged is two points, out of which are paid all costs such as appraisal fee and credit report. Only an actual cost, such as a recording fee or title insurance, may be charged over the two-point fee. A junior loan may be refinanced no more than once in every 12-month period and not more than twice during any five-year period. Consult the Commercial Law Article of the Maryland Annotated Code for details.

The Code permits balloon payments on second mortgages, but only deferred purchase-money second mortgages, and it permits a two-year, one-time postponement of the balloon. It also allows all fees, discounts, and points permitted or required under federal-related second mortgage purchase programs. However, the points and interest rate computed together may not exceed 24 percent.

Junior lenders in Maryland are prohibited from certain practices, including the following:

1 attempting to have the debtor waive his or her legal rights;
2 requiring accelerated payments, except in case of dafault;
3 having the debtor execute an assignment of wages for payment of the loan;
4 charging a fee to execute a release after the loan is paid.

Balloon Payments

As revised in 1984, the Maryland Secondary Mortgage Law requires private individuals who take back a second mortgage with a balloon clause to grant the borrower only one automatic one-time, six-month extension to the call date. Prior to July 1, 1984, the law required a 24-month extension.

Interest Rates

On or after July 1, 1982, and before July 1, 1985, a lender may charge interest not exceeding 24 percent per annum simple interest on a secondary mortgage loan, provided that: the interest is computed on the unpaid principal balances outstanding; the lender does not contract for, charge or receive any interest in advance or any compounded interest; and the lender conforms to other sections of the law.

ENTERPRISE DEVELOPMENT PROGRAM

The counties and municipalities of Maryland and Baltimore City are authorized to implement local enterprise development programs and establish funds in order to provide equity and to make and guarantee loans for the establishment and growth of enterprises, and to specify certain criteria and limitations for such equity investments, loans, and loan guaranties.

MARYLAND DEPARTMENT OF ECONOMIC AND COMMUNITY DEVELOPMENT

The Department of Economic and Community Development for the State of Maryland is the executive department with the principal authority for implementing legislative goals relating to housing. DECD is concerned with increasing the potential for Maryland families of moderate and limited income to rent or own decent housing at reasonable cost, to encourage and facilitate maintenance of the State housing stock, and to stimulate the flow of capital into the Maryland housing market. Within DECD there are three major divisions with housing responsibility: Community Development Administration, Maryland Housing Fund, and Division of Local and Regional Development. To obtain details about particular programs, and qualification criteria, contact DECD at 2525 Riva Road, Annapolis, MD 21401.

Elderly Housing Program (EHP)

State-appropriated funds are used to make deferred payment loans, subordinate to other financing, to approved applicants for the new construction or substantial rehabilitation of housing for the elderly.

Homeowner's Emergency Mortgage Assistance Act (HEMA)

HEMA provides financial counseling services and loans to certain unemployed homeowners who would otherwise be unable to make mortgage payments.

Maryland Home Financing Program (MHFP)

This state-sponsored plan provides low-rate loans to limited-income Maryland residents who are chosen by a lottery.

Maryland Housing Rehabilitation Program (MHRP)

The Maryland Housing Rehabilitation Program provides low-interest loans to finance the rehabilitation or renovation of houses and buildings.

QUESTIONS

1. In Maryland, mortgages:

   a. must be recorded in order to be valid between lender and borrower.
   b. may not be refused a person because of his or her religion.
   c. by law, must be for a minimum 10-year term.
   d. may be foreclosed by strict foreclosure if in default.

2. The FHA will insure a loan on real property in Maryland that is held subject to a ground rent:

   a. only in certain, specified areas of the state.
   b. and the FHA limit will not be reduced by the capitalized value of the annual rent.
   c. only to the in-fee value of the property.
   d. only in Baltimore City.

3. In Maryland, a land installment contract need not:

   a. be recorded by the vendor within 15 days after it has been signed by vendor and vendee.
   b. include all terms involved in the transaction.
   c. be signed by the grantor and grantee.
   d. be filed with the Real Estate Commission.

4. Ajax Savings and Loan gives Peter Taylor a loan to purchase a new home but fails to record the mortgage document. The mortgage does not give Ajax the power of sale in case of default. Which of the following is true?

   a. Ajax Savings and Loan will not be able to enforce the mortgage in a court of law should Taylor default on the loan.
   b. Should Taylor default on the loan, Ajax Savings and Loan cannot foreclose on the mortgage in court unless it is recorded.
   c. It is Taylor's obligation, as mortgagor, to record the mortgage.
   d. If Taylor defaults on the loan, Ajax Savings and Loan need not foreclose on the mortgage in court.

5. Liberty Loan Company gives Jane Alexander a 30-year loan to purchase a Baltimore condominium unit. Along with monthly payments of principal and interest, the lender requires Alexander to deposit funds in an escrow account for the payment of taxes and property insurance. Which of the following is true?

   a. Liberty Loan must pay Alexander interest on these escrow deposits when the loan is paid off.
   b. Alexander may require the lender to maintain her escrow account in an interest-bearing depository.
   c. Liberty Loan must credit Alexander's account for interest earned on her escrow deposits annually.
   d. Alexander must pay the loan company a minimum of three percent interest for maintaining such an account on her behalf.

16

Leases

MARYLAND GROUND RENTS

As mentioned in Chapter 7 of the text, an estate or interest in land can be owned or held as either a freehold estate or leasehold estate. A person who wishes to erect a building can acquire the land on which to build by either of these two estates. Such a person could purchase the owner's fee simple estate--that is, acquire the owner's freehold interest in the parcel of land--and then erect the improvement or building on it and be the fee simple owner of land and building. Another choice is available, as he or she could also lease from the owner a parcel of unimproved land--acquire a leasehold interest in it--for a long term, and then erect the building on the leased land. This kind of leasehold estate is usually created by a ground lease and the rent paid by the tenant is called ground rent. The ground owner owns a fee simple estate and the tenant owns the leasehold estate and the building.

Ground leases are generally net leases that require the lessee to pay rent, as well as real estate taxes, insurance, upkeep, and repairs. They can run for terms of fifty years or longer. As with all leases, the tenant's rights under a ground lease are considered by law to be personal property. Ground rents are payable in arrears, usually in semiannual payments.

History

In most states, ground leases are created for some industrial and/or commercial sites. As a holdover from Maryland's colonial days, however, some of the urban land in the state--residential as well as commercial and industrial--is occupied by persons owning leasehold estates who pay ground rent to the owners of the fee simple estates.

The basic concept of leasing ground dates back to the time of Moses. During the Middle Ages, it was refined as part of the political system of feudalism in which the tenant owed the overlord (and thus the king) loyalty and service as well as rent. The custom of paying a tribute, or rent, such as farm products, military service, or money, was well-established in England when Maryland was founded.

In the Charter of Maryland, dated 1632, King Charles I of England gave Lord Baltimore (and his heirs) the right to hold the land by the charter in his own name. A condition of the charter, however, created a ground rent of two Indian arrows from Maryland and one-fifth of all the gold and silver that was mined in the colony, which Lord Baltimore was to pay the King every year on the Tuesday of Easter week at Windsor Castle. The charter also gave Lord Baltimore the right to "sublet" land, which he did with enthusiasm, encouraging people to migrate to the colony.

The Revolutionary War brought an end to the feudal concept that the tenant owes the landlord loyalty and tribute as well as rent, but the system of long-term leases remained firmly established in Maryland.

As early as 1742, private citizens began to lease property under terms similar to those used today, for 99-year terms or longer. Buyers were attracted to the terms, which included an annual ground rent to be paid but no down payment. The first recorded 99-year lease with a clause for renewal was dated approximately 1770 and concerned property located in the Fell's Point section of Baltimore.

Creating a Ground Rent

Ground rent can be defined as that money paid to a landlord by a tenant when that tenant holds the landlord's land by virtue of a lease that was executed in the tenant's favor. Such a document usually leases the land to the tenant for 99 years and can be renewed forever at the tenant's option. A leasehold interest can be sold, mortgaged, or subleased. However, the leaseholder cannot impair the building, which is security for the ground rent. The lease is assigned to the purchaser of the leasehold by a document that specifically indicates that the estate is less than freehold and is regarded as personal property rather than real property.

Ground rent is created when a fee simple owner executes a ground lease. This creates a leasehold interest, or right, that is conveyed to the tenant and a reversionary interest, or right to possession, that the fee simple landowner retains. Possession of the land reverts back to the fee simple owner when the lease finally expires, is terminated by the tenant's default, or is not renewed.

Anyone who owns unencumbered fee simple property can create a leasehold estate. The worth of the reversion is based on the capitalized value of the ground rent. Although any amount of ground rent can be charged for a property, the rent should be reasonable in order to make the property marketable. Ground rent amounts are usually set by rents charged for comparable lots (competitive rents) in the neighborhood or simply "what the market will bear." The student should be aware that capitalization of the annual ground rent amount does not necessarily represent the true value of the piece of land. (Capitalization of rent or income is covered in Chapter 18 of the text.)

The expenses involved in originating or creating a new ground rent include the following:

1 charge for recording the lease--$2 or $2.50 per page and $.50 or $1 a name in Maryland counties and Baltimore City respectively
2 Maryland revenue stamps--approximately $1.10 per $1,000 of the capitalized value; also transfer tax of one-half percent or more of value
3 notary fees
4 legal fees for drawing the lease.

The Right of Redemption

In the past, leaseholders of residential properties had no right or privilege to purchase the land they held and thereby own it in fee simple (unless the lease specifically provided for this). Maryland state law now provides that all ground rents reserved by leases of residential land for periods of longer than 15 years are redeemable at the option of the tenant. This means that the tenant may purchase the fee simple estate from the landlord. Note that this redemption right applies only to residential property, whether single family or duplex.

To redeem a lease, the tenant must give the landlord one month's notice and then pay the landlord a sum of money equal to the capitalization of the rent at a rate that does not exceed that established by law. The redemption price, or capitalization figure, is calculated by dividing the annual rent by the percentage. For example, if the annual rent is $120, and that sum is 6 percent of the capitalized value, the capitalized value would be:

$$\frac{\text{Annual Rent}}{\text{Percentage}} = \text{Capitalized Value}$$

$$\frac{\$120}{.06} = \$2{,}000 \qquad .06\,\overline{)120.00}\ \ 2000.$$

If the lease was executed on or after July 1, 1971, it is redeemable at any time after the expiration of three years from the date of the lease. The redemption schedule for leases dated before July 1, 1971, is based on the date of the lease, as follows:

1 If the lease was executed between July 1, 1969, and July 1, 1971, the reversion is redeemable after five years from the date of lease, with one month's notice to the landlord at a six percent capitalization of the rent.

2 If the lease was executed before July 1, 1969, the reversion is redeemable at any time, with one month's notice to the landlord at a six percent capitalization of the rent. Leases executed between April 8, 1884, and April 5, 1888, may be redeemed at the redemption price specified in the lease, not to exceed four percent of the capitalization of rent.

3 If the lease is executed after July 1, 1982, the reversion is redeemable after five years from the date of the lease, with one month's notice to the landlord at a rate not exceeding 12 percent capitalization of the rent.

Leases executed prior to April 9, 1884, are irredeemable. Some ground rents that were created then are still in existence today.

Note that the statutory redemption rate has increased from "not more than four percent" in 1884 to "not more than six percent" on and after April 5, 1888, which has had the effect of reducing the tenant's cost to redeem. An annual rent of $120 is redeemable at four percent for $3,000.

$$\$120 \div .04 = .04\,\overline{)\$120.00}\ \ 3000. = \$3{,}000$$

The same rent redeemable at six percent requires only $2,000.

$$\$120 \div .06 \;=\; .06\,\overline{)\,120.00}^{\;2000.} \;=\; \$2,000$$

So, the limitation "not more than" was inserted to protect the landlord or fee owner from a tenant bargaining for a higher redemption rate and, thereby, a lower redemption price.

The legislature enacted this section of the code giving tenants the right to redeem for the purpose of breaking up long, irredeemable leases, rather than to give special consideration to lessees. In practice, it is often more profitable for a lessee to retain the leasehold estate. The lessee who redeems (purchases) a $120 per year, six percent ground rent for $2,000, will save $120 per year. But the lessee could save more money by putting that $2,000 into a savings account offering more than six percent interest on deposits. The lessee who deposits $2,000 in a savings account at seven and one-half percent will earn $150 interest per year, enough to pay the rent and still have a $30 profit.

Redemption fees. The fees incurred in redeeming a ground rent are similar to those for creating a new one. Transfer tax must also be paid on the transaction. In addition, the legal fees are usually higher because they cover the cost of searching the full chain of title.

Benefits to homeowners. Through the years, the concept of ground rent has changed in nature from a tax to a charge that is beneficial to homeowners. A person who buys a residence that is a leasehold will have to pay the ground rent, so the cost of the residence property is less than if the land were being bought outright. Before mortgage money was easily available, home builders and developers used the ground rent system as a method of reducing the amount of cash a buyer needed to acquire a home.

A ground rent is, in effect, a first lien on the property. To illustrate the effect of a ground rent on the cost of a house, consider a house and lot with a market value of $60,000. A purchaser could buy the fee simple interest from the seller for $60,000. If similar lots in the neighborhood were under ground rents of $360 per year, at the state redemption rate of six percent, the capitalized value of the land would be $6,000. If the seller were to create a ground rent, the sale price of the property could be reduced by $6,000 to $54,000. However, in that case the buyer would be purchasing a leasehold estate, which is a ground rent and not a fee simple. After paying $54,000 for the property, he or she would have to pay the annual ground rent of six percent of $6,000 ($360), and that rent would be payable forever--or until the buyer redeemed the ground rent by paying the $6,000 to buy the fee simple estate in the land.

Ground Rent Disclosure

When property is sold subject to a ground rent, the seller, by law, must give the buyer notice of this ground rent at the time of settlement. The seller must further inform the new leaseholder that nonpayment of the ground rent will entitle the holder of the ground rent to bring an action of ejectment against the leaseholder in court, after which the holder of the ground rent may own the property free and clear.

MARYLAND RESIDENTIAL LEASES

Maryland law provides that leases for terms of three years or less need not be in writing; those for more than three years but less than seven years must be in writing, but they need not be recorded; leases for seven years or more must be in writing, acknowledged, and recorded. Note, however, that even when such leases have not been properly recorded, they are still valid and binding between the original parties, against their creditors, and against their successors and assignees who have actual notice of the lease or who acquire the property when a tenant is in actual occupancy.

Possession of the property by a tenant under a lease for seven years or less gives notice of the tenant's rights.

Although the law requires leases for terms of more than seven years to be recorded, a memorandum of lease may be recorded instead. This memorandum must be executed by all persons who are parties to the lease and must contain certain pertinent information about the lease. Recording a memorandum of lease ensures that the lease itself is valid and binding against all persons, not just the parties previously mentioned.

Application for a Lease

An application for a lease must contain a statement explaining the liabilities incurred by the tenant upon signing the application, including the tenant's obligation to exercise the lease if the application is accepted. If the landlord requires any fees other than a security deposit--such as for a credit check based on information in the application--and these fees exceed $25, the landlord is required to return the fees in excess of the actual amount spent. This applies to landlords who offer five or more rental units on one parcel of property but not to seasonal rentals or condominiums.

Security Deposits

In Maryland, landlords may not require security deposits of more than two months' rent or $50, whichever is higher. Such deposits must be placed and maintained in a special account in a Maryland banking or savings institution within 30 days of receipt. The landlord must give the tenant a receipt for the deposit; failure to do so makes the landlord liable to the tenant for the sum of $25.

When a lease is terminated, the landlord must return the tenant's security deposit within 45 days, including simple interest at the rate of four percent per year. Interest accrues at six-month intervals from the day the tenant gives the security deposit. For deposits received before July 1, 1972, the tenant is entitled to the interest accrued from what date (the date on which state law concerning security deposits took effect).

Security deposits may be withheld by the landlord to cover the following expenses:

1 unpaid rent
2 damage due for breach or violation of lease terms (the landlord is entitled only to the actual loss caused by the breach)

3 cost of repairs of damage to leased premises in excess of ordinary wear and tear.

A landlord who wishes to withhold deposits to cover the cost of repairs due to damage to the premises must present to the tenant, within 15 days of the termination of the lease, a written list of the damages and the actual repair cost incurred. Failure to comply with this could make the landlord liable to the tenant for three times the amount of the security deposit, plus a reasonable sum for attorney's fees, and unpaid rent which could be reasonably withheld. An action pertaining to security deposits may be brought at any time during tenancy, or within two years after its termination.

Records System

State law requires that every landlord maintain a records system showing the dates and amounts of rent paid by tenants and that a receipt of some form was given to each tenant for each cash rent payment.

Flood Plain Area

Note that Baltimore County and City landlords must give tenants of multifamily dwellings notice that they are located in flood plain areas, as discussed in Chapter 4 of the text.

Rental Unit Registration

Owners of residential units in Baltimore City must file an annual registration statement with the Baltimore City Commissioner of Housing and Community Development, whether the units are occupied or not. The registration is to be accompanied by a $10 fee per residential rental unit. Failure to register is a misdemeanor subject to criminal prosecution and a fine of up to $300 for each day of violation. Other jurisdictions also have registration requirements.

Owner Identification

Owners of residential rental property are required by state law to post in a conspicuous place a sign listing the name, address, and telephone number of the property owner or managing agent. In lieu of such sign, this information may be included in the lease or the rent receipt.

Sale of Leased Premises

Unless specified to the contrary in the lease, the purchaser of a property that is occupied by a tenant under a lease is bound by the conditions and terms of that lease just as was the original landlord. If such purchaser does not wish to become a landlord, he or she should include a clause in the contract of sale with the seller requiring that the premises be delivered unoccupied and vacant at the time of settlement. Public local law of Baltimore City now requires a landlord to give the tenant the right of first refusal before the leased premises can be conveyed to a third party.

Termination of Tenancies

Any lease. A leasehold estate may be terminated by any of the following circumstances:

1 expiration of the lease term in itself provides notice to the lessor and the lessee; no further notice of termination is required
2 the lessee's purchase or redemption of the fee simple estate from the lessor, or the lessee's acquisition of title to the estate that is superior to that of his lessor
3 mutual agreement between the lessor and lessee
4 destruction of the premises by fire or unavoidable accident (except where the property can be restored by ordinary repairs in a few days or within a stipulated period); NOTE: This termination is effective if the lease is for a term of seven years or less and if the lease did not provide otherwise.
5 cancellation as provided by law at the option of the aggrieved or injured party when there has been a breach of any covenant or condition of the lease
6 eviction of the tenant as a result of a litigation
7 by paying 60 days' advance rent, a tenant in Baltimore City may dissolve or terminate any residential lease.

Year-to-year or renewable tenancies. The requirements to terminate tenancies from year to year differ throughout the state. In all the counties except Montgomery County and Baltimore City, the landlord must give the tenant written notice to terminate, as follows:

1 one week for a week-to-week tenancy
2 one month for a month-to-month tenancy
3 three months for a year-to-year tenancy.

A tenant's oral notice is sufficient to terminate such tenancies; notice from the landlord is not necessary. In Montgomery County, the parties may agree in writing on longer or shorter periods. The local laws of Baltimore City generally require a landlord to give the following written notice to terminate:

1 sixty days for a tenancy of less than one year, at sufferance, or "pur autre vie"
2 ninety days for a year-to-year tenancy
3 thirty days for all other cases.

A tenant may terminate any of these tenancies by giving the landlord thirty days' notice.

Holding over. When a landlord consents to a holdover tenant remaining on the premises, as described in the text, the holdover tenant becomes a periodic week-to-week tenant if the lease status was week-to-week prior to the holdover; in all other cases, the tenant becomes a periodic month-to-month tenant unless the lease specifies otherwise and this provision is initialed by the tenant. A tenant under a lease who unlawfully holds over beyond the termination of the lease is liable to the landlord for actual damages that may be caused by the holding over.

Dispossession. A landlord who gives the required notice or has a court order for termination of tenancy may dispossess a tenant and repossess the property by a simple court suit before a district court judge.

The length of notice the landlord must give the tenant before beginning dispossession proceedings is generally one month in renewable monthly tenancies or in tenancies with a fixed term and no provision for renewal. For automatically renewable yearly tenancies, this notice (with certain exceptions) is three months; for renewable weekly tenancies, it is one week. If the tenant or person in possession refuses to comply with the written request to remove from the property, the landlord may make a complaint in writing up to the district court of the county where the property is located. The court issues a summons, which is served by the sheriff to the tenant, to appear before the court, and an attested copy is affixed to the property in a conspicuous place. This is considered sufficient notice.

Failure to Pay Rent

In any action of summary ejectment for failure to pay rent where the landlord is awarded a judgment allowing restitution of the leased premises, the tenant has the right to redemption of the premises at any time before the actual execution of the eviction order by tendering in cash, certified check, or money order all past-due rent to the landlord, plus all court costs awarded.

Back Rent on Renewal of Lease

If a tenant named in a lease or an assignee applies to his or her landlord for a renewal under a covenant in the lease giving the tenant the right to renew, and if the tenant cannot produce vouchers or evidence showing payment of rent accrued for three years preceding this demand and application, the landlord, before executing the renewal of the lease, is entitled to demand and recover not more than three years' back rent, in addition to any renewal fine that may be provided for in the lease.

If there is no demand or payment of rent for more than 20 consecutive years, the landlord not only loses the rent but also the reversion of the property. If the landlord is under any legal disability when the 20-year period expires, he or she has two years after the removal of the disability within which to assert his or her rights. Failure to demand rent for 20 years could result in a fee simple title being vested in the tenant.

Tenant Receipt

In Anne Arundel County, unless the tenant makes payment by check or rents the property for commercial or business purposes, the landlord is required to give the tenant a receipt showing the amount of payment and the time period it covers. On conviction of violating this section of the law, any person or agent forfeits the rent for the period in question.

Surrender of Premises

When a lease contains a covenant or promise by the tenant to leave, restore, surrender, or yield the leased premises in good repair, this does not bind the tenant to erect any similar building or pay for any building destroyed by fire or otherwise without negligence or fault on the tenant's part.

Distress. A landlord may ask the courts to seize and sell a tenant's personal property for unpaid rent by filing a petition with a district court. This legal procedure is known as distress, and the taking of a tenant's property by the court is called distraint. A landlord may do this only if the tenancy has continued for longer than three months (by written lease or periodic tenancy) or was a tenancy at will.

Note that if a rental agreement does not clearly state such information as when tenancy expires, when rent accrues, or whether rent is to be paid in advance or in arrears, the lease's terms may be considered by the courts to be too vague because of ambiguous wording, and no distress will be allowed.

Prohibited Residential Lease Provisions

In Maryland, the following provisions are prohibited for use in residential leases:

1 A provision that allows any person to confess judgment against the tenant on a claim arising from the lease (this would allow a creditor to get a speedy judgment against the lessee by simply having an attorney file an affidavit with the court--no further legal proceedings would then be necessary).
2 A provision whereby the tenant agrees to waive or forego any rights or remedies against the landlord as provided by law.
3 A provision allowing the landlord to charge a penalty for late payment of rent in excess of five percent of the amount of rent due for the period in which the rent is delinquent. For weekly rentals, this late charge may not exceed $3.00 per week, nor may such charges exceed $12 per month.
4 Any provision whereby the tenant waives his or her right to a jury trial.
5 Any provision whereby the tenant agrees to a period for the landlord's notice to quit (in the event that the tenant breaches the lease terms) that is less than the period prescribed by law. Both parties, however, are free to agree to a period that is longer than is prescribed by law.
6 Any provision authorizing the landlord to take possession of the leased premises or any of the tenant's personal property unless the lease has been terminated by operation of law, and such personal property has been abandoned by the tenant.
7 Any provision intended to exempt or hold the landlord harmless from liability to the tenant or any other person for any injury, loss, damage, or liability arising from the landlord's omission, fault, negligence, or other misconduct on or about the leased premises contrary to public policy in areas that are under the tenant's control. This includes stairways, elevators, hallways, and so forth. These types of provisions are called exculpatory clauses and are void.
8 A provision allowing the automatic renewal of the lease term, unless the tenant has specifically acknowledged that section of the lease. Any such provision not signed or initialed by the tenant is unenforceable.
9 No lease may require that the tenant give the landlord a longer period of notice to terminate the tenancy than the period granted the landlord to likewise notify the tenant.

All of the preceding provisions, if inserted into a Maryland lease, are considered unenforceable.

Withholding Rent--Hazardous Conditions

State law requires that a landlord provide and maintain premises for tenants that are free of defects and do not present substantial and serious threat of danger to the life, health, and safety of the tenants. Where hazardous conditions exist on leased property, a tenant may give the landlord written notice by certified mail of the conditions and wait a period of 30 days. If the hazardous conditions are not corrected, then a tenant can withhold rent from the landlord or pay it into an escrow account for necessary repairs. Such conditions include fire or health hazards or other defects that may threaten the safety or occupancy of renters, such as:

1 lack of adequate sewage disposal facilities
2 infestation of rodents in two or more dwelling units
3 the existence of lead-based paint on surfaces within the unit.

The Baltimore City Code provides by a warranty of habitability that the premises must be fit for human habitation and further provides for remedies available to tenants if the premises are unsafe or dirty to the extent that tenants' health is threatened. The warranty of habitability differs from rent escrow laws in that tenants have the use of their rent money to make these repairs the landlord has failed to complete. Under the rent escrow, rent must be paid into an account where it is held until the repairs are made.

Note that minor, not dangerous, defects or housing code violations that go uncorrected are not just cause for nonpayment of rent.

Rent Escrow Account

The District Court can order tenants to pay rents into an escrow account of the court or administrative agency of the county. If the tenant fails to pay rent accrued or as it becomes due, the court, upon certification of the account, can give judgment in favor of the landlord and issue a warrant for possession. Upon final disposition of the action, the rent escrow account is distributed in accordance with the judgment or hearing.

Housing Discrimination - Elderly

A landlord, real estate broker, or real estate agent is prohibited from refusing to rent or sell a house to a person 62 years or older solely on the basis of age.

Form of the Lease

There are a number of lease forms available from local Boards of Realtors®, property owner associations, and tenant organizations. Any landlord who offers more than 4 dwelling units for rent on one parcel of property or at one location and who rents by means of written leases substantially increases the requirements concerning the form of written lease.

Retaliatory Evictions

A landlord may not evict a tenant, increase rent, or decrease any of the services to which a tenant is entitled for any of the following reasons:

1 the tenant has filed a written complaint with the landlord or with a public agency against the landlord
2 the tenant has filed a lawsuit against the landlord
3 the tenant is a member of a tenants' organization.

Smoke Detectors

Smoke detectors must be installed by January 1983 in all multifamily buildings and hotels constructed prior to 1975 and having four to nine units. The landlord is responsible for the installation, repair, or replacement of the detector. An occupant of a one-, two-, or three-family residential dwelling constructed prior to July 1975 is required to equip the apartment with at least one approved smoke detector, and to maintain it.

Lease Option Agreements

A lease option agreement includes any lease that contains a clause giving the tenant the option to purchase the landlord's interest in the property before some specified date. In Maryland, no lease option on improved residential property, with or without a ground rent interest, is valid unless it contains the statement, "THIS IS NOT A CONTRACT TO BUY" in capital letters, and also contains a clear statement of the option's purpose and effect with respect to the ultimate purchase of the property.

Sources of Assistance

Baltimore Neighborhoods, Inc., a private nonprofit civil rights agency working for fair housing and tenants' rights in the Baltimore area, publishes guides to laws covering tenant/landlord relations in Baltimore City, the counties, and the state. These guides, revised annually to incorporate new laws, may be purchased from the organization at 319 East 25 St., Baltimore, MD 21218.

MOBILE HOME PARKS

Title 8A of the Maryland Code, Real Property Article, sets forth the rights and responsibilities of mobile home tenants and owners. It sets forth provisions regarding such matters as park rules, maintenance, and tenancy. Although the particulars of this law are too detailed for this Supplement, a licensee planning to own or manage a mobile home park should be familiar with its provisions.

QUESTIONS

1. Mary Tenant has owned her residence for five years, subject to an annual ground rent of $120.

   a. Mary can redeem her ground lease by a payment of $1,500 after giving ten days' notice to the owner of the fee.
   b. Mary must give one month's notice to the fee owner and can then redeem her ground rent for $2,000.
   c. Mary can require the fee owner to redeem her ground rent for less than the capitalized value.
   d. Mary must give one month's notice to the fee owner and can then redeem her ground rent for $1,000.

2. The ground rent on a residence is $180 a year, and the lease has been in effect more than five years.

   a. A redemption at five percent will require $3,200.
   b. A redemption at six percent will require $3,000.
   c. A redemption at ten percent will require $6,400.
   d. A redemption at twelve percent will require $6,000.

3. John Builder has just completed a new house, which he is offering for sale at $68,000 for fee simple title. If, to satisfy an immediate buyer, he creates a ground lease requiring $240 a year ground rent at an eight percent redemption rate, then:

   a. the property may not be redeemed for at least 50 years.
   b. he can reduce the price to $65,000.
   c. he can reduce the price to $56,000.
   d. the in fee price would be $71,000.

4. Arthur Buyer is interested in buying a residence for $40,000 with a ground rent of $180.

   a. Arthur will receive a deed conveying to him a fee simple interest.
   b. Arthur will receive a deed conveying to him a leasehold estate subject to an annual ground rent of $180.
   c. Arthur will receive no deed until such time as he redeems the ground rent.
   d. Arthur will receive a fee simple deed after paying ground rent for five years.

5. Since 1970, John Commercial has owned a store building and lot subject to an annual ground rent of $240. If he gives one month's notice to his lessor:

   a. he can redeem his lease for $4,000.
   b. he may not necessarily redeem his lease.
   c. he can redeem his lease for $2,000.
   d. he can redeem his lease for $6,000.

6. A man who owns and occupies his home and pays a semiannual ground rent owns an estate in the real estate which is called a:

   a. fee simple estate.
   b. leasehold estate.
   c. estate at will.
   d. estate at sufferance.

7. Ground rents are sometimes originated in order to:

   a. reduce the amount of cash required to purchase a property.
   b. force the tenant to keep the property in good repair.
   c. provide further assurances to the mortgagee.
   d. prevent the lender from foreclosing.

8. A tenant signed an apartment lease calling for $250 rent per month; the landlord can also require:

   a. a $500 security deposit.
   b. a $550 security deposit.
   c. three months' rent as a security deposit.
   d. the tenant to post a bond equal to one year's rent as security.

9. A landlord holding a tenant's security deposit of $500 is required to:

   a. credit the deposit account $20 a year interest.
   b. allow the tenant five percent simple interest per year.
   c. return the deposit within 30 days after termination of the lease.
   d. give the tenant a receipt or be liable to the tenant for a sum of $250.

10. Sampson sold a house he owned which was occupied by Rawlins under a one-year lease having six months to run. Therefore:

    a. Rawlins must vacate at the closing of the sale.
    b. Rawlins' lease continues until its expiration.
    c. the lease terminates at closing.
    d. the lease is not binding on the new owner.

11. A tenant is entitled to occupy the landlord's property:

    a. after the lease term expires.
    b. until the tenant defaults and the lease is terminated by notice or a court orders the tenant to vacate.
    c. as long as the tenant continues to pay the rent.
    d. until the property is foreclosed.

12. A year-to-year tenancy:

    a. may be terminated without notice.
    b. expires without notice on the expiration date stipulated on the lease.
    c. may be terminated by giving the landlord seven days' notice.
    d. is terminated by a tenant's oral notice.

13. Which of the following leases need <u>not</u> be in writing, acknowledged, and recorded in Maryland?

    a. two-year residential lease
    b. twenty-year industrial lease
    c. eight-year commercial lease
    d. three-year apartment lease

14. The legal procedure by which the courts may seize and sell a tenant's personal property for unpaid rent is called:

    a. ejectment.
    b. distress.
    c. dispossession.
    d. distraint.

15. Which of the following provisions, if included in a residential lease in Maryland, is enforceable?

    a. a provision whereby the tenant agrees to pay the landlord a five percent penalty for late rent payments
    b. a provision whereby the tenant agrees to let the landlord use his or her pass key to take possession of the tenant's property if the tenant becomes more than one month behind in rent payments
    c. a provision whereby the tenant agrees to waive or forego any rights or remedies against the landlord as provided by law
    d. any provision whereby the tenant waives his or her right to a jury trial

21

Fair Housing Laws and Ethical Practices

MARYLAND FAIR HOUSING LAW

Article 49B of the Annotated Code of Maryland, which prohibits discrimination in many areas and provides for the creation of a Human Relations Commission to enforce the law, became effective July 1, 1971. Included in this article are several sections on "discrimination in housing" that prohibit discrimination in the following ways on the basis of race, color, sex, religion, national origin, marital status, or physical or mental handicap:

1 Refusing to sell or rent after a bona fide offer has been made, refusing to negotiate, or otherwise making a dwelling unavailable to any person
2 Changing the terms, conditions, or services available for different individuals as a means of discrimination
3 Being responsible in any way for a statement or advertisement concerning the sale or rental of a dwelling that indicates a preference, limitation, or discrimination
4 Discriminating against any person by representing that a dwelling is not available for inspection, sale, or rental when in fact it is available
5 Denying any person access, membership, or participation in any multiple listing service, real estate brokers' organization, or other facility relating to the sale or rental of dwellings as a means of discrimination, or changing the terms of such for any individual
6 Including any restrictive covenants that discriminate in any transfer, sale, rental, or leasing of housing, or honoring any such restrictive covenants
7 Refusing to consider both applicants' income when both marriage partners seek to buy or lease any dwelling
8 Refusing to consider alimony or child support awarded by a court and received by an applicant as a valid source of income, where that source can be verified as to its amount, length of time received, and regularity of receipt
9 Requesting or considering information about birth control practices in evaluating any prospective buyer or lessee of a dwelling
10 Inducing another person to transfer an interest in real property or discouraging another person from doing so by mentioning the existence or potential nearness of real property that is owned or used by certain persons or by representing that such nearness may result in:
   a. the lowering of property values
   b. a change in the racial, religious, or ethnic composition of the area in which the property is located

c. an increase in criminal or antisocial behavior in the area
d. a decline in the quality of the schools serving the area

11 Soliciting the listing of dwellings for sale or lease by any means for the purpose of changing the racial composition of the neighborhood
12 Denying a loan for the purchase, construction, improvement, or other maintenance of a dwelling to any person or changing the terms of such loan for an individual as a means of discrimination when the prospective lender is a bank, savings and loan institution, credit union, insurance company, or other person regularly engaged in the business of making such loans.

Housing discrimination - Elderly. Solely on the basis of age, a landlord, real estate broker, or real estate agent may not refuse to rent or sell housing to a person 62 years of age or older.

Exemptions. The following are exempt from compliance with the Maryland Fair Housing Law:

1 Any religious organization or nonprofit institution or organization that is operated by or in conjunction with a religious organization may give preference to persons of the same religion, when the dwellings in question are used for other than a commercial purpose, unless membership in such religion is restricted on the basis of race, color, sex, or national origin
2 A private club which is a bona fide club and which is exempt from taxation under the Internal Revenue Code may restrict the rental or occupancy of lodgings it owns to its members, as long as the lodgings are not operated commercially
3 Any person may refuse to sell, rent, or advertise any dwelling that is planned exclusively for, or occupied exclusively by, individuals of one sex, to any individual of the opposite sex
4 Any person may sell, rent, or advertise any dwelling to aged or elderly persons only, or if the dwelling is planned exclusively for or occupied exclusively by a specified age group
5 With respect to discrimination based on sex or marital status alone, it does not apply to the rental of rooms within any dwelling in which the owner maintains his or her principal residence or to the rental of any apartment in a dwelling containing not more than five units and in which the owner maintains his or her principal residence.

Many of these provisions are based upon the provisions of the Federal Fair Housing Act of 1968; by enacting its own fair housing law, Maryland has affirmed its commitment to eliminate housing discrimination and has ensured that all such complaints will be directed to the state authorities.

Blockbusting and steering. The unethical practice of blockbusting, as described in the text, is prohibited by the Maryland Real Estate License Code (Article 56, Sections 230A and 230B of the Annotated Code). Blockbusting and steering were discussed in detail in Chapter 14.

Conservation areas. Section 230C of the license law empowers the Real Estate Commission to determine and designate, after prior public hearing, certain localities as conservation areas. See Chapter 14 for a detailed discussion.

Enforcement. Fair housing complaints in Maryland are referred to and investigated by the state agencies. The Maryland Fair Housing Law is enforced by the Commission on Human Relations. Individuals may file complaints with the Commission; also, the Commission may initiate complaints on its own. The Commission will investigate all complaints and seek to eliminate discrimination by conference conciliation, and persuasion. It is empowered to call public hearings and issue orders to cease and desist. Court actions may be taken to enforce a Commission order. The Commission may also obtain temporary injunctions from the courts to "preserve the status quo." The Commission is required to forward a written copy of the findings of any investigation on a real estate licensee to the Real Estate Commission for appropriate action.

Judicial review. The staff of the Human Relations Commission investigates complaints of discrimination and provides written copies of its findings to the complainant and the persons named in the complaint. If the finding is that there is probable cause to believe the complaint to be correct, the staff tries to eliminate the discrimination by means of conference, conciliation, and persuasion. A copy of the findings is also forwarded to the Real Estate Commission if a licensee is involved.

Any agreement reached between the complainant and the respondent is put in writing and signed by the respondent. The Commission then enters an order setting forth the terms of the agreement. If no agreement is reached, the Commission makes a written finding to that effect.

If the Commission denies a request for reconsideration of a finding of no probable cause, the denial is a final order appealable to the circuit court, unless the U.S. Equal Employment Opportunity Commission has jurisdiction over the subject matter of the complaint.

In addition, provisions of the real estate license law, including the Code of Ethics and the regulations, are enforced by the Maryland Real Estate Commission, as discussed in Chapter 14 of this Supplement.

Complaints may be filed with the following agencies:

State of Maryland
Commission on Human Relations
701 St. Paul Street
Baltimore, Maryland 21202

Fair Housing
Department of Housing and
Urban Development
Washington, D.C. 20410

Real Estate Commission of Maryland
501 St. Paul Place
Baltimore, Maryland 21202

Fair Housing
HUD Area Office
Baltimore, Maryland 21202

Discrimination in Financing

It is unlawful for any bank, savings and loan institution, credit union, insurance company, or other person regularly engaged in the business of making mortgages or other loans for the purchase, construction, improvement, or repair or maintenance of dwellings: (1) to deny such a loan to a person applying, or (2) to discriminate against him or her in the fixing of the down payment, interest rate, duration, or other terms or conditions of such a loan because of the race, color, religion, creed, marital status, sex, national origin, or physical or mental handicap of such person, or of any member, stockholder, director, officer, or employee of such person, or of the prospective occupants, lessees, or tenants of the dwelling for which the loan appliction is made.

Antisolicitation Ordinances

Baltimore City law prohibits the solicitation of residential properties for purchase or sale by general door-to-door solicitation, in person, or by telephone, or by the mass distribution of circulars. There are no exceptions to the law. Solicitations as a result of personal referrals, general knowledge that a property is for sale, or offerings by an owner constitute violations of the law. The court has added that any uninvited call or visit could constitute violation of the ordinance.

Canvassing. Baltimore County law provides several methods of canvassing that are not considered solicitation. They include advertisements in bona fide newspapers of general circulation, radio or television; literature distributed through the U.S. mail; legitimate personal referrals; contacts with property owners resulting from the owner having personally advertised the property for sale; and solicitation for the purpose of obtaining information for appraisals for similar collecting of general sales or market data.

Enforcement. Violation of either the Baltimore City or Baltimore County law would be punishable as a misdemeanor, upon conviction, and could result in a fine, imprisonment, or both.

Educational Requirement

The Maryland Real Estate Commission places strong emphasis on fair housing. Regulations .13, .16, and .22 of the Commission require that all applicants for licensing as a real estate broker or salesperson must be instructed in:

> Human relations aspects of the practice of real estate, including study of fair housing laws and the effects of undesirable practices such as exploitation, steering, blockbusting, prejudicial solicitation, and related activities....

HUD Fair Housing Advertising Guidelines

In early December 1983, many brokers received notice from the Maryland Human Relations Commission of formal complaints from Baltimore Neighborhoods, Inc. These problems stemmed from misuse or lack of use of the Department of Housing and Urban Development's Fair Housing Advertising Guidelines. Following the guidelines printed here will assure compliance in advertising. It is imperative that licensees understand and utilize these guidelines.

A. All advertising of residential real estate for sale or rent to contain an equal opportunity logotype statement or slogan.
B. A simple formula to guide the real estate advertiser in using the equal opportunity logotype or slogan:
    1. If other logotypes are used in the advertisement, the equal housing opportunity logotype should be of a size equal to the size of the largest other logotype.
    2. If no other logotype is used in the advertisement, the following guidelines should be used:

Size of Advertising	Size of EHO Logo Including Slogan
1/2 page or larger	2" x 2"
1/8 page to 1/2 page	1" x 1"
4 column inches to 1/8 page	1/2" x 1/2"

3. The use of words, phrases, sentences, and visual aids which have a discriminatory effect in residential real estate advertising are not to be used.
4. The selective use of advertising in various media and with respect to various housing developments or sites can lead to discriminatory results and should be avoided. Such selective use may involve the strategic placement of billboards, brochure advertisements distributed within a limited geographic area by hand or in the mail, or advertising in particular geographic coverage editions of major metropolitan newspapers, or in local newspapers which are mainly advertising vehicles for reaching a particular segment of the community, or in displays or announcements only in selected sales offices.

D. In all space advertising which is less than 4 column inches the "equal housing opportunity" slogan should be used.

E. Whenever human models in photographs or drawings are used in display advertising, the models should be clearly definable as reasonably representing both majority and minority groups in the metropolitan area. Models, if used, should indicate to the general public that the housing is open to all without regard to race, color, religion, sex, or national origin and that it is not for the exclusive use of one such group.

QUESTIONS

1. A private club, by limiting the rental or occupancy of its lodgings to club members, as long as the club is not operated as a commercial hotel, is violating:

   a. the Federal Fair Housing Act of 1968.
   b. the Maryland Fair Housing Law.
   c. the Real Estate License Law.
   d. none of the above

2. Licensees must refrain from stating that a change in neighborhood racial characteristics may result in:

   a. a lowering of property values.
   b. a decline in the quality of the schools.
   c. an increase in criminal or antisocial behavior.
   d. any of the above

3. To attempt to induce an owner to sell his residence because of a possible change in the racial or ethnic character of the area:

   a. is called "blockbusting."
   b. is ethical and legal.
   c. is called "steering."
   d. is unethical but not illegal.

4. A salesperson is working on a residential listing in a changing neighborhood that was formerly all white. The salesperson:

   a. is proper in not showing this listing to white prospects.
   b. violates state and federal laws when he or she determines whether or not to show a listing based on a prospect's race.
   c. need not introduce into the neighborhood anyone not of the predominate race of the neighborhood.
   d. should have a salesperson of the same race as the prospect show the property.

5. James and Frances Miller, who are black, tell the real estate salesperson that they need a three-bedroom house in the $50,000 to $55,000 price range that is within walking distance to an elementary school. The salesperson, after identifying the Millers as genuine prospects, finds a house on Judson Street that meets all the Millers' requirements, but the salesperson knows that the residents of that neighborhood are unhappy about blacks moving into the area. The agent should:

   a. omit telling the Millers about this particular house.
   b. tell them about the house, but suggest that they would be happier in another neighborhood.
   c. file a complaint with the Human Relations Commission.
   d. inform the Millers about the availability of the house and arrange to show them the listing.

23

Closing the Real Estate Transaction/ Closing Statement Problem

EVIDENCE OF TITLE

In Maryland, the buyer has the obligation of examining the title to the real estate being purchased. In some cases, the buyer's attorney examines the records and indicates the condition of the title being purchased by preparing a certificate of title.

The attorney may first prepare an abstract from the county records and from this, prepare his or her opinion of the title. Or, such abstract may be used by a title company attorney as the basis for a title insurance commitment. The buyer's attorney will usually obtain such a title insurance commitment as of the date of settlement to protect the client.

CLOSING THE TRANSACTION

Most purchase and sale agreements are closed in the office of the title insurance company, the buyer's attorney, the mortgage lender or, occasionally, the real estate broker.

The escrow procedure for handling real estate closings is not generally practiced in Maryland.

Disbursement of Funds

In order to be valid between the parties or any third party, a purchase money mortgage or deed of trust involving Maryland land must contain, or have endorsed on or attached to it before recordation, the oath or affirmation of the party secured, or his or her agent, by the instrument stating that, at a time no later than the execution and delivery of the instrument, the actual sum of money advanced at the closing was paid over and disbursed either to the borrower or to the person responsible for disbursement of funds in the closing transaction.

Closing Statements

In preparation for the closing of a real estate purchase transaction, the buyer's or seller's attorney will prepare the necessary closing statement. The broker should possess the necessary knowledge to prepare such a statement in order to more accurately estimate the expenses of a sale and give the seller an estimate of the property's net sale proceeds. The buyer must be prepared with the proper amount of money to complete the purchase, and the broker should also be able to assist the buyer by making a reasonably accurate estimate of the cost. Closing costs are divided according to local custom, which varies throughout Maryland.

The real estate broker normally attends the closing of a sale, although the action is principally between the attorneys for the parties and/or the attorney for the mortgage lender. The broker is available for such service as he or she may be asked to render and, of course, to receive the commission.

Closing Problem

This closing problem example uses the procedures involved in an actual transaction. Note that a closing statement problem such as this does not appear on the state licensing exam. Broker applicants, however, are expected to answer questions on closing theory, prorations, transfer taxes, and so forth. The problem addressed in this chapter provides the student with practice in these areas. To that end, a settlement statement worksheet, rather than an actual closing statement is used, since it best illustrates the various expenses and charges involved in a real estate transaction. The material in the study problem is also presented, however, on actual closing forms at the end of the chapter.

Completing the worksheet. To use the worksheet most efficiently, follow these steps:

1 As the information given for the problem is read, list the types of expenses included in the transaction in the first column of the worksheet.
2 Go through the list of expenses. Consider those expenses related to the buyer, make any necessary proration computations, and record each buyer-related expense as either a debit to the buyer (an amount the buyer owes) or a credit to the buyer (an amount the buyer has already paid, promises to pay in the form of a loan or note, or will be paid).
3 Then go through the list of expenses and consider those expenses related to the seller. Make necessary proration computations and record each seller-related expense as either a debit to the seller (an amount the seller owes) or a credit to the seller (the selling price of the property and any prorated expenses the seller has prepaid).
4 Total the buyer's debit and credit columns and subtract the lesser from the greater total to determine what amount the buyer must pay at the closing (if debits exceed credits) or what amount the buyer will be paid at the closing (if credits exceed debits).
5 Total the seller's debit and credit columns and subtract the lesser from the greater total to determine what amount the seller will pay at the closing (if debits exceed credits) or what amount the seller will be paid at the closing (if credits exceed debits).

Read through the example information that follows and list all expense categories on the worksheet. Don't fill in any other columns yet.

Data describing the real estate transaction. Sam Soloman, an agent for the XYZ Real Estate Company (broker number 0000), which is a member of the local Realtors'® multiple listing service, secured a six-month exclusive-right-to-sell listing on September 13, 1984, from Robert Owens and his wife Lucy. The listing was for their home at 29 South Maple Avenue, Hometown, Maryland 00030 (Randolph County).

The house is a two-story colonial with a full basement. The first floor includes a living room, 12 feet by 15 feet; a dining room, 10 feet by 12 feet; a kitchen with breakfast space; and a tiled powder room. The second floor includes three bedrooms with two full baths; the bedrooms measure 12 feet by 11 feet, 12 feet by 14 feet, and 11 feet by 13 feet. The basement has a paneled recreation room and a laundry room, 10 feet by 12 feet; there is a forced hot air furnace (oil fuel) and an electric water heater. City water and sewer services are provided, and the house uses natural gas. There is no attic.

The house was built in 1960 but only owned by sellers since 1977. It is of brick construction and there is a detached frame garage with a side drive on the property. There is also a large cement patio adjacent to the rear of the house. The Owens own the property in fee; there is no ground rent. They have agreed to include the gas cooking range, the electric refrigerator, the gas clothes dryer, and the electic washer in the total selling price of $160,000.

The current real estate taxes of $1,750 have been paid. The broker's commission agreed upon is 6-1/2 percent of the gross sale price. The lot measures 60 feet by 150 feet. The legal description is Lot 3 in Block R of the Hilldale subdivision, as taken from the deed to the Owens, which is recorded in Liber 720, Folio 25. The house contains 2,364 square feet of floor space.

The Hometown Bank holds a mortgage on the property with an unpaid balance of $57,260, as of September. Interest is charged at the rate of 8-1/2 percent per annum, with the final payment to be made by 1997. The bank has indicated that this mortgage may be assumed by a qualified buyer. Monthly payments of $607.48 are applied first to the interest, then to the balance of the principal.

On November 15, 1984, the agent obtained a bona fide offer from Harry and Mary Barnett to purchase the property for $150,500. The offer was on the basis of 30 percent in cash, the buyers' assumption of the balance of the existing mortgage and the seller taking back a second purchase-money mortgage for the remainder of the purchase price, to be paid over five years at 12 percent interest. Possession was desired as of the date of closing, which was to be no later than December 15, 1984. The offer was accompanied by a check for $1,000 and the Barnetts agreed to increase the earnest money to 10 percent when their offer was accepted. The sellers accepted the offer and a contract was prepared on the basis of the Barnetts' terms.

The expenses for closing the transaction outlined above also included the following:

1 Title examination - $852
2 Title insurance policy - $301 (owners)

SETTLEMENT STATEMENT WORKSHEET

Property ____

Seller ____

Buyer ____

Settlement Date ______________________

	BUYER'S STATEMENT		SELLER'S STATEMENT	
	DEBIT	CREDIT	DEBIT	CREDIT

3 Preparation of deed - $50 (This is generally the buyer's expense, but local practice may vary.)
   3a Preparation of assumption agreement - $35
4 Preparation of second purchase-money mortgage - $50
5 Termite inspection - $50
6 Transfer tax (state tax, no county tax) - 1/2% of sales price
7 Revenue stamps (state and county total) - $1.65 per $500 (varies between $1.10 to $3.50 per $500)
8 Premium for fire and hazard insurance - $409.10
9 Recording charges of $18 each for deed and purchase-money mortgages and assumption agreements (this also varies by number of signatures and pages being recorded) - $54
10 Notary public fee - $5.50
11 Lien certificate - $20
12 Settlement charge - $75
13 Assumption fee - $30

Sellers and buyers will each pay one-half of the transfer tax and revenue stamps.

Itemized expenses on Settlement Statement Worksheet. At this point, you should have listed the following information on the settlement worksheet:

Purchase price
Earnest money deposit
Assumed mortgage principal
Prorated mortgage interest
Second Purchase-money mortgage
Real estate tax
Broker's commission
Title examination
Title insurance policy
Preparation of deed
Preparation of purchase-money mortgage
Preparation of Assumption Agreement
Termite inspection
Transfer tax
Revenue stamps (Recordation Tax)
Fire and hazard insurance
Recording fees (deed, purchase-money mortgage, and assumption agreement)
Notary fee
Lien certificate
Settlement charge

If you left any items out, add them to the worksheet at the bottom of your list. (The order of the items is not important.) When your list is complete, work through it, considering only those expenses that affect the buyers and record the result of your computations in the proper column. Then work through the list again, considering those expenses that affect the sellers and make those entries. NOTE: Compute all prorations on the basis of a 30-day month.

Check all your completed entries and computations against the following explanations.

PURCHASE PRICE. A debit to the buyers because they have promised to pay in cash or otherwise account for the entire agreed-upon price of the property. A credit to the sellers because they will be reimbursed for the selling price of the property.

EARNEST MONEY DEPOSIT. The buyers have paid 10 percent of the $150,500 purchase price, or $15,050, so this amount is credited to them. (Since the $15,050 was paid to the broker, rather than the sellers, this amount is not part of the sellers' statement.)

ASSUMED MORTGAGE PRINCIPAL AND INTEREST. The unpaid balance of the sellers' mortgage was $57,260 as of September 1 (the listing was taken September 13). However, since the sale was closed on December 15, three more monthly payments were made by the sellers and the balance reduced as follows:

DATE	BALANCE
September 1	$57,260.00
October 1	57,058.11
November 1	56,854.79
December 1	56,650.03

Therefore, the unpaid balance of the assumed mortgage on December 15 was the December 1 balance, and the prorated interest is based on that figure. Interest proration is for interest from December 1 to 15, or one-half month:

$56,650.03 x 8-1/2% = $4,815.25 per year
$ 4,815.25 ÷ 12 = $ 401.27 per month
$ 401.27 ÷ 2 = $ 200.64

Since the buyers agree to assume the sellers' remaining mortgage debt, the balance of the principal remaining is credited to them, as well as the interest that accrued on that principal while the sellers had possession of the property during half of the month of December. Since the sellers are relieved of their indebtedness for both the remaining principal and the interest for that part of December in which they were in possession of the property, both amounts are debited to them. In effect, the sellers are paying off their indebtedness with part of the purchase price of the property.

SECOND PURCHASE-MONEY MORTGAGE. The buyers are paying 30 percent in cash and assuming the existing mortgage. The sellers are taking back a second purchase-money mortgage for the remainder of the purchase price.

Purchase Price		$150,500.00
Less: 30% Cash	$45,150.00	
Assumed Mortgage	56,650.03	101,800.03
Second Purchase Money Mortgage		$ 48,699.97

Since the buyers agree to pay the amount of the purchase-money mortgage at a future date, that amount will be credited to them. Since the sellers agree to accept part of the purchase price in the future, that part of the purchase price must be debited to them, to be subtracted from the amount they receive on the day of closing.

REAL ESTATE TAX. In Maryland, real estate taxes are paid in advance on July 1 for the year ending the following June 30. Therefore, the prorated tax credit to the sellers is from December 15 through June 30 of the following year, or 6-1/2 months.

$1,750.00 ÷ 12 = $145.8333 per month
$145.8338 x 6-1/2 = $947.9164

The sellers will be credited with the prorated tax amount they have prepaid, and the buyers will be debited with that amount since they must pay taxes that have been assessed for the time during which they will own the property, taxes that the sellers have prepaid.

BROKER'S COMMISSION. The sellers must pay the broker his commission rate of 6-1/2 percent of the selling price of $150,500, or $9,782.50. Since the sellers owe the broker this amount, it is a debit to the sellers. The buyers will not pay the broker a commission.

TITLE EXAMINATION, TITLE INSURANCE POLICY, PREPARATION OF DEED, PREPARATION OF PURCHASE MONEY MORTGAGE, FIRE AND HAZARD INSURANCE, RECORDING FEES FOR BOTH DEED AND PURCHASE MONEY MORTGAGE, NOTARY FEE, LIEN CERTIFICATE, AND SETTLEMENT CHARGE. As agreed, the buyers will pay these expenses, so they are debited to the buyers.

TERMITE INSPECTION. As agreed, the sellers will pay this expense, so it is debited to them.

TRANSFER TAX. The transfer tax is one-half percent of the selling price of $150,000, or $752.50. Since the buyers and sellers have agreed to share this expense, each couple will be debited $376.25.

REVENUE STAMPS (Recordation Tax). The rate in Randolf County is $1.65 per $500 or fraction thereof of the purchase price. $150,500 divided by $500 is $301, which multiplied by $1.65 is $496.65. Since the buyers and sellers have agreed to share this expense, each couple will be debited with $248.33/.32.

Totaling debit and credit columns. BUYER OWES. Add all of the buyers' credits. Then add all of the buyers' debits. In this case, since the debits are greater than the credits, subtract the credits from the debits and the remainder is the amount owed by the buyers.

Total Buyers' Debits	$153,954.10
Total Buyers' Credits	120,600.64
Buyer Owes	$ 33,353.46

BALANCE DUE SELLER. Add all of the sellers' credits. Then add all of the sellers' debits. In this case, since the credits are greater than the debits, subtract the debits from the credits and the remainder is the balance due the sellers.

Total Credits	$151,447.92
Total Debits	116,007.71
Balance Due Seller	$ 35,440.21

Check all of your entries against the completed statement worksheet on page 162.

SETTLEMENT STATEMENT WORKSHEET

Property 29 South Maple Avenue, Hometown, Maryland 20030
Seller Robert Owens and Lucy Owens
Buyer Harry Barnett and Mary Barnett
Settlement Date December 15, 1984

	BUYER'S STATEMENT		SELLER'S STATEMENT	
	DEBIT	CREDIT	DEBIT	CREDIT
Purchase Price	$150,500			$150,500
Earnest Money Deposit		$15,050		
Assumed Mortgage Principal		$56,650.03	$56,650.03	
Prorated Mortgage Interest		$ 200.64	$ 200.64	
Second Mortgage		$48,699.97	$48,699.97	
Real Estate Tax	$947.92			$947.92
Broker's Commission			$9,782.50	
Title Examination	$852.00			
Title Insurance Policy	$301.00			
Preparation of Deed	$50.00			
Preparation of Purchase Money Mortgage	$50.00			
Termite Inspection			$ 50.00	
Transfer Tax	$376.25		$376.25	
Revenue Stamps	$248.33		$248.33	
Fire and Hazard Insurance	$409.10			
Recording Fees, Deed and Purch. Mon. Mort.	$ 54.00			
Notary Fee	$ 5.50			
Lien Certificate	$ 20.00			
Settlement Charge	$ 75.00			
Total of Debits and Credits	$153,954.10	$120,600.64	$116,007.72	$151,447.92
Due from Buyer to Close		$33,353.46		
Due to Seller to Close			$35,440.21	
	$153,954.10	$153,954.10	$151,447.92	$151,447.92

Using Standard Forms

Pages 164 and 165 show the closing statement information you have just completed transferred to a standard form currently used in much of Maryland. Some settlement attorneys prefer the HUD form shown beginning on page 166. Compare the information required on the buyers' and sellers' statements with the itemized listing on your worksheet. The information needed for this transaction is exactly the same in both instances, although the standard form must have many more items listed to accommodate other transactions, as well. The third standard form shows all items except the broker's payment of the earnest money ($8,100) to the sellers.

SETTLEMENT FOR: BUYERS

Lot #3 , Block R

On December 15 , 19 84

Subdivision Hilldale, Randolph County

29 South Maple Avenue

State of Account in re: Harry Barnett and Mary Barnett

Address

No liability is assumed by attorney for the accuracy of any information furnished by others or for any matter not of record when examination is made. Responsibility is not assumed for any monies due or payable, which at time of settlement are contingent upon assignment of funds not at such time available; said settlement and the payment of proceeds and disbursements hereunder are subject to receipt of such assignments. Attorney will receive a share of any title insurance premium paid by you.

	Debits		Credits	
Price/~~Loan~~	150,500	00		
~~Commission~~/Deposit Held by XYZ Real Estate Company			15,050	00
First ~~Deed of Trust~~/Mortgage Hometown Bank (assumed)			56,650	03
Interest accrued from 12-1-84 to 12-15-84 @ 8 1/2 %			200	64
Second ~~Deed of Trust~~/Mortgage Sellers			48,699	97
Interest accrued from to @ %				
Release notification				
Lien Certificate	20	00		
Long Distance Telephone Calls				
Trustees Release Fee $ Assumption Fee $ 30.00	30	00		
Escrows: Tax Fire Insurance F.H.A.				
Origination/Placement Fee to Lender				
Appraisal/Inspection Fee $ Credit Report $				
Fire & Ext. Cov. Ins. Paid to @ for yrs.	409	10		
Termite Certification				
Taxes: Transfer Tax-State @1/2 % ; County @ % (1/2)	376	25		
State & County 12-15-84 to 6-30-85 @ $1,750.00 pd. per annum	947	92		
Sanitary District @ $ per annum				
City Taxes @ $ per annum				
Special Assessments				
Water Bill / Escrow				
Survey				
Title Insurance – Lendor's Owner's $301.00	301	00		
Condominium Fees				
Notary Fee ~~and Copies~~	5	50		
Title Examination	852	00		
Prepare Deed $50 ~~Trust~~/Mortgage $50 Release $ Other (Assump. Agree.) $35	135	00		
Recording Deed $18 Trust/Mortgage $18 Release $ Other $18	54	00		
Settlement/~~Closing~~ fee	75	00		
Recordation Tax (Revenue Stamps) County & State $1.65($500)(1/2)	248	33		
Assignment from seller to				
Balance Due: to seller $ from buyer $33,353.46			33,353	46
	153,954	10	153,954	10

THIS SETTLEMENT SUBJECT TO FURTHER ADJUSTMENT IN EVENT OF ANY ERROR IN CALCULATION.

CERTIFIED TO BE A TRUE COPY

Approved and copy hereof received:

Closing Attorney

Harry Barnett

Mary Barnett

SETTLEMENT FOR: Sellers

On December 15, 19~~X~~84

Lot #3, Block R

Subdivision Hilldale, Randolph County

29 South Maple Avenue

State of Account in re: Robert Owens and Lucy Owens

Address

No liability is assumed by attorney for the accuracy of any information furnished by others or for any matter not of record when examination is made. Responsibility is not assumed for any monies due or payable, which at time of settlement are contingent upon assignment of funds not at such time available; said settlement and the payment of proceeds and disbursements hereunder are subject to receipt of such assignments. Attorney will receive a share of any title insurance premium paid by you.

	Debits		Credits	
Price/~~Loan~~			150,500	00
Commission/~~Deposit~~ XYZ Real Estate Company	9,782	50		
First ~~Deed of Trust~~/Mortgage Hometown Bank (assumed)	56,650	03		
Interest accrued from 12-1-84 to 12-15-84 @ 8 1/2 %	200	64		
Second ~~Deed of Trust~~/Mortgage from Buyers	48,699	97		
Interest accrued from to @ %				
Release notification				
Long Distance Telephone Calls				
Trustees Release Fee $ Assumption Fee $				
Escrows: Tax Fire Insurance F.H.A.				
Origination/Placement Fee to Lender				
Appraisal/Inspection Fee $ Credit Report $				
Fire & Ext. Cov. Ins. Paid to @ for yrs.				
Termite Certification	50	00		
Taxes: Transfer Tax-State @1/2 % County @ % (1/2)	376	25		
State & County 12-15-84/6-30-85 @ $1,750.00 (pd.) per annum			947	92
Sanitary District @ $ per annum				
City Taxes @ $ per annum				
Special Assessments				
Water Bill / Escrow				
Survey				
Title Insurance – Lendor's Owner's				
Condominium Fees				
Notary Fee and Copies				
Title Examination				
Prepare Deed $ Trust/Mortgage $ Release $ Other $				
Recording Deed $ Trust/Mortgage $ Release $ Other $				
Settlement/Closing fee				
Recordation Tax (Revenue Stamps) County & State $1.65($500)(1/2)	248	32		
Assignment from seller to				
Balance Due: to seller $ 35,440.21 from buyer $	35,440	21		
	151,447	92	151,447	92

THIS SETTLEMENT SUBJECT TO FURTHER ADJUSTMENT IN EVENT OF ANY ERROR IN CALCULATION.

CERTIFIED TO BE A TRUE COPY

Approved and copy hereof received:

Closing Attorney

Robert Owens

Lucy Owens

INSERT 'C'

A. U.S. DEPARTMENT OF HOUSING AND URBAN DEVELOPMENT **DISCLOSURE SETTLEMENT STATEMENT**	**B. TYPE OF LOAN** 1. ☐ FHA 2. ☐ FMHA 3. ☐ CONV. UNINS. 4. ☐ VA 5. ☐ CONV. INS. 6. FILE NUMBER 7. LOAN NUMBER
If the Truth-in-Lending Act applies to this transaction, a Truth-in-Lending statement is attached as page 3 of this form.	8. MORTG. INS. CASE NO.

C. **NOTE:** This form is furnished to you prior to settlement to give you information about your settlement costs, and again after settlement to show the actual costs you have paid. The present copy of the form is:

☐ ADVANCE DISCLOSURE OF COSTS: Some items are estimated, and are marked "(e)". Some amounts may change if the settlement is held on a date other than the date estimated below. The preparer of this form is not responsible for errors or changes in amounts furnished by others.

☐ STATEMENT OF ACTUAL COSTS Amounts paid to and by the settlement agent are shown. Items marked *"(p.o.c.)"* were paid outside the closing; they are shown here for informational purposes and are not included in totals.

D. NAME OF BORROWER	E. SELLER	F. LENDER
Harry Barnett and Mary Barnett	Robert Owens and Lucy Owens	

G. PROPERTY LOCATION	H. SETTLEMENT AGENT	I. DATES	
Lot #3, Block R Hilldale, Randolph County 29 South Maple Avenue	John Smith, Esquire	LOAN COMMITMENT	ADVANCE DISCLOSURE
	PLACE OF SETTLEMENT Smith, Jones & Brown Hilldale Office	SETTLEMENT 12-15-84	DATE OF PRORATIONS IF DIFFERENT FROM SETTLEMENT

J. SUMMARY OF BORROWER'S TRANSACTION

100.	**GROSS AMOUNT DUE FROM BORROWER:**	
101.	Contract sales price	150,500.00
102.	Personal property	
103.	Settlement charges to borrower *(From line 1400, Section L)*	2,506.18
104.		
105.		
	Adjustments for items paid by seller in advance:	
106.	City/town taxes to	
107.	County taxes to 6-30-85	947.92
108.	Assessments to	
109.	to	
110.	to	
111.	to	
112.	to	
120.	**GROSS AMOUNT DUE FROM BORROWER:**	153,954.10
200.	**AMOUNTS PAID BY OR IN BEHALF OF BORROWER:**	
201.	Deposit or earnest money	15,050.00
202.	Principal amount of new loan(s)	
203.	Existing loan(s) taken subject to	56,650.03
204.	Accrued Interest 12-1/15-84	200.64
205.	Second Mortgage - Sellers	48,699.97
	Credits to borrower for items unpaid by seller:	
206.	City/town taxes to	
207.	County taxes to	
208.	Assessments to	
209.	to	
210.	to	
211.	to	
212.	to	
220.	**TOTAL AMOUNTS PAID BY OR IN BEHALF OF BORROWER**	120,600.64
300.	**CASH AT SETTLEMENT REQUIRED FROM OR PAYABLE TO BORROWER:**	
301.	Gross amount due from borrower *(From line 120)*	153,954.10
302.	Less amounts paid by or in behalf of borrower *(From line 220)*	120,600.64
303.	**CASH REQUIRED FROM/OR PAYABLE TO/BORROWER**	33,353.46

K. SUMMARY OF SELLER'S TRANSACTION

400.	**GROSS AMOUNT DUE TO SELLER:**	
401.	Contract sales price	150,500.00
402.	Personal property	
403.		
404.		
	Adjustments for items paid by seller in advance:	
405.	City/town taxes to	
406.	County taxes to 6-30-85	947.92
407.	Assessments to	
408.	to	
409.	to	
410.	to	
411.	to	
420.	**GROSS AMOUNT DUE TO SELLER**	151,447.92
	NOTE: The following 500 and 600 series sections are not required to be completed when this form is used for advance disclosure of settlement costs prior to settlement.	
500.	**REDUCTIONS IN AMOUNT DUE TO SELLER**	
501.	Payoff of first mortgage loan	
502.	Payoff of second mortgage loan	
503.	**Settlement charges to seller** *(From line 1400, Section L)*	10,457.07
504.	**Existing loan(s) taken subject to**	56,650.03
505.	Interest accrued 12-1/15-84k	200.64
506.	Second Mortgage - Buyers	48,699.97
507.		
508.		
509.		
	Credits to borrower for items unpaid by seller:	
510.	City/town taxes to	
511.	County taxes to	
512.	Assessments to	
513.	to	
514.	to	
515.	to	
520.	**TOTAL REDUCTIONS IN AMOUNT DUE TO SELLER:**	116,007.71
600.	**CASH TO SELLER FROM SETTLEMENT:**	
601.	**Gross amount due to seller** *(From line 420)*	151,447.92
602.	**Less total reductions in amount due to seller:** *(From line 520)*	116,007.71
603.	**CASH TO SELLER FROM SETTLEMENT**	35,440.21

HUD-1 (5-75)

L. SETTLEMENT CHARGES	PAID FROM BORROWER'S FUNDS	PAID FROM SELLER'S FUNDS
700. **SALES/BROKER'S COMMISSION based on price** $150,500 @6 1/2%		
701. Total commission paid by seller Division of commission as follows:		9,782.50
702. $ to		
703. $ to		
704.		
800. **ITEMS PAYABLE IN CONNECTION WITH LOAN.**		
801. Loan Origination fee %		
802. Loan Discount %		
803. Appraisal Fee to		
804. Credit Report to		
805. Lender's inspection fee		
806. Mortgage Insurance application fee to		
807. Assumption refinancing fee	30.00	
808.		
809.		
810.		
811.		
900. **ITEMS REQUIRED BY LENDER TO BE PAID IN ADVANCE.**		
901. Interest from to @ $ /day		
902. Mortgage insurance premium for mo. to		
903. Hazard insurance premium for yrs. to		
904. yrs. to		
905.		
1000. **RESERVES DEPOSITED WITH LENDER FOR:**		
1001. Hazard insurance mo. @ $ /mo.	409.10	
1002. Mortgage insurance mo. @ $ /mo.		
1003. City property taxes mo. @ $ /mo.		
1004. County property taxes mo. @ $ /mo.		
1005. Annual assessments mo. @ $ /mo.		
1006. mo. @ $ /mo.		
1007. mo. @ $ /mo.		
1008. mo. @ $ /mo.		
1100. **TITLE CHARGES:**		
1101. Settlement or closing fee to	75.00	
1102. Abstract or title search to		
1103. Title examination to	852.00	
1104. Title insurance binder to		
1105. Document preparation to	135.00	
1106. Notary fees to	5.50	
1107. Attorney's Fees to		
(includes above items No.:		
1108. Title insurance to	301.00	
(includes above items No.:		
1109. Lender's coverage $		
1110. Owner's coverage $		
1111.		
1112.		
1113.		
1200. **GOVERNMENT RECORDING AND TRANSFER CHARGES**		
1201. Recording fees: Deed $ 18 ; Mortgage $ 36 Releases $	54.00	
1202. City/county tax/stamps: Deed $; Mortgage $	248.33	248.32
1203. State tax/stamps: Deed $; Mortgage $	376.25	376.25
1204.		
1300. **ADDITIONAL SETTLEMENT CHARGES**		
1301. Survey to		
1302. Pest inspection to		50.00
1303. Lien Certificate	20.00	
1304.		
1305.		
1400. **TOTAL SETTLEMENT CHARGES** *(entered on lines 103 and 503, Sections J and K)*	2,506.18	10,457.07

NOTE: Under certain circumstances the borrower and seller may be permitted to waive the 12-day period which must normally occur between advance disclosure and settlement. In the event such a waiver is made, copies of the statements of waiver, executed as provided in the regulations of the Department of Housing and Urban Development, shall be attached to and made a part of this form when the form is used as a settlement statement.

Signature ____________________

Date ____________

Signature ____________________

N. J. PASS BOOK CO. ORANGE N. J.

The Real Estate Licensing Examination

The Maryland Real Estate License Examination is prepared and administered by an independent testing service - Assessment Systems Incorporated, of Philadelphia, Pennsylvania, under the supervision of the Maryland Real Estate Commission. A number of states subscribe to the ASI testing program. In each state, the program is adapted to local real estate laws and practices and the priorities of the state's licensing agency. All questions are multiple choice and the exams are machine scored, so answers are marked on answer sheets.

The examinations for both brokers and salespeople are given in two parts. These examinations are continuously being updated. The first section on either examination is called the General Examination and contains 80 questions on general real estate knowledge. There is a passing grade requirement of 75 percent on this section for both brokers and salespeople. The second section, the Maryland State-Unique Examination, consists of questions on Maryland laws and practices, including the Real Estate License Law, Rules and Regulations, the Condominium Act, and the fair housing law--all discussed in this supplement. There are 30 state-unique questions on the salesperson examination and 40 state-unique questions on the broker examination. Passing grade requirement for the state-unique examination is 75 percent on the broker's examination and 66-2/3 percent on the salesperson's examination. The passing grade, referred to as the "cut score," is established by the Real Estate Commission.

The General Examination contains questions in five major content areas: real estate law; ownership/transfer; brokerage/agency; concepts of appraising and finance. Sample real estate transaction and real estate instruments (listing agreement, sales agreement, and settlement statement worksheet) are no longer included, although real estate contracts and settlement procedures are still covered.

The fee for each examination (original and reexamination) is $15.45. The candidate's guide containing instructions and application form may be obtained from the institution where the student fulfilled his or her educational requirements. It is mailed to the address shown on the form together with a check or money order made payable to Assessment Systems Incorporated. Failure to follow the instructions on the registration form could result in a student not being scheduled for the examination requested.

A person who wishes to take the examination, but has not preregistered for a particular test date, may report to any designated walk-in testing site, register, and take the test on the same day. Walk-in candidates are processed on a first-come, first-served basis. The fee for walk-ins is $25.45, which must be paid at the test center by check or money order. All candidates must bring positive identification. Questions concerning testing should be addressed to:

REAL Program
ASI Processing Center
210 South Fourth Street
Philadelphia, PA 19106
Tel: 215/592-8900

The Attorney General for Maryland has interpreted the license law to mean that a broker or salesperson candidate must pass the required course or courses before taking the examination for licensure.

License candidates can take either the state or the general sections of the examination individually if they so qualify. When a candidate first takes the real estate exam he or she is required to sit for both sections. If the candidate has already taken the state exam, however, but has failed one of the two sections, he or she will be permitted to retake only the section--state or general--that was failed. If a candidate fails one section of the exam three times, he or she must retake the entire exam. Both sections must be passed in a six-month period or the applicant must retake the entire exam. Candidates must pass both sections of the exam before becoming eligible to receive a Maryland real estate license.

The ASI approach to testing is designed to test reasoning processes as well as real estate knowledge. In the examination, there are questions on general real estate information and the Maryland Real Estate License Law and Rules and Regulations, as well as math problems and several kinds of comprehensive problems. Examples of such questions and problems have been included in this supplement so that you will become familiar with them and be better prepared for the examination.

Types of Questions on the Exam

Only one multiple choice answer format is used. An incomplete statement or a question is presented and is followed by four possible answers, only one of which is correct. For example:

10. During the period of time after a real estate sales contract is signed but before title actually passes, the status of the contract is:

    a. voidable.
    b. executory.
    c. executed.
    d. implied.

In answering this type of question, consider each answer carefully and eliminate the least likely ones, instead of randomly selecting an answer. It is better to guess the answer than leave a blank. If you have correctly answered the question and filled in your answer sheet properly, the line for that answer will appear as follows:

10.	A	B	C	D
	[ ]	[ ]	[■]	[ ]

The purpose of the examination is to provide a measure of your knowledge of real estate, and thereby allow you to demonstrate your qualification for licensure. You should try to answer all questions without spending too much time on any one question. Such words as NOT, EXCEPT, LEAST, MOST, etc. are underlined to help you avoid misreading a question.

Mathematics. Math problems relating to real estate transactions generally comprise approximately 20 percent of the examination. The problems are included as part of other content areas and include the following calculations: financing, tax assessment, commissions, area calculations, settlement statements, profit and loss, tax ramifications, and general basic calculations. The Maryland Real Estate Commission permits the use of silent, non-printing, hand-held, battery-operated calculators during the broker's and salesperson's license examinations.

Preparing for the License Examination

We have tried to prepare you for the Maryland Real Estate License Examination by including in this supplement the kinds of items usually found on the test. Familiarity with the form of the test, however, will not in itself ensure a passing score. Your most important preparation for this examination involves studying real estate principles and practices.

Concentrate on learning the material by studying the text and this supplement, by working all the tests and exercises, and by making sure that you can now solve any problems you missed.

Real Estate Education Company publishes three self-instructional workbooks specially designed to aid you in passing the licensing exam: Mastering Real Estate Mathematics, Fourth Edition, by Ventolo and Allaway; Principles and Practices of Real Estate, by Gaddy; and Study Guide for Modern Real Estate Practice, by Gorzelany. If copies of these books are not available through your local bookseller, you may purchase them directly from the publisher, using the order form at the back of this book.

FINAL EXAMINATION

The following questions are similar to those found on Maryland real estate licensing exams. Use this 70-question exam as a final evaluation of your real estate knowledge. Consider 50 or more correct answers to be a passing grade.

1. A contract agreed to under duress is:

   a. voidable.
   b. void.
   c. unenforceable.
   d. enforceable.

2. The landlord of tenant A has sold the building to the state so that an expressway can be built. A's lease is up, but the landlord is letting A remain until the time the building will be torn down; A continues to pay the same rent as prescribed in the lease. A's tenancy is called:

   a. holdover tenancy.
   b. month-to-month tenancy.
   c. tenancy at sufferance.
   d. tenancy at will.

3. When a form of real estate sales contract has been agreed to and signed by a purchaser and spouse and given to the seller's broker with an earnest money check:

   a. this transaction consitutes a valid contract in the eyes of the law.
   b. the purchaser can sue the seller for specific performance.
   c. this transaction is considered an offer.
   d. the earnest money will be returned if the buyer defaults.

4. A person must perform according to the terms of a contract within a time limit if:

   a. a specific time date is mentioned in the contract.
   b. the clause "time is of the essence" appears on the contract.
   c. unenforceable.
   d. none of the above

5. A seller gives an open listing to several brokers, specifically promising that if one of the brokers finds a buyer for the seller's real estate, the seller will then be obligated to pay a commission to that broker. This offer by the seller is a(n):

   a. executed agreement.
   b. discharged agreement.
   c. unilateral agreement.
   d. bilateral agreement.

6. When an unlicensed salesperson negotiates his or her first sale of real property, the commission is payable to:

   a. the broker only.
   b. no one.
   c. the salesperson only.
   d. the broker and the salesperson.

7. If a license is issued on September 20, it will expire:

   a. two years from the date of issuance.
   b. on September 20 in the licensing year.
   c. at the end of the biennial license term.
   d. on April 30, 4 years later.

8. The maximum commission allowed by the Real Estate Commission is set at:

   a. 6 percent.
   b. 10 percent.
   c. 7-1/2 percent.
   d. none of the above

9. A salesperson's license must be:

   a. kept in a safe place by the salesperson.
   b. carried by the salesperson.
   c. retained by his or her broker.
   d. maintained in the salesperson's personnel file by the broker.

10. A 40-acre tract was sold for $1,200 per acre; the seller realized a 14.5% profit from the sale. What was the original cost of the tract?

   a. $41,040.00
   b. $42,876.31
   c. $39,987.96
   d. $41,921.40

11. For the past twenty years, Joe and Maria Spinelli have operated a neighborhood grocery store in Illville. Last week, the local zoning board passed an ordinance that prohibits packaged food sales in the area where the Spinellis' grocery store is located. The Spinellis' store is now an example of a(n):

   a. outlawed classification.
   b. nonconforming use.
   c. dilapidated structure.
   d. depreciated improvement.

12. The amount of money that would be paid for property by a buyer to a seller, both being ready, willing and able to act and both being fully informed, represents that property's:

   a. exchange value.
   b. tax value.
   c. market value.
   d. equalized value.

13. Which of the following is not credited to the buyer at time of settlement?

    a. sale price
    b. buyer's earnest money
    c. an assumed mortgage
    d. a purchase money mortgage

14. When the license of a broker is suspended or revoked, his or her salespeople must:

    a. find a new employer.
    b. continue listing and selling.
    c. stop listing and selling.
    d. obtain a broker's license.

15. Membership on the Real Estate Commission includes:

    a. licensed salespersons only.
    b. licensed brokers only.
    c. unlicensed persons and licensed brokers and salespersons.
    d. those persons appointed by the Attorney General.

16. Licenses are issued:

    a. by the Real Estate Board.
    b. to all applicants who have successfully passed the required course.
    c. to all brokers who have successfully passed the required courses.
    d. by the Real Estate Commission.

17. The maximum amount that a claimant may collect from the guaranty fund is:

    a. unlimited.
    b. $250,000.
    c. $25,000.
    d. $10,000.

18. Ethical standards which must be observed by all licensees in real estate transactions are determined by:

    a. the National Association of Realtors®.
    b. the Real Estate Commission.
    c. the Maryland Association of Realtors®.
    d. the local Boards.

19. Which of the following is not a method of calculating depreciation?

    a. structural depreciation method
    b. declining balance method
    c. staight-line method
    d. sum-of-the-years'-digits method

20. Which of the following is <u>not</u> characteristic of value?

   a. utility
   b. scarcity
   c. transferability
   d. cost

21. A qualified veteran wants to buy a property with five rental units. He could obtain <u>all but</u> which one of the following loans?

   a. VA loan
   b. FHA loan
   c. conventional loan
   d. credit union loan

22. A developer desiring to convert a building which is more than five years old into a timeshare project in Maryland:

   a. must give each tenant 180 days' notice.
   b. must give each tenant 120 days' notice.
   c. need not give tenants any notice.
   d. must notify each tenant within 10 days after filing the public offering statement.

23. The street address of a property is:

   a. a formal land description.
   b. an informal land description.
   c. a legal land description.
   d. legally sufficient to describe a parcel of land on a deed.

24. The authority under the federal Fair Housing Act rests with:

   a. the Attorney General.
   b. the FBI.
   c. the Federal Housing Authority.
   d. the Secretary of Housing and Urban Development.

25. James Johnson is a salesperson working for broker Sally Best. Johnson sells a multiple listed property for $80,000. The commission rate is 7 percent of the selling price. The referral network that referred the buyer receives 10 percent of the total commission. The listing broker receives 30 percent, and the selling broker receives 60 percent. Johnson's agreement with his broker calls for 50 percent of the commission on any sale he negotiates. For this transaction, broker Best will pay Johnson:

   a. $1,680.00.
   b. $1,880.00.
   c. $3,360.00.
   d. $2,800.00.

26. An option:

    a. requires the optionee to complete the option.
    b. keeps the offer open for a specified period of time.
    c. gives the buyer an easement on the property.
    d. makes the seller liable for a commission to broker if option is not exercised.

27. A quitclaim deed conveys:

    a. only fixtures and easements.
    b. an uninsured title to real property.
    c. any interest the grantor may have.
    d. as good a title as warranty deeds.

28. Which of the following is not normally referred to as real property?

    a. water rights
    b. appurtenances
    c. air space rights
    d. furniture

29. The distinguishing trait of real property, as distinguished from personal property, is that it:

    a. can be mortgaged.
    b. is considered immobile, fixed, and permanent.
    c. can be freely transferred.
    d. is always taxed at a higher rate.

30. The money used for FHA loans is supplied by:

    a. Fannie Mae.
    b. qualified lending institutions.
    c. the Federal Housing Administration.
    d. Freddie Mac.

31. The maximum amount that may be loaned to a qualified veteran on a VA-guaranteed loan is limited to:

    a. the assessed value of the property.
    b. 60 percent of the appraisal.
    c. $27,500.
    d. the amount shown on the Certificate of Reasonable Value (CRV).

32. Which of the following is not characteristic of an easement?

    a. It is an interest which can be protected through a court against interference.
    b. It is created by conveyance.
    c. It is an encumbrance to the servient tenant.
    d. It can be terminated at will by the servient tenant.

33. A mechanic's lien is a right granted by statute. All of the following statements are true except:

  a. It is based on the enhancement of value theory.
  b. It is a voluntary lien.
  c. It gives security to those who perform labor or furnish material in the improvement of real estate.
  d. The rights of the claimant are controlled by the laws of the state in which the real estate is located.

34. Which of the following is not essential in order that a contract for the purchase of real estate be valid and enforceable?

  a. reality of consent
  b. legal capacity to contract
  c. acknowledgment of the contract
  d. offer and acceptance

35. In an amortized mortgage loan, how are the monthly payments credited?

  a. credit to principal balance increases as interest decreases
  b. credit to principal balance decreases as interest decreases
  c. credits to principal and interest remain constant
  d. credits to principal increase as interest increases

36. A building sold for $124,000; the buyer paid $12,400 earnest money payment. The buyer obtained a loan for the balance. The mortgage lender charged a fee of 2 percent of the loan. What was the total cash used by the buyer for this transaction?

  a. $14,640 c. $2,240
  b. $14,880 d. $2,480

37. A mortgage loan that requires monthly payments of $175.75 for 20 years and a final payment of $5,095 is known as:

  a. a wraparound mortgage. c. a balloon mortgage.
  b. an accelerated mortgage. d. a variable mortgage.

38. By paying the debt before a foreclosure sale, the mortgage has the right to regain his or her property. Such right is called:

  a. acceleration. c. reversion.
  b. redemption. d. recovery.

39. A mortgage loan that allows a borrower who is paying off an existing mortgage to get additional financing from a second lender is called:

  a. a wraparound mortgage. c. a balloon mortgage.
  b. an open-end mortgage. d. an accelerated mortgage.

40. The responsibilities of a real estate agent do <u>not</u> require:

    a. dealing fairly with the third party.
    b. competence on the part of the broker.
    c. the broker to give legal interpretations.
    d. loyalty to the principal.

41. A properly drawn property management contract should include all of the following <u>except</u>:

    a. a legal description of the property.
    b. the terms and conditions of the employment.
    c. a statement that the management agreement has been incorporated into the corporate minutes.
    d. how the manager is to be paid.

42. The selling price of a property is $72,500. This can be financed if the buyer can put 10 percent down and pay 1.5 points. How much money must the buyer have for this transaction?

    a. $8,770.80   c. $8,055.37
    b. $8,228.75   d. $8,617.35

43. A woman sold her property for $88,000. If she made a profit of 10 percent, what was the original cost of the real estate?

    a. $80,000   c. $79,200
    b. $79,000   d. $61,000

44. Which of the following best describes the term <u>procuring cause</u>?

    a. one who works for another
    b. one who procures for legal consideration
    c. one who originates or starts an action which results in a desired transaction
    d. one who acts as a trustee and has the legal duty to procure in a confidential manner in behalf of another person

45. A buyer of a $75,000 home has paid $2,500 as earnest money and has a loan commitment for 70 percent of the purchase price. The balance of cash needed by the buyer to close the transaction is:

    a. $9,000.   c. $20,000.
    b. $9,500.   d. $20,500.

46. The kind of deed that carries with it five covenants is a:

    a. warranty deed.   c. grant deed.
    b. quitclaim deed.   d. deed in trust.

47. An insurance premium has been paid in advance by the seller of a house. The policy, worth $50,000, has a premium of $400 for a three-year period, beginning January 1, 1982, ending on December 31, 1984. The closing date for the sale of the house is July 15, 1983. The amount to be reimbursed is:

 a. $206.59. c. $201.00.
 b. $215.00. d. $ 95.00.

48. In some states, a lender is the owner of mortgaged land. These states are known as:

 a. title-theory states. c. both a and b
 b. lien-theory states. d. neither a nor b

49. You sell a property that you have listed for $150,000. The commission rate is 7 percent. Your agreement with your broker calls for you to receive 25 percent of the total commission for listing and 35 percent of the total commission for selling. How much commission does the broker retain?

 a. $2,625 c. $4,200
 b. $3,780 d. $6,300

50. Capitalization rates are:

 a. determined by the gross rent multiplier.
 b. the rates of return a property will produce on the owner's investment.
 c. set by the Real Estate Commission.
 d. set by the State Banking Commissioner.

51. A is a salesperson working for Broker C. A sells a house for $25,000 which was listed with B's office through the multiple listing service. The commission is 6 percent of the selling price. From this commission, 5 percent is payable to the listing service; 35 percent to the listing broker, and 60 percent to the selling broker. C has employed A on the basis that A will receive 40 percent of the commission accruing to C's office. A is entitled to receive:

 a. $490. c. $ 360.
 b. $315. d. $1,500.

52. A seller wants to net $63,000 on a house after paying the broker's fee of 6 percent. The gross selling price of the house should be:

 a. $67,021. c. $67,035.
 b. $68,093. d. $66,091.

53. An acre contains:

a. 160 square feet.
b. 160 square rods.
c. 360 degrees.
d. 640 square feet.

54. A specific parcel of real estate has a market value of $60,000 and is assessed for tax purposes at 20 percent of market value. The tax rate for the county in which the property is located is 25 mills. The tax bill will be:

a. $300.
b. $250.
c. $600.
d. $150.

55. A listing contract in which the broker's commission is contingent upon the broker's producing a buyer before the property is sold by the owner or another broker is a(n):

a. open listing.
b. net listing.
c. multiple listing.
d. exclusive-right-to-sell.

56. Amount of commission set in a listing agreement is determined by:

a. state law.
b. local board of Realtors®.
c. mutual agreement.
d. Real Estate Commission.

57. A parcel of property was sold in a state in which the stamp tax rate is $.50 for each $500 paid in cash at the time of transfer. If the total price of the property is $67,500 and the buyer assumed a $42,250 mortgage, what is the amount of transfer tax paid?

a. $25.25
b. $26
c. $25.50
d. $25

58. The clause that requires a mortgagor to immediately pay the entire mortgage debt, interest, and charges is called:

a. escalation.
b. alienation.
c. acceleration.
d. lock-in.

59. The current value of a piece of property is $35,000, and the assessed value is 40 percent of its current value. The tax rate is $4 per $100. What is the amount of the tax?

a. $705
b. $625.40
c. $560
d. $526.15

60. A person who has absolute control of a parcel of real estate is said to own a:

 a. leasehold estate.
 b. life estate.
 c. fee simple estate.
 d. fee determinable.

61. Two adjacent lots having equal depth were purchased for a total of $22,000. One lot has a frontage of 100 feet and sold for $140 per front foot. The other lot has a frontage of 80 feet and sold for $1 per square foot. What is the depth of these lots?

 a. 100 feet
 b. 150 feet
 c. 180 feet
 d. 280 feet

62. A tract of land containing 871,200 square feet was purchased by a developer for $10,000 per acre. Streets and sidewalks will take up 10 percent of the property. One fifth of the property is under water. The balance of the property was divided into one-half acre lots and sold for $8,000 per lot. How much profit did the developer make?

 a. $24,000
 b. $60,000
 c. $77,800
 d. $84,800

63. Property with a market value of $74,000 is assessed at 37 percent of the market value. The taxes are $1,300.55. What is the tax rate?

 a. $1.75/$100
 b. $5.75/$100
 c. $7.50/$100
 d. $4.75/$100

64. Deposit money received by a salesperson must be:

 a. deposited in the broker's trust account by the salesperson.
 b. given to the seller of the property.
 c. placed in the broker's safe.
 d. given to the broker for deposit in her/his trust account.

65. Under Maryland Real Estate License Law, Section 224 (Suspension-Revocation of License), the Commission may impose a penalty per violation. The penalty is:

 a. $500 and/or 1 year in jail.
 b. $5,000.
 c. up to $2,000.
 d. up to $1,000 and/or 1 year in jail.

66. Jane and Jim Jones own their home as tenants by the entirety. All of the following statements are true except:

   a. If one spouse dies, the survivor automatically becomes the owner in severalty.
   b. Neither spouse has a disposable interest in the property during the lifetime of the other.
   c. Should they divorce, they would become joint tenants.
   d. The property cannot be attached by a creditor unless the creditor is the creditor of both spouses.

67. If any unity of joint tenancy is broken, the law will regard the estate as:

   a. a tenancy at will.
   b. a tenancy in common.
   c. an estate in severalty.
   d. an estate for years.

68. Which of the following is not a party to a will?

   a. testator
   b. devisee
   c. demisee
   d. legatee

69. A means of voluntary alienation of real property is best described as:

   a. adverse possession or eminent domain.
   b. deed or mortgage.
   c. foreclosure or partition.
   d. condemnation or escheat.

70. A lot measuring 100 feet wide by 200 feet deep sold for $50 per front foot. What would the salesperson's 60 percent of the 10 percent commission be on the sale?

   a. $300
   b. $500
   c. $ 600
   d. $1,200

Index

Answer Key

These answers are given for each chapter in order to help you make maximum use of the tests. If you did not answer a question correctly, restudy the course material until you understand the correct answer.

Chapter 5
1. b
2. c
3. c
4. b
5. b

Chapter 6
1. a
2. a
3. b
4. d
5. d
6. a
7. a
8. a
9. c
10. b

Chapter 7
1. d
2. b
3. a
4. a
5. a

Chapter 8
1. b
2. c
3. a
4. a
5. a
6. b
7. a
8. d
9. b
10. b

Chapter 9
1. d
2. c
3. d
4. c
5. c
6. d

Chapter 10
1. d
2. b
3. d
4. c
5. b
6. a
7. b
8. d
9. d
10. a

Chapter 11
1. a
2. a
3. b
4. d
5. b

Chapter 12
1. b
2. b
3. b
4. b

Chapter 13
1. d
2. b
3. b
4. a
5. c

Chapter 14
1. a
2. c
3. a
4. b
5. c
6. c
7. b
8. c
9. c
10. a
11. b
12. c
13. c
14. c
15. c
16. b
17. c
18. b
19. b
20. b
21. b
22. a
23. b
24. a
25. d
26. a
27. b
28. b
29. a
30. d
31. a
32. b
33. a
34. b
35. a
36. d
37. c
38. a
39. a
40. a
41. c
42. c
43. d
44. a
45. a
46. c
47. b
48. d
49. a
50. d

Chapter 15
1. b
2. a
3. d
4. b
5. c

Chapter 16
1. b
2. b
3. b
4. b
5. b
6. b
7. a
8. a
9. a
10. b
11. b
12. d
13. a
14. b
15. a

Chapter 21
1. d
2. d
3. a
4. b
5. d

Final Examination
1. a
2. d
3. c
4. b
5. c
6. b
7. c
8. d
9. c
10. d
11. b
12. c
13. a
14. c
15. c
16. d
17. c
18. b
19. a
20. d
21. a
22. b
23. b
24. d
25. a
26. b
27. c
28. d
29. b
30. b
31. d
32. d
33. b
34. c
35. a
36. a
37. c
38. b
39. a
40. c
41. c
42. b
43. a
44. c
45. c
46. a
47. a
48. a
49. c
50. b
51. c
52. a
53. b
54. a
55. a
56. c
57. a
58. b
59. c
60. c
61. c
62. a
63. c
64. d
65. c
66. c
67. b
68. c
69. b
70. a

REAL ESTATE EDUCATION COMPANY

GUIDE TO PASSING THE REAL ESTATE EXAM

By Lawrence Sager

Guide to Passing the Real Estate Exam is the only manual designed specifically for the ACT salesperson and broker exams. Provides additional test-taking drills . . . helps you review important topics . . . and gives the additional confidence you need to pass the ACT real estate exam.

This ACT-style exam manual features . . .

- point-by-point outlines in sections corresponding to the four topic areas of the exam—real estate law, valuation, finance, and special fields
- alphabetical glossary
- diagnostic tests that aid you when identifying areas that require additional study
- hundreds of ACT-style practice questions
- one sample sales and one sample broker exam—both with the answers fully explained
- math review
- section on exam strategies—how to prepare mentally and physically—how to follow directions . . . how to develop a strategy for studying . . . and how to guess.

Check box #2 on the order card $14.95 order number 1970-02

FUNDAMENTALS OF REAL ESTATE APPRAISAL, 3rd edition

By William L. Ventolo, Jr. and Martha R. Williams. James Boykin, Consulting Editor

Thorough and concise explanation of real estate appraisal. Covers—in detail—the cost approach . . . market comparison approach . . . and income approach to appraising. NEW TO THIS EDITION . . .

- information on the ways financing techniques affect appraised value—provides numerous examples to give a hands-on feel for this critical element in current appraisals
- section on solar heating added to aid understanding of this form of developing technology as it relates to an appraiser's everyday work
- complete, up-to-date discussion of zoning and depreciation and the way each affects a parcel's value

Numbers and figures have been updated throughout the text to reflect current costs and values of real estate. Features end-of-chapter exams plus glossaries of appraisal and construction terms.

Check box #3 on the order card $28.95 order number 1556-10

ESSENTIALS OF REAL ESTATE FINANCE, 3rd edition

By David Sirota

Popular real estate finance book includes current, up-to-date information—text has been completely revised to include complete coverage of financing methods and instruments in use today. Includes comprehensive discussion of the sources and techniques of financing. Book is clearly written and well organized, while workbook format encourages note-taking.

Special features of the third edition of *Essentials of Real Estate Finance* include . . .

- text revised to reflect changes in laws—you won't have to search for up-to-date information to use . . . Everything you need is included!
- over 50 graphs, charts and tables have been completely updated—emphasize basic principles and apply them to current market conditions
- sample forms and contracts have been incorporated into the appropriate sections for easy reference
- glossary of real estate terms included for quick review

Check box #4 on the order card $28.95 order number 1557-10